Anglo-Hispania beyond the Black Legend

Anglo-Hispania beyond the Black Legend

British Campaigns, Travellers and Attitudes towards Spain since 1489

Mark Lawrence

BLOOMSBURY ACADEMIC
LONDON • NEW YORK • OXFORD • NEW DELHI • SYDNEY

BLOOMSBURY ACADEMIC

Bloomsbury Publishing Plc, 50 Bedford Square, London, WC1B 3DP, UK
Bloomsbury Publishing Inc, 1385 Broadway, New York, NY 10018, USA
Bloomsbury Publishing Ireland, 29 Earlsfort Terrace, Dublin 2, D02 AY28, Ireland

BLOOMSBURY, BLOOMSBURY ACADEMIC and the Diana logo are trademarks of
Bloomsbury Publishing Plc

First published in Great Britain 2023
This paperback edition published in 2025

Copyright © Mark Lawrence 2023

Mark Lawrence has asserted his right under the Copyright, Designs and Patents Act, 1988,
to be identified as author of this work.

For legal purposes the Acknowledgements on p. vi constitute an extension of this
copyright page.

Cover images: Map Of Europe © Nicholas Free/iStock. UK flag
© janaluchenko/Adobe Stock. Spanish flag © Tarik GOK /Adobe Stock.
Cover design: Annabel Hewitson

All rights reserved. No part of this publication may be: i) reproduced or
transmitted in any form, electronic or mechanical, including photocopying,
recording or by means of any information storage or retrieval system without
prior permission in writing from the publishers; or ii) used or reproduced in any
way for the training, development or operation of artificial intelligence (AI)
technologies, including generative AI technologies. The rights holders expressly
reserve this publication from the text and data mining exception as per
Article 4(3) of the Digital Single Market Directive (EU) 2019/790.

Bloomsbury Publishing Plc does not have any control over, or responsibility for, any
third-party websites referred to or in this book. All internet addresses given in this
book were correct at the time of going to press. The author and publisher regret any
inconvenience caused if addresses have changed or sites have ceased to exist, but can
accept no responsibility for any such changes.

Every effort has been made to trace the copyright holders and obtain permission to
reproduce the copyright material. Please do get in touch with any enquiries or any
information relating to such material or the rights holder. We would be pleased to rectify
any omissions in subsequent editions of this publication should they be drawn to our
attention.

A catalogue record for this book is available from the British Library.

A catalog record for this book is available from the Library of Congress.

ISBN: HB: 978-1-3503-6622-0
PB: 978-1-3503-6626-8
ePDF: 978-1-3503-6623-7
eBook: 978-1-3503-6624-4

Typeset by Newgen KnowledgeWorks Pvt. Ltd., Chennai, India

For product safety related questions contact productsafety@bloomsbury.com.

To find out more about our authors and books visit www.bloomsbury.com
and sign up for our newsletters.

Contents

Acknowledgements — vi

1. Introduction — 1
2. Anglo-Spanish relations and the Black Legend between the Habsburg alliances, 1489–1714 — 13
3. Eighteenth-century Anglo-Hispania — 37
4. The Peninsular War and its aftermath — 51
5. Anglo-Hispania and the first Carlist War (1833–40) — 75
6. Anglo-Hispania and the world — 97
7. Anglo-Hispania between disaster and civil war — 109
8. Anglo-Hispania during civil war and world war — 121
9. Anglo-Hispania and Franco's Spain — 149
10. Conclusion — 161

Notes — 165
Bibliography — 205
Index — 235

Acknowledgements

This book has been on my mind for years. So many Spanish friendships and experiences over the years kept alive the idea of writing an entangled history. But I needed the granting of research leave from the University of Kent School of History, as well as the opportune help of colleagues, librarians and archivists, to bring this project to fruition. My thanks go to the anonymous reviewers who gave feedback on my original proposal. I am especially indebted to Gregorio Alonso, a reviewer who also read the first draft of the manuscript. His corrections and insights have been invaluable. Any surviving errors are entirely my own. My thanks also go to Conxa Rodríguez Vives, who kindly acquainted me with her work on Ramón Cabrera. My colleagues at Kent, PhD candidate Jacinta Mallon and Humanities librarian Emma Furderer, made available digitized servicemen's newspapers from the Second World War, which proved of immense help. The staff at the Archivo Histórico de las Palmas (Gran Canaria) did the utmost to accommodate me during a whistle-stop tour of the Canary Islands in April 2022. As ever, Rhodri Mogford and his colleagues at Bloomsbury have been encouraging and professional in their support throughout. Last but not the least, my thanks go to my family, Susana and Nicole, for making all this worthwhile.

Canterbury, February 2023

1

Introduction

Britain and Spain are traditionally viewed as antagonistic rivals in history. Comparable in some ways as composite monarchies, successive projectors of European global power and embodiments of peculiarly patriotic expressions of Christianity, in other ways Britain and Spain seemed worlds apart in their respective corners of the European continent. British Protestants excoriated Spain in a 'Black Legend' and Catholic propagandists dismissed rising English power as the work of pirates and heretics. But the two countries were joined in surprising alliances in the nineteenth century and a great international cause in the twentieth. Cultural exchanges flourished amidst the growth of travel and new ideas in the eighteenth century. Whereas Spaniards feared or admired Britain for its successful political and fiscal system, Britons romanticized Iberia for its supposed failures. British campaigns in the 1700s and 1800s established a Romantic Spain in memoir culture, which the twentieth century gradually dissolved in the ideological cauldron of the 1930s and the advent of mass tourism. By the late twentieth century, both Spain and especially Britain found their soft power magnified via the global reach of their languages. The ongoing presence of hundreds of thousands of young Spaniards in Britain, and a similar amount of British retirees in Spain, has created a transnational diaspora culture largely unaltered by the Brexit process.[1]

The historical profession over the course of the past twenty years has been characterized by growing interest in processes like migration and climate change, which extend beyond national borders. Such varieties of history as the transnational and the environmental have challenged the assumption that the nation is the main object of analysis. Yet, historians continue to begin their research with a premise rooted 'somewhere' and typically in the modern nation or its previous incarnations even as they examine cross-border, regional or trans-continental phenomena. Nation states may now be seen as unequal to the challenges of globalization, public health and climate change. But multinational organizations seldom achieve the support or legitimacy for common enterprises. Rather, international bodies and attitudes continue to preserve nations as the pinnacle of legitimacy and identity.

European nations, despite two centuries of modernization, world markets and globalization, have never fallen out of favour with commentators and historians. Modern methods of understanding history, despite their universal applicability, in many ways reinforced nationhood. Eighteenth-century *philosophers* prized objectivity in their understanding of history, bestowing the nineteenth century with an emerging corpus of professionalized history across Europe.[2] Some historians, such as the geographically minded French of the twentieth century, thought in terms of regions. Most recently, the 'global turn' in history has revived the interests of scholars in the field of intellectual history, who in turn have made a formidable contribution by adding some missing pieces to the puzzle while challenging the established ethnocentric historiography. Especially, Maurizio Isabella in *Risorgimento in Exile* has explored exile as an 'intellectual experience' and its impact on the Italian national movement in terms of cultural transfer.[3] But the bordered European nation state continues to be a popular object of study in the Anglosphere. Even the avowedly scientific analyses of Marxist historians tended to explain social transformation within borders, accepting universality in material terms but dismissing anything more abstract as superstructure.[4]

The nation continues to motivate world politics. Present-day authoritarian regimes cherish selective stories about their past, often in contrast to their neighbours and in support of an inherited right to interfere in their 'near abroad'. For example, eleventh-century chroniclers in Kyiv wrote an early history of Rus, creating a foundational story of the Russian people. To this day, Ukraine and Russia are divided by a shared story of a common past.[5] Even in democratic Spain, the lack of a consensus about such burdens from the past as the Civil War or the ending of Islamic Spain is evident in the way extremists on the political left and right have tried to insist on their own exclusive forms of Spanishness, drawing selectively on lessons from the past and from other countries. Santiago Abascal, leader of the far-right *Vox* party, for example, dismissed a long-standing current of Hispanophobia known as the 'black legend' as 'the work of the enemies of Spain'.[6] This assessment is essentially true, and yet it is not hard to imagine how any far-right government in power would silence its critics by labelling them 'enemies of Spain'.

The intrinsic qualities of nations have concerned not only politicians but also popular culture. Beyond the academy, nations have continued to be defined with reference to supposedly different neighbouring countries. For example, Bohemian

(Czech) villages (*böhmische Dörfer*) are an idiom in the German language for something incomprehensible. Polish economy (*polnische Wirtschaft*) is a pejorative term for waste and chaos. Stereotypes about neighbours are natural. But images of countries not immediately on the borders, or even on separate continents, are harder to evaluate. In German, 'Spanish' behaviour acquired the meaning of behaviour out of character. *Das kommt mir spanisch vor* ('that seems Spanish to me') is an admonition for unexpected or unnatural behaviour and phenomena. In Britain, 'Spanish practices' described irregular customs favouring employees' interests that had to be tolerated by their employers. The term, now passé, probably originated in the taboo of Catholic (viz. 'Spanish') practices in Elizabethan England. Spain, perhaps more than most European countries, continues to evoke strong symbols, and not just within Europe. The land of the fiesta, siesta, flamenco and bullfighting has resonated abroad since at least the advent of Romanticism two centuries ago. Even now, in a recent survey of Japanese opinion, some 30 per cent of correspondents identified bulls and 12 per cent flamenco as the symbols they most associated with Spain.[7] Generations of intellectuals abroad either ignored or embraced Spain precisely because of its distinctive culture and apparent eccentricity from a supposed European mainstream. Spain was a country, in the words of the Duke of Wellington, where 'two plus two do not equal four'.[8] Over a hundred years later, another British campaigner in Spain, George Orwell, indulged national stereotypes:

> National characteristics are not easy to pin down, and when pinned down they often turn out to be trivialities or seem to have no connection with one other. Spaniards are cruel to animals, Italians can do nothing without making a deafening noise, the Chinese are addicted to gambling ... Obviously, such things do not matter in themselves. Nevertheless, nothing is causeless, and the fact that Englishmen have bad teeth can tell something about the realities of English life.[9]

Stereotypes are hallowed through the ages. Even historians, avowedly objective professionals loathe to fall into the lazy trap of stereotypes, study contemporary prejudices and encomiums with a view to understanding what was considered possible and impossible in bilateral relations. The nation-centred historiographical approach has continued to flourish as part of the increasing popularity of global, transnational and comparative history.[10] This book offers a political, cultural and military study of the encounters between Britain and Spain since the dawn of the Tudor and Catholic monarchies in the late fifteenth century. This start in the early modern period is well chosen, seeing that first Spain and then England projected much of the Western power of the age, especially across the Atlantic.[11] The cumulation and decline of first Spanish and then British pre-eminence offered rich legacies to impress military, political and cultural encounters. For this reason, the book is weighted more substantially towards the modern than the early modern era. *Anglo-Hispania* is liberal in its definition. Often England looms larger than Britain, as Castile sometimes does with Spain. But in other places, regions and nations stand out. The Basque country dominates much of the treatment of British views of Carlism. Scotland and Catalonia dominate comparisons in several places, especially during the events surrounding the negotiated Anglo-Scottish political union of 1707 and the imposed Castilian domination of Catalonia and Aragón in the wake of the Spanish Succession War (1701–14). Given that the constitutional question continues to dominate politics in Scotland and Catalonia, this perspective offers contemporary relevance as well as pathways to more focused studies.[12]

Anglo-Hispania blends political, social, cultural and military history in an attempt to reveal the multifaceted entanglements across the Bay of Biscay. The gist of this volume is entangled history rather than transnational. It studies Anglo-Hispanic exchanges mostly, but not exclusively, from north to south, and does not confine itself to the impact of one-time events, personalities or ideas. The structure is broadly chronological, although the pace of narrative and retrospective views of fiction and memoirs sometimes require flexibility with dates. The varieties of history shift in accordance with the salient nature of the entanglements, from cultural and dynastic in the build-up to the advent of Bourbon Spain in 1700, to military, imperial and cultural in the eighteenth century, to military and cultural in the nineteenth, and to the widest range in respect of the accelerated Anglo-Spanish interactions of the civil war and the world-war era. The main focus is Anglo-Spanish, bilateral and European interactions. But given the elasticity of the terms 'Spaniard' and 'Briton' in the context of both countries' extensive non-European empires, this book occasionally includes the wider British empire, the United States and Latin America in its consideration. Anglo culture often confused Old and New Spain, racializing 'Spanish' Americans amidst indigenous and mestizo populations, while Spaniards in turn referred to the United States as 'Angloamérica' until well into the nineteenth century.[13] Given the Spanish empire's role in fostering the 'Black Legend' and given the Anglo-Hispanic entanglements of slavery and anti-slavery, the American angle is present in most chapters. The vast Spanish empire in the Americas was a focus for British traders, adventurers, pirates and mercenaries for over two hundred years.

The book adopts varying political, cultural, social and diplomatic approaches to Anglo-Hispanic entanglements and is also diverse in its use of sources. It is lavish in its use of British travel memoirs, especially because they portrayed different kinds of preconceptions. The Romantic interest in the picaresque side to life played by bandits and smugglers was overhauled by politically engaged accounts of revolution and reaction in the twentieth century. Most chapters include British perceptions on military campaigns in Spain, and I am pleased to offer diarists of various backgrounds the benefit of doubt. Even if dates and locations may be inaccurate, the real value of first-hand testimony lies in what it reveals of attitudes and values, as well as the visceral experience of fear, hunger and exposure in a strange land. They answer lofty war aims with the reality on the ground.

Besides, historians would do well to let sources speak for themselves. As Ilya Berkovich argues in his recent study of early modern military campaigns, 'Unless there are reasons to doubt the authenticity of a particular source, the statements of the authors are taken as they stand ... it is presumptuous to assume that they should always know better what were the actual thoughts, feelings and acts of the people whom they study.'[14] As the military Hispanist, Charles Esdaile, has noted, 'Neither diaries, letters nor, a fortiori, memoirs can be regarded as reliable guides to past events, but, read en masse, they are at least suggestive of past mentalities, whilst at the same time affording us with a window on human experience that is otherwise unattainable.'[15] On a grander scale, too, a priori choices in events whose outcomes belied those decisions – whether Philip II's decision to banish English heresy in 1588, a British volunteer's choice in 1936 to halt fascism in Spain or Franco's pro-Axis policies in the Second World War – are particularly impactful when witnessed in contemporary memoirs and propaganda.

A particular theme in *Anglo-Hispania* is the repeated transnational interaction of soldiers and strategy in major wars. I offer plebeian accounts in increasing amounts as the chapters progress, not least because interactions between Britons and Spaniards increased in the context of protracted wars in the nineteenth and twentieth centuries, especially in the tourism boom of the second half of the twentieth century. A large volume of research explains foreign experiences in the Spanish Civil War, a reasonable amount in Spain's War of Independence (1808–14), but little concerning either Spain's Carlist War of the 1830s, or the War of Spanish Succession (1700–14). A lot remains to be said about Spain's role as a non-belligerent during the Second World War. Most of the Anglo-Hispanic entanglements in all the five wars concerned not just volunteers, strategy and propaganda, but also the vital British possession of Gibraltar. A rock won almost absent-mindedly during the Succession War of the early eighteenth century would go on to dominate Anglo-Spanish relations and British defence anxieties in the twentieth.

Equally, I use literary sources on occasion. Novels and plays have no serious claim to historical accuracy. But they can reveal attitudes and prejudices, reflecting selective views of Anglo-Hispanic interaction, which in turn fed their own likes and prejudices. Ultimately, Anglo-Hispanic attitudes were not about reality or what was really happening, but what was believed to be real or really happening. This includes historical agents other than political, military or cultural leaders and an exploration of perceived difference.

The persistence of the nation and the rise of British Hispanism

Even though Spain's history has been largely 'normalized' by two generations of recent historical scholarship,[16] most of the early modern and modern period witnessed European attitudes of Iberia as exotic and obscurantist. The sway of Romanticism persisted whenever historians looked south across the Pyrenees. Foreign intellectuals continued to particularize Spain even as their Iberian colleagues opened up to wider European influences and debates. The term 'Hispanist' ('hispanista') was used in Spain from the late nineteenth century, and by 1914 it was accepted as a word by the Spanish Royal Academy. Tellingly, by 1956 its meaning had solidified into an outsider's view. 'Hispanism' had become the preserve of foreign intellectuals working on Spanish history and culture.[17]

While Spanish intellectuals yearned to break out of the claustrophobia or exile imposed by the Franco regime, foreign intellectuals continued to see Spanish history and its culture as sui generis. The British war correspondent, John Langdon-Davies, published some of the more objective accounts of life in the republican zone of the Spanish civil war (1936–9), a conflict which had an international appeal like no other. But his interest in Spain was stimulated by his Romantic belief in the egalitarian and harmonious nature of the Catalan culture.[18] British historians like Hugh Thomas, Gerald Brenan and Ian Gibson were appreciated in Spain because they were both profoundly interested in the Iberian Peninsula on a personal basis and they provided an objectivity that only foreign historians could attain for much of the twentieth century.[19] British historians operating during the Franco era had things one way. Spanish historians tended to have French, rather than English, as their main foreign language, and the Franco regime provided them with neither the resources nor intellectual freedom to conduct archival research.[20] Non-Hispanist historians, for their part, tended to footnote Spain as a frontier in studies of Europe and the Western world, or to merge it into wider phenomena like the Napoleonic empire or the origins of the Second World War. The study of the country tended to skew towards phenomena which had wider impact, such as the reconquest, conquest of the Americas, or the Spanish civil war. Iberia abroad was a frontier in the mind, as much as a frontier of the Roman, Islamic and European world.

Spain as a European frontier

Iberia has been considered a European borderland for most of the time since the northern kingdom of Asturias began the 'Reconquest' in the eighth century. The frontier extended southwards through Islamic Spain, then via dynastic lands in wider Europe and then via the vastness of the Americas. When, in the 1790s, the dissenting Mexican priest, Servando Teresa de Mier, was exiled to Spain, the historical jumble of frontiers in the Spanish empire was symbolized in response to the young man's way of speaking. Mier's accent was considered 'foreign' in northern Spain. It was mistaken as Andalucían in Castile and as Portuguese in Andalucía.[21] The confusion of languages, dialects and accents throughout Iberia and the Iberian Americas attested to their plurilingual and multi-ethnic make-up across the centuries. This diversity began from humble beginnings in the early modern period.

For most of Europe's medieval period, Spain was the frontier of Christendom. Crossing the Straits of Gibraltar in 711, the Moors defeated and killed the last Visigothic king of Iberia and rapidly advanced through the peninsula, taking Córdova, Toledo, Mérida and Zaragoza. Having overrun most of Spain, the Moors pressed on to invade France. Initially successful, they were defeated at the Battle of Tours in 732 or 733 at the hands of the Frankish leader, Charles Martel. This thwarted Umayyad invasion was celebrated by the anonymous chroniclers on the Christian side not as a 'Christian' victory, but as 'European'. As the Arab invasion of France had come from Iberia, the territory now comprising Spain would gradually become indelibly marked as non-European. Almost a millennium later, the French literary trope 'Africa begins at the Pyrenees' continued to peripheralize Spain.[22] The dismissive tone concealed Spain's central position in ancient and medieval history. The classical world, which had the Mediterranean at its centre, made Hispania its western bulwark. Christendom pushed north of the Mediterranean into non-classical Scandinavia and Slavic lands while losing ground in Africa. Iberia was its central fault line.

'Spain' was a geographical expression for much longer than foreigners accepted its existence as something more.[23] The Christian kingdoms in the eighth century began a lengthy, almost eight-hundred-year, process, of recovering the Iberian Peninsula from Muslim rule. The incremental occupation of the peninsula was baptized as a 'reconquest' of lost lands. It was popularized by nineteenth-century nation-builders, and politicized by the Franco regime, in both cases using the Castilian myths of Pelayo and Covadonga in contrast to other Iberian narratives. Castile was depicted as the messianic kingdom on a mission not only to absorb the polities in Iberia, but also to establish strong central government and Catholic uniformity. The completion of the *Reconquista* in 1492 was immediately followed by a process of *Conquista*, this time in the Americas. But 'Conquest' barely fitted the reality of Spanish imperialism in the New World any more than 'Reconquest' fitted medieval Iberia. Despite the fame of Hernán Cortes and his *conquistadores*, America was not 'conquered' by Spaniards alone. Rather a few hundred Spanish adventurers were a vanguard which mobilized discontent amongst the Tlaxcala to overthrow the Mexica empire.[24] Meanwhile, the advent of Habsburg Spain in 1516 ushered in almost two centuries of world power, encompassing dynastic lands in central Europe and the Netherlands, along with Italy and Portugal, and ultimately huge stretches of the Americas and Asia. The Spanish empire, especially after Philip II's acquisition of the Portuguese throne in 1580, had an unprecedented range among major global powers. The death of the last Habsburg ruler of the Spanish empire in 1700 set in motion a War of Succession (1701–14), which divorced Spain from its dynastic lands in most of the rest of Europe, turning Austria into an exclusively European power while the new Spain of the Bourbons governed and expanded the territories in the Americas and Asia.

Spain's military prestige from the mid-seventeenth century faded amidst the general rise in British perceptions of its obscurantism. The forbidding spectacle of Spain's baroque royal and Church architecture, designed to overawe rather than enlighten, symbolized the imperial mission. Religious and royal buildings swelled with undulating facades and wreathed columns. The artistic and architectural patronage bestowed by monarchs like Philip II and Philip IV on palaces, academies and monasteries, followed by Italian Filippo Juvarra's architecture, showed the investment made by Habsburgs and Bourbons alike in the sponsorship of culture. The unusual power vested in Spanish monarchs over the Catholic church reinforced its propaganda fide that was established in the seventeenth century to supervise missionary activity throughout the world.

Yet early modern Spain was in many ways more enlightened than other European monarchies. Its global imperial standing made its monarchs worldly. Nineteenth-century historian, Modesto Lafuente, contrasted the metaphysics of the thirteenth-century king of Castile, Alfonso the Wise (famous, amongst other things, for commissioning a book cataloguing the heavens), with Isabel the Catholic and her successors, 'who had to manage heaven and earth simultaneously'.[25] The 'Catholic Monarchs' eschewed much of the supernatural legitimacy surrounding other royal dynasties. They did not think their office sacred, claimed no powers to heal the sick – even when French monarchs reserved this supernatural power as late as the 1820s – and Spanish monarchs enjoyed no special ceremonies for births, coronations and deaths. Nor was early modern Spanish monarchism especially absolutist. Attempts to gain power over regional liberties were certainly no greater than those elsewhere in Europe. When the Spanish Jesuit, Juan de Mariana, claimed in 1621 that the king has 'no absolute power', his comments were condemned in Paris and London, but not in Madrid.[26] Later liberals, many of whom were also historians, celebrated an earlier 'Golden Age' of Spanish liberties. For the president of Spain's Second Republic, Manuel Azaña, Spain's real golden age ended in 1521, with the rise to power of Carlos V and his suppression of the comunero rebellion.[27] But regional and corporate liberties mostly in fact survived in Habsburg Spain.

Likewise, Spanish imperialism, despite its Black Legend, was the product of dynastic diplomacy, peripheral tensions and local stakeholders as much as a sense of mission. The last feature, which was wrapped up with a self-image of justice, was common to both English and Spanish efforts to evangelize the Americas.[28] Much of the Hispanophobic 'Black Legend' centred on the New World of the colonizers. The Black Legend was negative propaganda starting in the sixteenth century and spread by rival powers depicting Spain as fanatical and cruel. Indirectly, it has also pervaded historical scholarship, as historians until well into the twentieth century sought explanation for Spain's supposed historical backwardness. But the legend has been long and satisfactorily revised by academics.[29] The revisionist historiography had a daunting task in the Anglosphere literature. Richard L. Kagan coined the 'Prescott Paradigm', which was based on the prolific writings of nineteenth-century American historian, William H. Prescott. Prescott orientalized Spain and Spanish America as an antitheses to US notions of liberty and modernity.[30] Nineteenth-century Anglo thinkers believed either tacitly or explicitly that Spain's decline and internal chaos were caused by the legacy of religious bigotry and political despotism. In general, US travellers tended to complement rather than counter British condescension towards Spain. George Ticknor, Harvard's first professor of modern languages, wrote of his visit to Spain in the early nineteenth century: 'Imagine a country so deserted and desolate, and with so little travelling and communication, as to have no taverns' that was found wanting for both 'cultivation and refinement'.[31] American poet Henry Wadsworth Longfellow once remarked in a personal letter, 'there is so little change in the Spanish character, that you find everything as it is said to have been two hundred years ago.'[32]

Spain's timeless character abroad became associated with a militant Catholic zeal, impermeable to foreign influences and inured to the relative poverty of the Castilian tableland. Iberia's climate and aridity confirmed northern Europeans in a view of an intractable culture south of the Pyrenees. The underproductive nature of the Spanish meseta was different from fertile France, and campaigns in Iberia suffered accordingly. Henri IV (1553–1610) remarked how 'large armies invading Spain starve whereas small ones are swallowed up by a hostile population'.[33] A nineteenth-century study of the War of the Spanish Succession (1702–14) stressed the impossibility of Castile's open plains and population for any would-be conqueror: 'Castille may soon be over-run, but never subdued. It is an easy morsel to swallow, but hard to digest; which, instead of nourishing, oppresses its devourer.'[34] The Spanish Civil War poem *Spain* by W. H. Auden described the country as an 'arid square, that fragment nipped off from hot Africa, soldered so crudely to inventive Europe'.[35] The association made on foreign campaign memoirs between Spain's unyielding geography and forthright human character was especially marked in British testimonies over the course of four major military interventions between 1700 and 1939. Victor Pritchett, a British literary critic who toured Spain on foot in the 1920s, thought that Spaniards had no 'inner life' or fantasy life, unlike the introspective Anglo-Saxons.[36]

These orientalizing narratives reveal more about their authors than about Spain. In fact, only a highly selective reading of foreign intervention in Spain would reveal, for instance, the unyielding Spanish xenophobia beloved of British writers. Foreign intruders succeeded when Spanish support turned them into allies. The French Duke of Berwick triumphed in the War of Spanish Succession (1700–14) against the Habsburgs, and again in 1719 against his erstwhile Bourbon ally, Philip V. A hundred years later, Napoleon failed in his invasion in 1808; yet in 1823, a French army was welcomed as liberators against an unpopular liberal regime. Foreign interventionists, like travellers and migrants, could be welcome in Spain as long as they fitted into the needs and desires of local culture and the life of the 'pueblo'. In Anglo-Hispanic terms, the themes of diplomacy clashing with culture began at the start of this study. Both monarchies liked to cloak dynastic ambition in the name of spreading Christianity, a policy which entailed more pitfalls than glory. Six hundred English archers, an elite force esteemed in Europe, arrived in Cádiz in 1511 to support Ferdinand of Aragón's *Empresa de África*, a campaign aimed ultimately at conquering the Holy Land. Yet, the men never saw service. In a story recognizable to later generations of interventionists, the northerners discovered a fondness for Andalucían wine and were disbanded before they left Europe.[37] The ups and downs of individual soldiers, travellers, exiles and diplomats belied the lofty aims of war, peace and propaganda.

2

Anglo-Spanish relations and the Black Legend between the Habsburg alliances, 1489–1714

Despite the abiding image of Spain and England as natural historical enemies, for much of the late medieval and early Tudor period, Spain was a natural counterbalance for England's repeated wars in France. Eleanor of Castile (1241–1290), beloved wife of a British pseudo-Caesar, Edward I, was commemorated with a dozen 'Eleanor crosses' across the East Midlands of England. English attitudes derived from a situation of comparative weakness, which was often overlooked by later writers. The Tudor dynasty which triumphed in the War of the Roses (1455–87) governed a bloodied England which in European terms appeared like a barbaric periphery. A British study of the firebrand Golden Age Cardinal Francisco Cisneros (1436–1517), published in the 1930s when Britannia was still at global pre-eminence and Spain about to descend into civil war, marvelled at the contrast between the two countries in the fifteenth century:

> It is sobering to an Englishman's historical pride to read for instance the despatches embodying the negotiations between England and Spain over the marriage of Catherine of Aragon with Arthur, Prince of Wales, and to realise that at that period England not only was a minor power as compared with Spain, but was ready to recognise the fact.[1]

For generations of early modern Englishmen, Spain was a land of wealth and opportunity. Fifteenth-century England was probably poorer than Spain, and its GDP per capita was only marginally higher than that of Spain between 1500 and 1650. The real divergence happened progressively after the mid-seventeenth century as Spanish Parliaments were curtailed and the British Parliaments empowered.[2] Nor was Spain solely a source of economic attraction – Golden Age playwrights like Lope de Vega and Tirso de Molina inspired British culture. As Barbara Fuchs has shown, English greats like Shakespeare and Marlowe were indebted to their Spanish forbears and contemporaries, often resentfully so, given the Hispanophobic climate in which they were writing.³

The crown of Castile weighed more heavily in the diplomatic calculations of the English court than was the case in reverse. The reign of Henry VII and even the early years of Henry VIII were also marked by an instinctively pro-Habsburg foreign policy. Even though the Anglo-Castilian alliance forged in the 1489 Treaty of Medina Campo was dragged out through complex marriage negotiations, Anglo-Hispanic relations grew ever closer. Henry VII went on to supply huge subsidies to Archduke Charles in a bid to make him king of Castile instead of the rival Ferdinand of Aragón. Vast sums were raised by special taxes on wealthy landowners and merchants and delivered in cash to Spanish territories in the Netherlands. Charles V's ability to expand the Spanish empire once he inherited the Habsburg crown in 1519 was thus in no small way linked to the English alliance.⁴ In 1493, the youngest daughter of the Catholic monarchs, Catherine of Aragón, was fatefully promised in marriage to Henry VII's eldest male heir. After Prince Arthur's death, this marriage passed to the future Henry VIII, setting in motion decades of Anglo-Spanish tension and religious upheaval. When Henry VIII became king of England in 1509, he inherited his late brother's marriage to Catherine of Aragón, in continuation of the dual Habsburg–Tudor pincers encircling France.

In 1505, King Ferdinand allowed foreigners, who had lived in Spain for at least fifteen years and settled with family and property, to trade on equal terms with the new Spanish empire as long as they employed Spanish intermediaries. Traders moved between Bristol, Seville and the Canary Islands with ease, intermarrying and exploiting the nascent Atlantic trade with the Americas. Both Britons and Spaniards gained cartographical knowledge and survival techniques sailing along Morocco's Atlantic coast, and there were even rival plans in England and Spain to colonize this stretch of north-west Africa which commanded access to the Mediterranean and Atlantic.⁵ Bristolians became the chief agents of Anglo-Hispanic trade. It was a hemisphere in which English explorers like Henry Hawks passed themselves off as Spaniards (Pedro Sánchez) when it suited their business.⁶ The allure of American silver and the fame of 'El Dorado' inspired English intellectuals. Thomas More, the Renaissance humanist venerated as a Catholic saint for his martyrdom in defiance of Henry VIII, was impressed by Spain's exploration of the New World. His sociopolitical satire *Utopia* (1516) was inspired by the imagined innocence of Peruvian society. In 1541, Henry VIII was presented with an English translation of the Spanish geographer Martín Fernández de Enciso's pioneering description of the American mainland, *Suma de geographia*.⁷

But relations frayed once it became clear that Catherine of Aragón would not produce a male heir. The fretful diplomatic and eventual religion schism caused by Henry's divorce from Catherine did not immediately produce Anglo-Spanish enmity. Even during Henry VIII's defiance of Papal authority, the crown of Castile continued to issue select permits to individual English tradesmen. But Tudor England remained an unlikely bedfellow to Spain. Spanish subjects were an almost invisible minority amongst the thousands of French, Flemish, Dutch and other nationalities who lived and worked in London's skilled trades and commerce. Of the alien heads of household in London in 1571, only seventeen were recorded as Spanish.[8] The vector of relations remained the realm of dynastic diplomacy. Once a Catholic (Mary I) briefly occupied the English throne from 1553 to 1558; her co-monarch, and designated regent of England in the event of his wife giving birth, was Philip II of Spain. An anti-Catholic revolt led by Sir Thomas Wyatt's army in 1554 was defeated by the crown, despite Wyatt's xenophobic appeals against the foreign co-monarch. But as the Catholic queen bore no children, the Anglo-Hispanic honeymoon in relations did not last long. The death of Mary in 1558 ended what had been a golden age of over half a century in Tudor–Habsburg relations.

The vacillations in Anglo-Habsburg relations shifted towards enmity only with the enthronement of Mary's Protestant half-sister. The ascent to the English throne in 1558 of Elizabeth I, a queen widely considered illegitimate, changed everything. Elizabeth's long reign was a source of consternation for Phillip of Spain. It became indelibly associated with piracy, arrogance and above all heresy. The latter feature influenced National-Catholic opinion in the Franco era, which liked to compare the sanctified Catholic Isabella I of Castile with her unworthy Tudor namesake.[9] A state of cold war developed, which would go hot in 1585. The scene was set for rivalry and a leading English share in the Hispanophobic 'Black Legend' which demonized the Spanish empire.

The 'Black Legend' was a diverse body of weaponized propaganda common across Protestant northern Europe which depicted Spaniards as cruel, fanatical and intolerant. The legend transcended its Elizabethan heyday. Hispanophobia was boosted in the wake of Spain's defeat to the United States in 1898, an event much jeered in the Anglo-American press – leading Spanish intellectuals, especially Julián Juderías, identified a litany of Hispanophobic propaganda in Protestant print and image culture.[10] As a premise, the Black Legend has been excised from serious historical scholarship. It lingered so long in part because even Spanish historians, anguished by their country's repeated civil wars and truncated modernization, accepted some of its premises.[11] It inspired one recent populist history which attributed the source of the legend to heretical Protestant Europe, with Perfidious Albion as the main culprit.[12]

Contemporaries and later writers represented Elizabethan England as an underdog and Spain as an overbearing empire rife with haughtiness and abuses. During the second half of the sixteenth century, in the words of Roca Barea, 'Hispanophobia became a constituent part of English identity'.[13] Thomas Nashe, the Elizabethan picaresque novelist, wrote that 'pride is the disease of the Spaniard' and that the 'Spaniard is born a braggart in his mother's womb'.[14] By contrast, English pirates were celebrated as patriotic underdogs taming the overbearing Spanish empire. English raiders flaunted Spanish liveries they had caught in battle proclaiming *non sufficit orbis* ('the world is not enough'). Around the same time of English privateering, the anti-slavery cleric, Bartolomé de las Casas, published widely disseminated critiques of the Spanish treatment of the American Indians, and his work was read avidly in Protestant Europe. Aztec emperor Moctezuma was largely seen as having been tricked into submitting to the *conquistadores*, which delegitimized Spanish imperial rule.[15] The root of the Black Legend lay in Las Casas's writings, in his defence of the indigenous population (nobody much noticed his vacillation on the question of African slaves). English piracy was thus laced with righteous indignation, such as when Francis Drake's chaplain condemned the 'whoredom and filth of Sodom which Spanish overlords spread among American natives'.[16] The prospect of untapped wealth in unworthy Spanish hands enticed a generation of English adventurers. Walter Raleigh, whose expedition to find the mythical El Dorado he later explained in part as a bid to deliver natives from the 'tyranny of the Spaniards', deemed Spain's unlikely American wealth to be fair game:

> For we find that by the abundant treasure of that country the Spanish king vexes all the princes of Europe, and is become, in a few years, from a poor king of Castile, the greatest monarch of this part of the world, and likely every day to increase if other princes forslow the good occasions offered, and suffer him to add this empire to the rest, which by far exceedeth all the rest. If his gold now endanger us, he will then be unresistible. Such of the Spaniards as afterwards endeavoured the conquest thereof, whereof there have been many, as shall be declared hereafter, thought that this Inca, of whom this emperor now living is descended, took his way by the river of Amazons, by that branch which is called Papamene.[17]

Elizabethan propagandists published sectarian treatises against Spanish Catholicism, including the former co-monarch of Mary's regime. The death in

1568 of the 23-year-old and mentally ill heir to the Spanish throne was attributed to the neglect and cruelty shown by Philip II. John Foxe's *Book of Martyrs* claimed the prince had been killed for 'having seen into the errors of popery, and abhorred the very name of the inquisition'. Prince Carlos, according to Foxe, 'inveighed publicly against the institution, ridiculed the affected piety of the inquisitors, did all he could to expose their atrocious deeds, end even declared, that if he ever came to the crown, he would abolish the Inquisition, and exterminate its agents'.[18] Propaganda, even in the early modern era, circumscribed a specific community and allowed all included to interact with an ideological structure – in this case, of patriotic Protestantism. Foxe's Protestant martyrology set a theme which survived long into the nineteenth century. British 'Black Legend' writers in the Victorian era continued to draw inspiration both from anti-Catholicism and wonder at the achievements of the conquistadores. Charles Kingsley's 1855 novel *Westward Ho!* contrasted the supposedly masculine and Protestant values of the Elizabethan privateers with the debilitating Marian femininity of their Spanish targets: 'They pray to a woman, the idolatrous rascals!, and no wonder they fight like women'.[19] Britain's Anglo cousins in the early United States shared this condescension. There was little popular knowledge of Spanish America beyond the era of Columbus and the conquistadores. One American schoolbook in the 1790s observed how Spain and Spanish Americans were 'naturally weak and effeminate' and 'dedicate the greatest part of their lives to loitering and inactive pleasures'.[20] Elizabethan England mixed fear at Spanish expansion with Protestant disdain for its Catholic and renegade ethnic make-up. The English Lord Lieutenant of Ireland, a few years before the launch of the Armada, called Spain a 'semi-morisco nation, sprung from the filth of Africa … and of base Ottomans and rejected Jews'.[21]

In 1585, Elizabeth I signed a series of treaties with the Protestant Dutch who were defying Spanish overlordship, setting in motion an undeclared war with Spain, which would last until 1604. Rumours spread that Francis Drake was preparing a fleet to attack Spain. Spanish ports were closed to English vessels, ruining bilateral trade. Of the 246 foreign ships calling in Sanlúcar de Barrameda (Cádiz) in 1578, 93 were English.[22] Spain's sudden world empire presented Elizabethan England with problems of rulership which extended beyond the direct threat of the famous Armada. The threat of Spanish invasion in 1588 was answered by popular rumours about Catholic Spanish brutality. Subsequent generations believed the myth that a successful Spanish invasion would have led to Protestant adults being killed and their children branded with 'L' for 'Lutheran'.[23] In the event, the English were spared this apocalypse.

The Spanish invasion was delayed by a year anyway, thanks to Francis Drake's 'singing of the King of Spain's beard' in raids on Cádiz and Portuguese outposts. When the Armada set sail in 1588, a combination of poor Spanish planning and leadership, appalling weather, and fighting by outnumbered English vessels prevented Admiral Medina-Sidonia from attempting a land invasion. Even though only 35 out of the Armada's 127 vessels were actually sunk, the survivors faced a hazardous and demoralized retreat to Iberian ports.[24]

Once the Spanish invasion fleet had been repelled, Elizabeth's personality cult peaked. Partly cultivated by court propagandists and partly the product of a popular patriotism, the cult of 'Gloriana' found itself at its pinnacle amidst the Spanish defeat of 1588. Thereafter, the reign of the Virgin Queen dimmed amidst socio-economic unrest, a legacy of ungovernable sailors and privateers and a major defeat at the hands of Spain. The fate of the 'English Armada' of 1589 was understated by generations of patriotic Britons dazzled by the events of 1588, in part because Elizabeth I ordered the suppression of news of the disaster. Even Spanish writers, accustomed to assuming British superiority at sea as much as Spanish prowess on land, tended to overlook the English calamity during the siege of La Coruña and attack on Lisbon. Francis Drake, the most famous privateer of his age, enraged his queen by ignoring her orders to attack the remains of the Armada in Spain's northern ports in 1589. But the English siege of La Coruña was a drawn-out failure, while a revolt in Portugal, which Elizabeth hoped would revive the traditional English alliance, was derailed by Spanish countermeasures. After the loss of forty ships, and at least ten times the casualties than those sustained by the defending Spaniards, the English fleet limped back to port.[25] One English account of disputed authorship, but likely penned by Devereux, Earl of Essex, on account of its criticism of the queen's preparations, noted how 'England hath not known wars, but of late, from whole Ignorance proceeded this Discomfort, which I hope will warn those who hereafter go to the wars to make preparation of such as may better preserve men's lives by the skill'.[26]

The defeat of 1589 restored the naval balance of power in favour of the Spanish. Counterfactually, an English triumph, according to Luis Gorrochategui, would have prized Portugal away from Spain, made England Europe's naval overlord and opened up early opportunities to expand in the Americas.[27] But England was too small to effect such a strategic revolution. Elizabeth I engaged in diplomatic negotiations with Ahmad al-Mansur, sultan of Morocco, about options for a joint attack on Spain's American territories, or even the colonization of Spain itself with lands attached to both English and Moroccan crowns (even if he proposed that his own subjects would fare better in the Spanish heat). Al-Mansur saw his power strengthened after his conquest of the Songhai empire and capture of Timbuktu. But Elizabeth I died before negotiations about a joint attack across the Atlantic could leave the drawing board.[28]

The last years of Elizabeth's life saw her regime adopt a defensive posture, dependent more than ever on unruly sea captains, including the rebellious Earl of Essex who had defied the queen's express orders not to sail on the 1589 expedition. An English attempt to avenge a Spanish raid on the south-west coast of England in 1595 was derailed once the privateer captains, Drake and Hawkins, disagreed about whether the Canaries or the Panamanian coast offered greater loot. The wealth of the Spanish empire dazzled the golden age of English piracy during Elizabeth's later reign. Robert Devereux, second Earl of Essex, defied his queen's vacillation in the war against Spain by sacking Cádiz in 1596. The huge debts Devereux amassed drove him to attempt a desperate personal invasion of the elderly queen's private chamber, as part of an arrogant bid to oust Elizabeth's key advisor, Sir Robert Cecil. Frustrated, Devereux made an attempt to raise London against the queen in 1601. He was executed for treason – his demise interwoven with his ambition and greed concerning the opportunities of war and piracy against Spain.[29]

The death of Spanish emperor Philip II in 1598, and that of Elizabeth I in 1603, opened up possibilities for an Anglo-Spanish peace. Scotland and England now shared a monarch in the person of James VII (James I of England). The new pan-British Stuart monarchy offered the prospect of better relations with Spain. Much of the Anglo-Spanish hostility had been either personal in nature, or caused by the question of the maritime northern Netherlands, a traditional concern for English foreign and trade policy. But the Netherlands had achieved de facto independence. The Treaty of London (1604) sealed peace between Spain and England in Europe, leaving the ongoing issues of pirates and adventurers in the Americas as a free-for-all. The English colony established at Jamestown in the Chesapeake in 1607 was a violation of Spain's claim to sovereignty over the whole New World. But, despite a flurry of activity in Madrid, including a decision to reinforce Fort St Augustine in Florida (out of confused intelligence that English settlement plans lay further south), no attack was made on the English outpost. In 1611, a crew of Spanish adventurers sailed as far as the Chesapeake but were spotted by English lookouts. After both sides captured hostages, the Spaniards sailed away, taking John Clark (of future *Mayflower* fame) with them. Spain's policy of keeping the Stuarts as friendly neutrals thus had a transformative impact in global history. The refusal to destroy Jamestown led to nothing less than the division of the Americas into vast Spanish-speaking and English-speaking worlds.[30]

Despite voicing protests over Jamestown, a settlement whose strategic legacy was not necessarily yet visible, Philip III could be content with Anglo-Hispania. The new royal union of Great Britain was turned, in the words of one historian, into 'a neutral territory for Spanish interests'.[31] In 1622, the English Catholic adventurer, Anthony Sherley, wrote a homily to Philip IV's chief minister, the Duke of Olivares, claiming King James I as a reincarnation of the Spanish apostle saint of Spain, 'Santiago'. But, mainstream public opinion remained steeped in the Hispanophobic and Anti-Catholic sentiment of the Elizabethan era. A graphic image in 1621 entitled 'Double Deliverance' depicted the Spanish Armada and the Gunpowder Plot as evidence of the threat of Popery.[32] Spanish ambassadors, aware of the profound impact of the Reformation, cultivated material rather than emotional attachments. Bribes and honours were lavished on merchants and courtiers, commissions awarded to British naval officers fighting under the Habsburgs against the Turks and the old demands for freedom of worship for British Catholics dropped in return for barring the Americas to routine English commerce. The Spanish crown sighed with relief at the failure of the Catholic Gunpowder Plot (1605), even though many in London, including protestors outside the residence of the ambassador, suspected malign foreign backing. The sums spent on keeping Jacobean Britain as a harmless neutral were considerable, but much less than the ruinous cost of the Armada campaign (1588) or the ongoing war against the Dutch.[33]

But there were limits to this Anglo-Hispanic rapprochement. Diego Sarmiento de Acuña, Count Gondomar, was the Machiavellian Spanish ambassador to King James's court during 1613–22. His embassy became a focus for British Hispanophobia as fears abounded of another Armada-style invasion in 1614. Gondomar interceded personally to ensure the execution of the explorer and veteran of 1588, Walter Raleigh, who had been judged guilty of breaking an agreement not to raid Spanish outposts in the New World.[34] Relations soured further when a plot to seal a Habsburg–Stuart alliance via marriage came to naught. Bold attempts by the new Anglo-Scottish union of crowns (1603) to marry a British prince to a Spanish Habsburg princess manifested in the affair of the 'Spanish Match' of 1623. Prince Charles, the later ill-fated King Charles I, travelled to Spain incognito as 'Jack Smith' with a companion in order to marry the Spanish king's sister. The prince's seven months in Madrid exposed him to Spanish arts, refining his famously good taste. But the negotiation ended in fiasco, as Charles left Spain humiliated, and the lengthy negotiations about an Anglo-Spanish alliance misfired.[35]

Amidst this humiliating spat, Anglo-Hispanic relations deteriorated to levels not seen in a generation. Thomas Middleton's Hispanophobic play *A Game at Chess* (1624) got rave reviews before being closed under the energetic pressure of Spanish ambassador, Gondomar. Partly as a consequence of the marriage failure, and partly out of a desire to lead public opinion by standing tall with the cause of Protestant Europe, Charles I (1625–49) ended the generation of Anglo-Spanish peace. His accession to the throne was followed by a failed attack against Cádiz in November 1625. This led, as a consequence, to the English Parliament impeaching the king's favourite who had bungled the operation, the Duke of Buckingham.[36]

The failed overture to war was of major significance. The Spanish military organization of 'tercios' was much envied and feared by English observers, given their decisive performance in such battles as the White Mountain in 1620 and later at Nördlingen in 1634.[37] The economic cost of war was severe not only on the domestic exchequer but also on British ships and private wealth caught on Spanish territory. Reprisals had extended to include the confiscation of all property held in private hands and from February 1627 they also targeted subjects of the kingdoms of Scotland and Ireland on account of the fact that their ships had been found carrying English goods.[38] At the same time, the costs of war created crises of indebtedness for Spain. Defaults entailed the transfer of burdens onto bankers and meant a compulsory rescheduling of debt.

The revolution and civil war which rocked the British Isles after 1642 did not much alter imperial rivalry with Spain. The War of the Three Kingdoms and subsequent Cromwellian Republic (1642–60) were accompanied by redoubled rivalry with the Spanish empire beyond Europe. The period 1638–60, according to one recent study, witnessed British commerce and power projection into the Spanish sphere of global influence, beginning the Anglo rise in Atlantic history and ushering in Spain's slow imperial decline.[39] During this period, the Anglo-Hispanic colonization of the Americas shared a Christian world view and sense of mission, which contrasted with the stark differentiation of the religious cold war in Europe. British Protestants and Spanish Catholics resorted to similar biblical justifications for holy violence and conversion during their dual conquest of the New World. Unlike Asiatic powers, neither Spaniards nor Britons had to worry about invasions from rival empires on their borders: only the 'savages' of the New World who would be converted, civilized and settled into European life.[40] The presence of Anglo-Hispanic colonizers, whether malign or benign in temperament, served as a model for the ideal colonized subject and an aid for Old World dominance. The shared view of the native was repaid in kind by the attitudes of the Indians, the vast majority of whom remained outside of the colonial power networks and dealt with the Old World only fleetingly. William Dampier, the English pirate and circumnavigator, recalled an incident at the Panamanian isthmus in the winter of 1684–5 when some Indians were taking a share of loot from a seized Lima galleon: 'Here an *Indian* Canoa came aboard with three Men in her. These Men could not speak *Spanish,* neither could they distinguish us from *Spaniards;* the wild *Indians* usually thinking all white Men to be *Spaniards*.'[41]

But in Europe, the distinctions between Spanish and British policy and culture were plain to see. Britain's outcast status as a regicidal republic (1649–60), cast Anglo-Hispania as continued counterpoint, when not outright enemies. Spain's relative decline in world affairs during the seventeenth century also shifted British geopolitical anxieties.

Seventeenth-century Spanish anxieties about England were not just political and imperial in nature, but also scientific. Spanish commentators were aware how the more industrious northern Europeans were applying discoveries in science to project power and commerce. The playwright, Jerónimo de Barrionuevo (1587–1671), upon learning of an innovation in English warships that threatened to make them even more formidable, commented laconically that 'human ingenuity can do anything'.[42] But Spaniards were also spared much of the political turmoil attendant upon Britain's mid-century. Lettered men like Saavedra Fajardo (1584–1648) and Solórzano Pereira (1575–1655) defended a sort of Habsburg consensus, vehemently opposed both to notions of absolutism coming from France, and to the strong state *Leviathan* advocated by Thomas Hobbes (1588–1679) in the wake of the execution of Charles I.[43] Seventeenth-century Spain may have been characterized by a weak central government and by a class of reformers agonized over the causes of, and remedies for, its decline. But its political stability was enviable when compared with the chaos of the Thirty Years' and English civil wars.

Oliver Cromwell, anti-Catholic victor of the War of the Three Kingdoms (1642–51), remarked how his focus on the power of Spain had blinded him to the rise of France. The ending of the Fronde revolt inside France around 1653 encouraged Louis XIV to seek a treaty with the English republic against Habsburg threats from Spain and the empire. Cromwell was happy to oblige, given the security of his Dutch ally and the threat he feared Spanish Catholicism posed to Protestant settlers in North America. Cromwell considered Spain in Elizabethan terms as possessed of immense real and potential wealth in the Americas with which to thwart Protestantism. He also feared Spain as a focus for plotting from England's tiny Catholic minority. He worried that clandestine English Catholic priests were being 'Spaniolized' and cultivating an enemy within. Thus, in November 1655, an Anglo-French defensive treaty was signed. Louis XIV's (at this time) toleration of the French Protestant minority gave Cromwell a clear conscience.[44] Cromwellian veterans of the civil wars allied with the French in defeating Spanish forces in Dunkirk at the Battle of the Dunes (1658), neutering the Spanish privateering threat to merchant shipping and what had been a royalist threat to penetrate the English republic.

The restoration of the monarchy in Britain in 1660 led to a series of pro-French policies. But the tilt towards Versailles rankled with Protestant notions of limited royal power. Enraged Whig opinion prevailed in 1688 when a new limited monarchy led by William and Mary replaced the absolutist pretensions of James II (1685–88). The Williamite monarchy in 1690 even joined in an alliance with Spain and most European powers against French expansionism. Spain had thus long fallen from the pedestal of beloved enemy in the Protestant imagination. The eighteenth-century growth of Francophobia in Britain displaced older Hispanophobia. 'Church and King' patriotism was centred on England but was mapped out across the rest of the British Isles. It took on an accelerated form amidst a thriving press culture and frequent wars with France.[45] The unification in 1707 of England and Scotland into a single state reinforced Britain as a Protestant great power, in strategic competition with France. Even though Spain had long since fallen from its role of England's chief antagonist, the country had a key role to play in British unification itself. The War of the Spanish Succession (1700–14) bonded English and Scottish troops together as veterans in the Habsburg cause, completing a military union even before the Scottish Parliament dissolved itself in Edinburgh and reconvened 400 miles south in London.[46]

Spain's Succession War thus eased the process of British unification, despite largely unexplored opportunities open to continental protagonists to divide and rule. The Scottish presence at Darién in Central America did not incline the Bourbons towards dividing and ruling their policy towards Britain.[47] Meanwhile an Anglo-Scottish veterans' union was pre-empting the political version. Ambitious Scots sought service in English regiments, like during the Nine Years' War (1688–97), which meant that the English and Scottish officer corps was already partly integrated before the Act of Union of 1707.[48] The unified Britain, which the Scottish ruling dynasty had long sought, became a reality, in a context of Anglo-Scottish comradeship in foreign wars and shared views of the Spanish empire. Scotland's ill-fated attempt at establishing a colony in the

Panamanian isthmus, the Darién scheme, was couched in the same moralistic and self-confident terms of English colonialism. A Scottish pamphleteer wrote that the Spaniards could not dispute the establishment of New Edinburgh because the local Dariens 'are in actual possession of their Liberty, and were never subdued, nor received a Spanish governor or garrison amongst them'.[49] Scottish Protestants feared the overbearing power of Catholic Spain as much as their southern royal neighbours. The failure of the scheme, and the ruinous losses it inflicted on Scottish investors, sweetened the pill of the Anglo-Scottish union in 1707 when London agreed to revalue the Scottish pound and some of the national debt.

The War of the Spanish Succession and the revival of the Anglo-Habsburg alliance

The War of the Spanish Succession (1700–14) in most respects resembled the 'cabinet wars' which dominated eighteenth-century Europe. In the eighteenth century, considerable investment was placed in the individual soldier, which ensured that European generals sought wherever possible to avoid battle and to win their campaigns by manoeuvre. In the War of Spanish Succession, for example, there were only about a dozen major battles. Yet 100 later in the Napoleonic Wars, there were at least forty major battles.[50] But even if the military character of the Succession War was unexceptional, its political impact for Britain and Spain was profound. It bound both powers together internally and externally and established a tradition of Spanish campaign memoirs in English.

When the childless King Charles II of Spain died in 1700, he offered his throne and possessions in the Netherlands, Italy and the Americas to Philip of Anjou. Philip was the grandson of Louis XIV, the king of France, Europe's greatest power. Other European powers were alarmed at the prospect of a Bourbon alliance of crowns. But England had the most to fear in terms of global policy from the prospect of a unified Franco-Spanish Bourbon monarchy, preferring instead the 'Habsburg model' of a weak central power. England, Holland, the Holy Roman Empire and Prussia supported a rival claimant to the Spanish throne, Archduke Charles, the younger son of the Habsburg emperor, Leopold I. The ensuing 'Grand Alliance' turned Iberia into the most protracted theatre of war, along with more concentrated battle-fronts along the Rhine and Danube. In many ways this War of Succession would be Spain's first internationalized civil war. Neither the Bourbon nor Habsburg claimants had been brought up in the Spanish court, and matters of bias and alliance politics led both men to surround themselves with foreign courtiers, French ones in the case of the Bourbon Phillip, and English, Dutch and German in the case of the Habsburg Charles.[51]

Spanish historians have tended to sideline the international dimension to the War of Succession, focusing instead on the way the Bourbon victors fundamentally reshaped Spain's political organization. More recent research on the war has tended to historicize the modern-day regional autonomy question, especially with regard to the defeat of Habsburg Catalonia in 1714.[52] Spanish unification proceeded more violently than in Britain. And British campaigners in the doomed cause of the Habsburgs were certainly impressed by the division in Spain between a pro-Habsburg periphery and a solidly pro-Bourbon Castile. James Stanhope, commander of British forces in Spain, remarked in 1706 that

> the continent [sic] of Spain is now divided into parties, as formerly into the crowns, of Castile and Aragón. All the latter we are possessed of; and, I believe, the provinces which compose it would be very well pleased to continue thus separated. But this is the thing in the world we ought to fear the most; since such a division would render Spain perfectly insignificant in the balance of Europe.[53]

Britain's alliance with Austria gave London a leading role in Mediterranean operations, bequeathing a strategic post-war gain with the award of Gibraltar in the Treaty of Utrecht (and thereby British control of the passage between the Mediterranean Sea and Atlantic Ocean). Despite the enduring British hold on Gibraltar, and the shorter-lived gain of Menorca, the English-language historiography has mostly studied two features of the war. It has concentrated first on the successes of John Churchill, Duke of Marlborough, along the Rhine and Danube, consigning the less glamorous Spanish campaign, in the words of one recent book on the subject, to the role of 'Marlborough's other army'[54] and second on the ways in which the war accelerated Britain's 'fiscal-military' state and domestic political divisions. The Whigs were more enthusiastic in their prosecution of the war against Louis XIV. The Tories, who had a minority Jacobite wing, were more ambivalent. They won the general election of 1710 with the aim of ending the war by accepting the Bourbon Philip V as King of Spain. This policy attitude doomed the pro-Habsburg Catalans whose resistance depended on Britain's naval support. The Tories ended Britain's participation in the war, but in doing so they lost control of its posterity. The Whig view – that the war was justified as a bid to halt Louis XIV's ruthless expansion – was accepted by subsequent historians, mostly markedly by George Macaulay Trevelyan (1876–1962). Otherwise, the Spanish side to Britain's grand struggle against Louis XIV lived on in literature. The late-nineteenth-century historical novelist, George Henty, included the War of the Spanish Succession in his nationalistic repertoire of British fighting in Spain.[55]

Britain's role in the war in Spain

Soon after British forces landed in Spain in support of the Habsburgs, they were met by a century-and-a-half of cultural alienation caused by the mutual black legend of Anglo-Hispania. Their chances were not helped by the notorious arrogance expressed by the Habsburg pretender towards his putative Spanish subjects. The 14,000 Anglo-Dutch troops who landed around on Cádiz in 1702 were defeated militarily. The Protestant allies dithered while the Spanish Bourbon defence mobilized cavalry and militia. But even without Bourbon resolve, the invaders' cause was not helped by the behaviour of their troops in Puerto de Santa María. Looting was expected behaviour by occupying armies, but the defacing of Catholic churches outraged civilians and acted as a rallying cry for the Bourbon militia, ending all hopes that an invasion might promote popular support for the Habsburg cause. Attempts by the Allies to entrench themselves around the coast were ineffective, and on 30 September 1702, five weeks after the disembarkation, the Allied troops withdrew to the sea once more.[56]

While Spanish civilians were enraged by heretical invaders, the war in Europe found its echo in Britain's public sphere. Print culture disseminated the Black Legend by attributing to Spain itself the cause of its ills. One English sermon in January 1705 reflected little on the immediate cause of the war, preferring instead to preach the historic 'cruelty' of Spain as witnessed in the Inquisition and its behaviour in the Indies as causes of the civil war.[57] English propaganda efforts emanated from Jamaica to Bourbon-held Cuba and mainland Spanish America, offering bribes and protection for governors to join the Habsburg cause. Spanish Americans, pamphlets alleged, would be subjected to French tyranny in the event of a Habsburg defeat.[58] In 1709, the Bourbons banned the import and circulation of an indigenous-language Bible which had been published in London and which intended to waylay 'simple Indians' and turn them away from 'the true religion'.[59]

English efforts foundered in Spanish America, and they made little headway in Spain itself. The Anglo-Dutch attempt to establish 'Carlos III' was proving difficult beyond coastal areas of Spain where the Allies' naval superiority could be brought to bear. Even Barcelona, finally seized for the Habsburg cause after an English-led siege in autumn 1705, had proved a difficult conquest.[60] The seas offered better chances. The Anglo-Dutch fleet scored a resounding victory at the Battle of Vigo Bay on 23 October 1702. A huge Spanish treasure convoy was intercepted, and the entire French and Spanish fleet either captured or destroyed. British-led forces seized Gibraltar in 1704. The strategic value of this rock on the Andalucía coast had long been mooted in seventeenth-century England. The English loss of Tangier in 1684 (which had been awarded to Charles II in 1661 as a Portuguese dowry) raised the attractiveness of the rock, and there were several discrete but influential voices (such as naval administrator, Samuel Pepys) in favour of seizing Gibraltar through fair means or foul.[61] The Allied assault which Sir George Rooke ordered on 2 August 1704 was therefore more than mere opportunism. The Spanish garrison commanded by Diego de Salinas amounted to only 100 men. Despite Salinas offering stiff resistance, English troops managed to climb the rock on its unguarded eastern face and to overwhelm the small Bourbon force. After Salinas surrendered with full military honours, the Allies left behind a garrison of 2,000 troops and sailed in search of more targets.[62]

But targets proved hard to secure the further inland Protestant troops ventured. An Allied march on Madrid in 1707 met with despondency at best and outright hostility at worst from the Spanish population. As an English commander confided to his senior, Lord Stanhope, in 1706, 'Assure yourself, that in Castile there is a most violent spirit against us, which appears to a degree that could not be believed'.[63] Even the Habsburg littoral remained insecure for the Allies. The kingdom of Valencia had been in turmoil ever since the anti-seigneurial rising of the *maulets* in 1704. The English occupation of the city of Valencia on 4 February 1706 was a form of counter-revolution, as a pro-noble viceroy accompanied the Allies to replace the pro-peasant, Juan Bautista Basset y Ramos.[64] Soon afterwards, the English commander, the Earl of Peterborough, was recalled to England, his reputation tarnished by suspicions that he was out of sympathy with the Habsburg cause in Spain. His downfall became a proxy for partisan rivalry between dovish Tories and hawkish Whigs. Five years of war had made Spanish affairs a domestic fault line in English politics.

Peterborough's unease at the indifference, or outright hostility, displayed by the Castilian population towards the Habsburg cause was exacerbated by the Spanish use of irregular tactics. In fact, Spain's enduring reputation as a seat of guerrilla warfare begins with the War of Succession, not the more famous Peninsular War (1808–14). The inability of the Allies to sustain large armies over protracted times made irregular tactics like ambush more attractive. During the Allies' retreat from Madrid, Castilian villagers grew alienated by the army's demands for provisions. But in marginal agricultural areas, like most of Castile, contractors failed to source sufficient local supplies. The pillaging of armies thus produced a major backlash that expressed itself in the outbreak of a savage guerrilla war. At the village of Campillo de Aragón, enraged locals massacred wounded soldiers from the Coldstream Guards. The Allies inculpated the local priest, hanging him at the door of his own church.[65]

While the Allies campaigned across Castile, Philip V's Spanish realm faced financial turmoil. The loss of the treasure vessel at Vigo, combined with the cost of war, led Philip V to rely increasingly on French arms and money for Spain's defence. The year 1706 had thus marked an *annus horribilis* for the Bourbon cause in Spain, with cities across Catalonia, Aragón and Valencia having fallen to the Allies. To the loss of Gibraltar in 1704 was added Barcelona in 1705, and Alicante, Ibiza and Mallorca in 1706. Bourbon attempts to recapture Barcelona were defeated. An English captain, George Carleton, managed to rally some retreating troops outside the city; reinforcements and supplies flowed incessantly into the city, and even a solar eclipse on 12 May 1706 was celebrated as 'the demise of the Sun King' (Louis XIV).[66] War, mobilization and commitment to their liberties had made Barcelona the centre of Habsburg gravity in Spain. But Habsburg fortunes did not last.

The Anglo-Scottish political union of 1707, marked an *annus mirabilis* for the Bourbons. An English attempt to seize the southern French port of Toulon failed – at the cost of the Bourbons scuttling most of their Mediterranean fleet. But landlocked Castile remained unconquered. Even though British naval control of the eastern Spanish seaboard guaranteed a safeguard for an Allied presence of some sort in Spain for the rest of the war, there were no navigable rivers permitting the landing of supplies and men in Castile.

Even worse for the Allies, on 25 April 1707, five months before their naval success at Toulon, their armies suffered a decisive defeat at Almansa (Albacete). The Bourbon victory at Almansa in 1707 rescued Philip's cause. The Duke of Berwick used his cavalry brilliantly. Even though an English-led counter-attack against the Spanish right flank almost succeeded, the Bourbons carried the day. The defeated Allied infantry could not keep pace with its cavalry in retreat, and barely 800 escaped death or capture. The Allies also lost all their baggage and all their twenty-four cannon.[67] The defeat was decisive for the Habsburg cause in Spain. Within a month of Almansa, the Duke of Berwick cleared virtually all of Valencia and Aragón of Habsburg control. The Bourbons began the task of imposing Castillian law onto these territories at the same time as a peaceful union between England and Scotland was established which respected the latter's different legal system.[68] The defeat was politically controversial in Britain. The Westminster Parliament debated why only 8,000 British troops were available to fight at Almansa, even though Parliament had approved an army of 29,000 to be sent to the Iberian Peninsula.[69]

Two years later, on the sanctified 5 November commemorating the defeat of the Catholic 'Gunpowder Plot', the entangled Anglo-Hispanic religious rivalry returned in the symbolism of sectarian politics. A High Tory Anglican clergyman provoked riots with a sermon attacking the supporters of the pro-war Whig party. Henry Sacheverell's sermon waxed furious at the dissenting Protestants represented by the Whig party and in the presence of thousands of Calvinist war refugees from Germany, but said very little about the old enemy, the Catholicism represented by Spain.[70] Whig attempts to prosecute Henry Sacheverell increased the tension to such an extent that in spring 1710, the Tories won a landslide in that year's general election, and Queen Anne replaced her Whig administration with one led by Tories.[71] The advent of the dovish Tories to power set the scene for a scaling back of British commitment to the land campaign in Spain and a concentration on cheaper and more lucrative naval warfare.

Meanwhile, only the fortified towns of Denia, Alicante and Xàtiva held out for the Allies. Whereas the former two could be resupplied by sea, Xàtiva was overwhelmed after a bitter siege and a brutal onslaught. Surrendered English troops were killed indiscriminately along with many civilians. And Xátiva was erased in the mass expulsion of its inhabitants and its renaming as San Felipe in honour of the Bourbons.[72]

After Almansa, Catalonia seemed poised to fall to the Bourbons. But threats to Louis XIV's eastern borders caused the withdrawal of Bourbon troops, especially during 1709, which gave the Habsburg forces a second wind. This opportunity was exploited by Lieutenant-General James Stanhope, Peterborough's replacement as commander of British forces in Spain. Stanhope was a cultural Hispanophile as a result of having spent his youth in Madrid. As he was the grandson of England's ambassador, he got acquainted with Spanish language and culture.[73] In 1706, he was appointed British plenipotentiary to Habsburg Spain, which enabled him to promote British commercial interests. He tried to emulate the advantages which Britain had secured in Portugal in 1703, most importantly via access to Spain's American markets.

Anglo-Hispania and the Habsburg rally

Fresh from capturing the island of Menorca in September 1708, Stanhope plotted to take advantage of Louis XIV's withdrawal of troops from Spain. In the summer of 1710, he led an Allied advance on Madrid. The city had been occupied once before – by the Portuguese in 1707 – but neither this occupation of the Spanish capital, nor its repeat in 1710, could persuade Castilians to yield to the Habsburg claim. Stanhope would discover, like many other conquerors before and since, that seizing Madrid could never induce the sort of despair in the country that the capture of Paris or London might in France and England respectively.[74] As Lord Stanhope's descendant and biographer remarked in the 1830s,

> In Spain it was shown in the War of the Succession, and again more lately in our own times that the possession of the chief city is of scarcely any avail either to the foreign enemy or to the native partisan. Twice did the archduke Charles three times did Joseph Bonaparte advance in triumph towards Madrid and as often did they learn that it is one thing to seize the Castle in capital and another thing to subdue the Castilian people. Thus what in France is the consummation of conquest with the Spaniards is hardly its commencement and thus under every possible disadvantage from wretched armies wretched generals wretched laws and wretched governments they have maintained will continue to maintain their independence.[75]

The British impression of Madrid being incidental rather than vital to the outcomes of war in Spain persisted into the twentieth century. Madrid, as the British poet, W. H. Auden, put it during another Spanish civil war two centuries later, was 'the heart (of Spain), but to keep it beating it had to exercise the sinews of modern warfare'.[76]

During the spring of 1710, James Stanhope visited London where he urged a greater British effort in Spain. By the summer, Allied forces in Catalonia finally matched those of the Bourbons, and offensive operations resumed. On 27 July 1710, at the Battle of Almenar (Lleida), the Bourbons were ousted from Catalonia. The Allies occupied a more elevated position with the sun at their backs on a very hot afternoon. The battle involved about 30,000 troops on both sides, as well as the presence of both claimants to the Spanish throne. Stanhope's victory allowed his cavalry to pursue the Bourbon retreat to Madrid.[77] Stanhope accused his subordinates of waiting too long to support his cavalry thrust that day, and of frustrating his plan to destroy the Bourbon field army.[78] But his campaign progressed nonetheless, capturing Zaragoza on 21 August 1710 and clearing Aragón of Bourbon control. Stanhope had hoped that the civilian population would now rally to the Habsburg cause. But this was not to be. As he complained in a letter of 4 July 1710, 'We expected an insurrection in Aragón, and that the enemies would have followed us, and marched out of the country; but neither is happening, and on the contrary, the enemies applying their thoughts to intercept our convoys'. The universality of popular resistance to foreign invaders left Stanhope in despair: 'I am sorry to say that we have very few deserters, and of those few hardly any are Spanish; and, from all that we can learn, we have good reason to be persuaded that nothing but force can dispossess … the Castillians'.[79] Ordinary British soldiers drew their own conclusions about the differences between the Castilians and their French allies. Spaniards acquired a brave and fanatical reputation amongst British veterans, at odds with the supposedly sophisticated, yet also bombastic and cowardly French. The shorthand British troops used for describing Spaniards as 'Dons' sounded less contemptuous in their ears than 'Monsieurs' describing the French.[80]

Even though the Allies rallied in 1710 with a new offensive through Aragón into Castile, the civilian population remained hostile. The Allies' capture of Madrid in 1710 was the high point of the Habsburg campaign in Spain. The presence even of the Habsburg pretender, Charles III, could not raise much public spectacle beyond the natural curiosity of the capital's street children. James Stanhope, British military commander and now plenipotentiary of Charles of Austria, tried in vain to curry favour with the capital's notables. In September 1710, he moderated an order to delegitimize all banknotes bearing the Bourbon seal of Philip V. Instead, their value would be honoured at the 1700 rate, the year of the last legitimate Bourbon king and before the onset of wartime inflation.[81] It was to no avail. The hostility of elites increased once Charles III expelled from the capital nobles who refused to switch their allegiance. The announcement of the death penalty for any expellee returning to the capital, combined with news of outrages committed by 'heretical' troops at religious sites, lost the Allies any hope of collaboration.[82] This poor impression, combined with the Allies' overextended supply lines, caused a crisis in the Allied command. Stanhope demanded an aggressive campaign to link up with his Portuguese allies in the west. The Allies still had the Bourbons on the back foot. Any enemy counterattack against the Allies' supply lines along the Pyrenees would be negligible anyway, as the rigours of winter forced troops to live off whatever they found in situ. The Portuguese forces lay around 200 kilometres west, at Almaraz (Cáceres). But a breakdown in alliance politics robbed Stanhope of his opportunity to link up with the Portuguese and cut Bourbon Spain in two.

Instead, the Bourbons manoeuvred to seize Almaraz and its bridge, pushing the Portuguese to withdraw towards their own frontier. Charles III ordered a general retreat from Madrid. At Brihuega (Guadalajara), the part of the Allies' retreating force commanded by Lord Stanhope was defeated and forced to surrender. While the British troops rested in the town, they were suddenly surrounded and outnumbered by Bourbon troops. The British fortified Brihuega, but they had no artillery, and the wall around the town was dilapidated. Bourbon superiority in cannon eventually broke the stubborn British defence, despite Vendôme's troops being bloodily repulsed in their first wave.[83] The surviving British troops surrendered just a day before a Habsburg vanguard arrived at Villaviciosa de Tajuña, only 5 kilometres from Brihuega, and mauled the Bourbon army. The Allies could not hope to keep the field in the wake of Stanhope's disaster. The name of Brihuega echoed in British military legend and even inspired a commentary by Ernest Hemmingway during the Spanish Civil War.[84] Despite the Allies' tactical victory nearby, the strategic result was a disaster and a withdrawal towards Catalonia.[85]

The Allies' turmoil thereafter was relentless. A strong position in Catalonia at the very least might have held indefinitely. The British navy controlled the Mediterranean in the wake of Toulon, and the Catalans saw in the Allied side their best hope for preserving their traditional liberties. But the death of the Habsburg emperor on 17 April 1711 changed strategic calculations. As the pretender, 'Charles III of Spain', was now also heir to the Habsburg crown in Vienna, the Allies were about to run the risk of replacing a domineering Franco-Spanish Bourbon monarchy with an overbearing Austro-Spanish Habsburg version. With the governing Tories in Britain keen on a compromise and secret peace feelers to the exhausted French bearing some fruit, the stage was set for Allied disengagement from Spain. During the peace talks of 1711, the French dominated Spanish affairs, thinly disguising their interest by claiming that Philip V's resolve in protecting his Spanish crown in war would be honoured also in peace. In any case, by 1711, Spain's war had embraced the popular classes: Spanish troops were forming the lion's share of the effort against the Allies in Spain.[86] The British-led counter-campaign, by contrast, had become the inverse of Napoleon's efforts in Spain a century later. The Allies dominated the seas and support in the Catalan-Valencian littoral. But the landlocked Spanish interior was dominated by Castilian power.

For the Allied powers, a Habsburg union of the Spanish empire with Austria seemed hardly preferable to a Spanish union with France. Britain, especially, was worried at the prospect of Habsburg domination in Europe and the Americas. By 1713, the Treaty of Utrecht ended the war between the Bourbon and Habsburg sides. British prisoners held at Burgos at the conclusion of peace could not believe the news that their government had agreed to a peace settlement which denied the Habsburg claimant the Spanish throne.[87] Early British impressions were disappointing. Viscount Bolingbroke, who led the British party to peace negotiations, commented that 'Gibraltar and Port Mahon (Menorca) will be all we have left to show for those immense sums which have been expended, and for that blood which has been shed, in those parts'.[88] Philip V was recognized as legitimate king of Spain and emperor of Spanish America. But he relinquished his claim to the French throne and Spanish territories in the Low Countries and Italy. Portugal retained its colonies and Britain retained Gibraltar, Menorca and significant trading rights with Spanish America. But the civil war in Spain was not yet over. One of the most remarkable features of the Habsburg war effort was its recourse to propaganda, especially printed pamphlets. One Bourbon riposte jibed that the archduke might have ended up with a much enlarged army if his printing budgets had been diverted towards munitions.[89]

The Allied newsreading classes were enervated in kind. Their abandonment of the Catalan cause led to rancour both in Barcelona and amongst pro-Catalan commentators, mostly Whigs, in Britain. Strong anti-Bourbon sentiment persisted in Catalonia owing to the violations of local laws under Viceroy Velasco, and the knowledge that the English and Dutch consumers were the best markets for Catalan textiles and spirits. Similar economic and anti-French reasons mobilized British public opinion behind Catalonia. A surge of pro-Catalan literature blanketed the coffee houses of London. One commentator, Michael Strubell, touched a nerve by publishing his *Deplorable History of the Catalans*. Strubell opened his invective shaming the newly unified Britain which, in its supposed love of liberty, had seen fit to abandon the liberty-loving Catalans to their fate: 'the very Revolution of the Barcelonians, looked at first so mad and desperate ... that their enemies flattered themselves that the first Bomb thrown into the town would frighten them into submission, but the World has a fresh Instance of the influence of Liberty upon generous Minds'.[90]

The Catalans fought on, despite the Anglo-French peace of 1713. The siege of Barcelona began on 25 July 1713. While the lower classes decided to resist, the nobility and the clergy went over to the Bourbon side. This radicalized the resistance even more, giving it airs of secessionism, if not inchoate republicanism. After nearly fourteen months of siege, on 11 September, after the death of thousands and the destruction of a third of the city's buildings, the city surrendered. The death of Queen Anne on 1 August 1714 came too late to effect a change in official British attitudes towards the Catalans. Even though Anne's successor, King George, Elector of Hannover, was more sympathetic, his attention was distracted by a renewed Jacobite attempt on the British throne in 1715. Barcelona was finally captured on 11 September 1714, a date hallowed in

Catalanism as the 'Diada'. The conquering Bourbons treated Barcelona harshly and stripped the city and the principality of most of its autonomy. A large citadel was built in Barcelona in 1715–18, which thereafter became a symbol of Bourbon oppression looming over the teeming city below, as well as an impregnable fortress against both attack and insurrection.

Thus the Anglo-Hispanic turmoil of the early eighteenth century resulted in the unification of the respective polities. Although Catalonia, as part of the kingdom of Aragón, had been linked to Castile as early as 1478 by the Union of Crowns, Spain like Britain contained features of being composite kingdoms.[91] Only Ireland and the Basque country remained outside the direct rule of London and Madrid for the rest of the eighteenth century, possessing the potential, if not always the reality, of self-rule via a Protestant Parliament in Dublin and the 'fueros' sworn in at the Tree of Gernika.

In Britain and Spain, the threat of regional backlash against centralization was solved respectively with the Anglo-Scottish Act of Union of 1707 and the Nueva Planta decrees of Philip V. The territories of the Crown of Aragon (Aragon, Catalonia, Valencia) underwent legal unification through the decrees of the *Nueva Planta*, (1707–16), contemporary to the Act of Union of Scotland and England. On the one hand, Scotland, unlike Catalonia, possessed a heritage of independent statehood.[92] But on the other hand, Jacobitism in Scotland (which in any case was unionist in theory if not in deed) never achieved the degree of support that *austracismo* had managed in Catalonia and Aragón. For all the actions in Spain, a hidden truth lingered on the British side of this Anglo-Hispanic entanglement. The War of the Spanish Succession was in many ways a second war of the British succession. An outright British defeat would probably have led to the restoration of the Jacobite line and a protracted civil war in the British Isles involving Spanish intervention. As recently as 1689, Britain had faced a major Jacobite revolt, and another followed peace in 1715.

England and Scotland were united even though Scotland's separate legal and religious structure was unaffected. The Bourbon victory in Spain, by contrast, suppressed much of Aragón's legal and political autonomy. It allowed the gradual militarization of the Spanish monarchy, including an increase in the intensity and regularity of conscription.[93] The War of the Spanish Succession also left a modernizing military impact in Britain. It helped the British regular army evolve from being little more than a royal bodyguard in 1660 into a major 'continental' army. In the words of Saul David, 'the British redcoat played a key role in his country's rise to greatness, (winning) no fewer than three great conflicts against France – the War of the Spanish Succession, the Seven Years'

War and the Napoleonic Wars – in just over a hundred years'.[94] Standing armies were celebrated again, in contrast to the previous century's upheaval of civil war and revolution, and Britishness became more martial in nature. National culture esteemed military values and archetypes, which would persist in times of peace.

Britain, as 'sole winner' of the 1701–14 war according to one diplomatic historian, secured strategic victory in the War of the Spanish Succession.[95] Britain gained Gibraltar, the coveted 'asiento' monopoly on the slave trade with Spanish America, and an enduring great power status in continental diplomacy. Yet, the stated aim of preventing a Bourbon occupying the Spanish throne eluded the Allies. The subsequent Anglo-Hispanic century was marked by a mutual rivalry and suspicion, along with a British travel boom in Spain inspired in part by the war, as the subsequent chapter shows.

3

Eighteenth-century Anglo-Hispania

The peace following Spain's Succession War lasted only a few years. The War of the Quadruple Alliance (1718–20) pitted Bourbon Spain against Britain and other major powers. A Spanish invasion of Britain in support of a renewed Jacobite rising failed as the exiles and Spanish troops landed at Stornoway proved too few and naval support was scattered in stormy weather.[1] The peace of 1720 left the Hanoverian regime in Britain intact and strengthened via a modern cabinet system of government. Robert Walpole's long premiership (1721–41) established a stable parliamentary system which combined some of the best parts of limited monarchy and representative government. In the words of a leading historian of eighteenth-century Britain, 'A nation once considered barbarous for its political instability was in the process of acquiring an enviable reputation of mature self-governance.'[2] Political stability unleashed a new era of conspicuous consumption. In 1714, the Anglo-Dutch philosopher, Bernard Mandeville, published *The Fable of the Bees*, a controversial thesis arguing that the 'private vice' of luxury and consumption led to the 'public virtue' of prosperous, orderly societies. Mandeville contrasted the progress of the English and Dutch, the latter of whom resisted 'Spanish Tyranny and Fury' during the era of Philip II, stress-testing their water-logged republic for future prosperity.[3]

Just as the Succession War had energized public opinion in Britain, that same Tory–Whig divide attained a relevance in the diplomatic affairs of continental Europe which would last over two centuries. Britain's advanced public sphere, with all its proclivities for shaping, changing and reshaping government policy, was often misread as unreliability in absolutist Europe. 'Perfidious Albion' grew as a motif for Britain as a self-interested ally or underhanded enemy. Meanwhile, the devastation caused by the war to Spain itself drove Philip V to make imperial trade concessions to the French as well as the British. Ultimately, his successor (Ferdinand VI, 1746–59) would set in trail the 'Bourbon reforms', which reduced the power of the church and imposed more efficient fiscal reforms and Iberian control in the Americas, aiming to increase revenue for the Spanish monarchy.[4]

The Treaty of Utrecht in 1713 granted Britain the coveted *asiento*, or contract, to supply a defined number of enslaved Africans to the Spanish Americas for a thirty-year period, along with a limited number of manufacturers to the annual Portobello market. It was conferred upon the South Sea Company which was headquartered in London with an outpost in the River Plate. The Atlantic had become a constantly shifting ocean of competition, linking metropolitan powers with protected markets and slavers along the African coast. Exaggerated hopes of new markets led to the bursting of the 'South Sea Bubble' in 1720. In practice, the asiento empowered provincial British ports like Liverpool which were already booming on the back of Britain's apogee in the slave trade in the first half of the eighteenth century. During the eighteenth century, the international slave trade broke new grounds in horror, as one of humanity's oldest industries was turned into a mass commodity by Europe's technological and commercial advances. British interest tilted across the Atlantic as the vast Spanish empire became a focus for British perceptions. The asiento also offered new opportunities for illicit British trade with the Americas.[5] One British captain in 1731 petitioned Prime Minister Walpole for an expansion of trade and colonies into Spanish lands, casting the incumbent overlords in contemptuous terms:

> Are we not a powerful People upon a fine Island? Is there a maritime power on the Globe that we need to fear? ... Spain may justly boast of Possessions in the Indies, for their Extent and natural Luxuriancy ... But what effects have these advantages had on her People? The Priests had made the People zealous and very superstitious, and such vast Wealth made them supine, indolent, careless and inactive.[6]

Excepting the asiento, the Spanish colonies in the Americas were formally all but closed to British trade. Beyond this, however, a whole universe of smuggling thrived around the Spanish American coastline as the demand for British manufactured goods soared amongst the criollo elites. The British pressed free trade as a means of penetrating rival empires. But Spanish policy understood 'free trade' largely as a means of creating an internal market for the benefit of the metropole. Even though Spain during the second half of the eighteenth century tried to bind its American empire more firmly to the motherland via a series of political and economic measures of the Bourbon reform era, these failed to dent criollo appetite for smuggled British goods. Spanish industry remained stunted by weak domestic markets, expensive capital, poor communications and poor productivity in the face of British competition. In 1724, the Spanish economist, Jerónimo Uztáriz, published his *Theory and Practice of Commerce and Maritime Affairs* which attacked generations of poor policy. Foreigners, according to Uztáriz, had been allowed to monopolize the commodities trade, scuppering Spanish industry and stunting maritime trade.[7]

The century thus beckoned in an economic cold war of Anglo-Spanish rivalry. The War of Jenkins' Ear (1739–48), so named because of the drawn-out recriminations following Spanish coastguard actions against a British smuggler in 1731 (and known in Spanish as the more anodyne 'War of the Asiento'), merged into the wider War of the Austrian Succession that would end in 1748. Commercial rivalry and pressure from economic interests in Britain allied with xenophobic public opinion in pushing a divided Parliament and cabinet towards war.[8] But the war of the severed ear was launched with high hopes from the British side. Penetrating Spanish America promised to counteract Bourbon gains in central Europe in the wake of the War of the Polish Succession (1733–5). War also inspired the providential wishful thinking common to Hispanophobic opinion of the era. The British public sphere abounded with opinion articles predicting a 'grateful' criollo population awaiting liberation and share of the 'rights' of Englishmen, along with plans to reroute the long-distance trade galleons operating between Cádiz, Lima and Manila via London instead.[9] British strategists hoped to secure Cuba and even Panama, where a Royal Navy seaman foretold that Spain's benighted subjects would 'bless their deliverers; their hearts and mines [sic] would be opened up to us'.[10]

In the event, the war proved indecisive. Spain failed to champion a Jacobite rising in Britain which, during 1745, showed brief promise of capturing London. In the aftermath of war, Britain's rights to the asiento were replaced with compensation and the award of different trading privileges. Anglo-Hispania would not come to blows again until Spain joined the first global war of 1756–63 on the French side. The final Hannoverian defeat of the Jacobites sent streams of compromised families into exile, including to Spain. The defeated Gordon clan left the Scottish highlands in the wake of the Hannoverian victory at Culloden (1746). By 1754, the Gordons had set up a sherry business in Jérez (Andalucía), generating an export-oriented industry geared towards British markets which thrived amidst war and anarchism over subsequent generations. Almost half of Spain's long eighteenth century (1700–1808) involved Britain either as an enemy in war or as an armed interventionary in civil war. As a consequence, thousands of Spanish prisoners of war saw out the intermittent conflict in so-called parole towns in Britain, which were mostly, but not exclusively, coastal settlements and fortresses. Whereas ordinary soldiers and sailors spent their captivity in prison hulks (pontoons), officers were given parole to remain in towns and to travel within a 1-mile radius. Sometimes officers achieved permission to travel further afield and to substitute their modest allowances with local employment. The British commissioners (known as the 'Sick and Hurt Board') were more concerned with Spanish contact with fellow French captives than with local civilians.[11]

The Seven Years' War entangled British and Spanish empires foremost. This conflict, more than the later French Revolutionary and Napoleonic Wars, lay claim to being the first and uniquely global in reach. The Seven Years' War turned Europe's colonies in the New World, Asia and Africa into a battlefield, on occasion, even *the* main battlefield. Spain initially remained neutral. The fall from power of several pro-French ministers at the outset spared Britain the enmity of France's most powerful ally. But by 1761, increasing British contraband and privateering along the Spanish American coastline decided Carlos III's hand. The 'Family Compact' affirmed a renewed Franco-Spanish alliance and Ambassador Edward Clarke, Earl of Bristol, left Madrid. From Britain, Clarke published an analysis of his embassy which offered sober reading for his countrymen now at war: 'Our trade with Old and New Spain is full one third less than it was about forty years ago, and the balance and exchange between Spain and Great Britain are more and more turning against the latter kingdom'.[12] The reasons, Clarke affirmed, lay in French encroachments on British import markets since the advent of the Bourbons, Britain's self-defeating greed in selling products at high prices, along with Spain's own advances in industry sustained by its lower labour costs.[13]

Clarke's anxieties would have come as a surprise to Spanish commentators. Spain's poor military performance during the remaining two years of the global conflict unleashed a series of military reforms and political soul-searching. In 1762, British troops disembarked in Cuba and captured Havana, managing to hold the island's capital against a counter-attack launched from Santiago, despite endemic disease decimating their ranks. But most of the island remained in Spanish hands, and peace negotiations over the course of 1763 saw the British happy to relinquish Havana in return for the cession of Florida. But the capture of the Cuban capital gave a warlike emphasis to the so-called Bourbon reforms in the empire after Cuba was returned to Spanish rule. The military imperative emboldened Spanish reformers at court and ushered in a generation of improvements in commerce, fortifications and army organization.[14] British prowess in 1762 inspired imitation of the Anglo model. During 1762, a series of political pamphlets under the title of *Estafeta de Londres* cast a shrewd eye towards the formidable enemy. Hoping to return Spain to the Golden Age of the fifteenth and sixteenth centuries, the *Estafeta* editor, Francisco Mariano Nifo, pleaded for an emulation of British economic models, including canals, welfare reforms, industrialization and improvements in ploughing techniques.[15] But the Anglophobic logic of the Bourbon alliance was unshakeable.

Spain's unsuccessful participation in the Seven Years' War led to British gains in the peace of 1763. Spain yielded Florida to Britain and granted rights of navigation in the Mississippi in return for the return of British conquests in Cuba and the Philippines. Carlos III's chief minister, Jerónimo Grimaldi, was annoyed at Britain's untrammelled commercial ambition and resented Spain's poor showing in the recent war. 'The English', he commented to the British ambassador, 'are an enterprising nation, and have views of commerce which cannot be borne'.[16] British merchants continued to be an open secret in Spain's empire. In 1787, the Inquisition in Mexico published an English-language catechism designed to help British converts to Catholicism.[17]

British attitudes, meanwhile, continued to be steeped in the Black Legend, albeit with Enlightenment philosophy mixed in. The Enlightenment liked to typecast Spain as an obscurantist counterpoint. Spain's outsized colonial expansion in the Americas seemed less a symptom of Spanish vitality and more a cause of Iberia's political and economic decline.[18] Spain, so eighteenth-century enlightened thinkers believed, had a culture of disdain for manual work. Joseph Townsend (1739–1816), a critic of the public provision of welfare, toured Spain between 1786 and 1791 and looked askance at the generous welfare offered by Spain's bloated Catholic church. Beggars were treated with 'excessive generosity', the bishop of Córdoba donating bread on a daily basis to 7,000 people.[19] Spain, Townsend thought with a kind of Malthusian logic, was proof that welfare was debilitating unless organized by workers themselves and that workers needed to work. The endemic view of 'lazy' Spaniards impressed more by honour than labour persisted in the eighteenth century. But archival research has shown that Spanish artisans were not particularly lazy or backward when compared to the rest of Europe.[20]

Only when foreigners travelled to Spanish America did they evince Iberian achievement. The Prussian scientist, Alexander von Humboldt, was an enlightened opponent of slavery. But contemporary racism led him to remark on the superiority of Spanish culture in Venezuela in 1800: 'settlers ... develop and strengthen in man the sentiment of liberty and independence; and give birth to that noble pride of character which has at all times distinguished the Castillian race'.[21] Europeans from all corners of the old continent felt superior in foreign climes. The 'constitutive other', which divided Anglo-Hispanic perceptions in Europe, united against pre-Columbine populations in the Americas.

The French Enlightenment philosopher, Montesquieu, was fascinated by British liberty and contrasted it with Spanish obscurantism. Montesquieu's *Spirit of the Laws* argued that climate, religion, laws, government and popular customs forge national character. Warm Spain placed its character in some ways in the positive realm of vivacity, passivity and sociability, unlike the dull and drunken northern Europeans. But other signs were ominous of what Montesquieu called the Inquisition-prone and priest-addled country: a warning of what 'goes wrong' when monarchs refuse to embrace the Enlightenment. Spain, according to Montesquieu, presided over the Western world's first intrinsically barbaric empire, which became the counter-model of a modern commercial society and a fanatical rejection of science. Whereas Voltaire believed that the Enlightenment could cure fanatics, Rousseau reserved a role for violence for destroying fanatics who refused to be 'free'.[22] Spain remained an implacable symbol of fanaticism. The significant reformist element in Spanish Catholicism was overlooked. The war against Napoleon placed reformist clerics on the wrong side of public opinion. Even more in Spain than in the rest of Europe, the French Revolution virtually eliminated the religious Enlightenment, while later attempts to rehabilitate the Enlightenment barely extended into the clerical sphere.[23] As Joseph Clark explains, 'the spectral figure of the fanatical cleric inciting his flock to revolt, "the crucifix held aloft in one hand and the dagger in the other", became a staple of political speeches, press reports and even sermons in 1792'.[24]

Eighteenth-century writers liked to dwell on the decline of empires. The idealized ancient Greek and Roman empires attracted growing fascination throughout the century. Eighteenth-century British readers, too, were fascinated by the works of Hume, Gibbon, and in the Spanish case, William Robertson. Literate readers invested time and concentration in lengthy tomes of scholarship, challenging themselves in moral and pedagogical ways, and committing their insights to marginalia, commonplace books and debate.[25] Foreign writers were less charitable about the decline of Spain. But the long economic and demographic decline of the seventeenth century, especially in the Castilian tableland, indelibly shifted foreign attitudes of Spain's poverty. As one late-eighteenth-century French traveller commented, 'any other traffic than that in wine and olive oil carried on the backs of mules and asses from one province to another ... and grain on beasts of burden'. The poor infrastructure, Bourgoing concluded, meant that 'materials needed by the factories, merchandise which passes from the frontiers and ports to the interior is almost always transported by the same slow and consequently expensive means'.[26]

Abbé Raynal's 1770 study of European trade with the Indies, a work which was widely read in Britain, criticized Spain for its backwardness. It accused Spain's empire of leaving no great economic, intellectual, cultural or scientific legacy.[27] Eighteenth-century British writers, particularly such Scottish Enlightenment figures as David Hume and Adam Smith, explained the paradox of a declining Spain in Europe in charge of a vast, and in some cases, expanding empire abroad as the product of outdated bullionism (preoccupation with owning precious metals) and mercantilism (restricting imports and maximizing exports). The Spanish empire remained trapped in cycles of inflation and weak credit markets. The vast wealth of the Americas thus remained poorly exploited.[28] By the eighteenth century, European intellectuals were excoriating Spanish backwardness but also American torpor and lethargy.[29] This cosy view made the vastness of a territory stretching from California to Patagonia all the riper for Anglo conquest.

Unlike the British monarchy's fiscal-military state, war disturbed the Spanish monarchy's attempts to improve revenue streams, not least because of Madrid's aversion to taking on public debt.[30] This internal market remained too small to encourage the virtuous cycle of economic growth. The Spanish empire, unlike the British colonies in North America, failed to secure inalienable property rights. Trade was monopolized, public offices sold and taxes corruptly farmed. Spain was unable to take advantage, therefore, of a critical historical juncture – the opening of the Atlantic to trade. Stagnation then spiralled into economic decline, whereas the British empire flourished on the Atlantic trade on the back of property rights and more inclusive institutions.[31] Only comparatively recently has the Spanish empire gained a more positive appraisal. Most historians now reject the pre-twentieth-century 'black legend' of economic backwardness, identifying instead a series of structural changes that paved the way for the dramatic modernization which Spain has experienced in the course of the past century-and-a-half.[32] Even so, no power could rival the efficiency of Britain's national debt in the eighteenth century. Even British defeats in the Americas could not dislodge the power of London. The independence gained by Britain's thirteen colonies, in part thanks to the intervention of Spain, did not disrupt the fiscal-military state.

Spain's role in Britain's defeat was vital. A Franco-Spanish fleet sailed up the English Channel, and Gibraltar was subjected to a lengthy siege. For three-and-a-half years (1779–83) the rock was blockaded from land and sea by Franco-Spanish forces. Water could be secured but bread was almost unobtainable, and meat, fish and vegetables were in short supply. The Spanish besieging forces in the Campo de Gibraltar did not bother to bombard the British, and instead relied on starvation to take its course. A British eyewitness recalled the mouth-watering frustration at seeing 'the Spanish hills covered with cattle, while we can scarce procure a piece of salt beef, and that at a price'.[33] A daring resupply effort led by Admiral Rodney succeeded in 1780, helping to stave off the worst of privations, and Gibraltar remained in British hands amidst so many other losses in the peace treaty of 1783. But British observers barely credited Spain's role in the defeat. Robert Watson's *History of the Reign of Philip II* was published at the end of the American Revolutionary War in 1783. It tacitly compared British intransigence towards the just demands of the Americans with the attitude of Philip II towards the rebellious Dutch. Even in defeat, the old Hispanophobic trope in British patriotism was reaffirmed.[34]

Spain's eighteenth-century rally

The publication in the Panckouke encyclopedia in 1782 of an article entitled 'Espagne' typified the general disdain held by Enlightenment thinkers north of the Pyrenees towards Spain. Curiously, the reaction of Spanish intellectuals to this negative image both hardened their sense of belonging to a community of 'Spain' and increased the appeal of British, rather than condescending French, civilization.[35] Despite the instinctive Anglophobia of Carlos III (reigned 1759–88) and British views of the peril of the Franco-Spanish 'Family Compact', British travellers who ventured to Spain were impressed by elements of progress which belied the general Black Legend. The English penal reformer, John Howard (1726–1790), considered Spanish prisons in Andalucía favourably in terms of their provisions, cleanliness and productive employment. A prison near Cádiz harbouring petty criminals impressed Howard as to its hybrid form of welfare:

> A number of men were at work also as tailors and carpenters, whilst fifty of the boys at least were under instruction in the school; so that the *lazy* Spaniards, as we are apt, with our national superciliousness, to call them, here set an example of training to habits of industry the idle and the dissolute, from which the *notable* English might learn a very useful lesson.[36]

British travellers who made it to Madrid were immediately reminded of the gin alleys and squalor of their capital city's own East End. But the Enlightenment zeal of Carlos III's reign left a deep impression on visitors and writers alike. William Coxe, an Anglican clergyman and historian, during the early nineteenth century, published a positive appraisal of recent Spanish history. But he stopped short of the generation of turmoil in which he was writing. He halted his narrative with the death in 1788 of the enlightened monarch, Carlos III, for 'the death of Charles in itself forms an epoch; because it took place at the very moment when that tremendous revolution began, which changed the face of continental Europe, altered the characters of nations and of individuals, and swept away the established institutions of moral and political society'.[37]

Spanish intellectuals, for their part, towards the end of the century, tended to approve of Britain's constitutional settlement. The greatest Enlightenment philosopher, Gaspar de Jovellanos (1744–1811), was influenced by British travellers and a friendship with the British consul at La Coruña, Alexander Jardine, even before the culmination of Anglo-Spanish collaboration of the Peninsular War.[38] But the geostrategic differences between the Spanish and British empires persisted, bestowing a binary relationship of resentment and predation. The British 'fiscal-military state' created for London a virtuous cycle of imperial and economic expansion. The Spanish monarchy, by contrast, continued to suffer a weak internal market which rendered war a burden rather than a boon.[39] Britain's view of the Spanish empire as a vast pool of untapped resources dictated a foreign policy aimed at getting even more access to the markets of the Hispanic world.[40]

Birth of travel literature

Spain's rustic and backward reputation marked it out as a special destination on the margins of the burgeoning market for travel literature in eighteenth-century Britain. But most British gentlemen performing the Grand Tour of the continent stayed north of the Pyrenees. This aristocratic tourism left Madrid off their itineraries of Paris, Rome and the Alps. When the aristocrat, Thomas Pelham, made an unusual tour of Iberia in 1775, he recorded making so many precautions 'as if he were going into Arabia'.[41] As Black Legend historian, William Maltby, noted, people in the Anglophone world 'rarely had an opportunity to discover that their notions of Spain and Spaniards were erroneous'.[42] But the exotic and excoriated land of the Christians and Moors was finally beginning to corner a market of its own. Henry Swinburne (1743–1803), a Bristolian Catholic of independent means, in 1779 published his *Travels through Spain, 1775 and*

1776. It was the first English antiquarian study of Spain and was refreshingly devoid of the affected and high-cultural priorities common to accounts of the Grand Tour. For all his admiration, Swinburne also expressed patriotism upon passing into Gibraltar, 'the honest pride of Englishmen, in admiring the tall, handsome figures, and spirited, martial presence of the soldiers, and in drawing very comfortable parallels between them and the dirty melancholy dwarfs we had seen mounting guard in the Spanish garrison'.[43]

Even British defeats in the Americas could not dislodge the power of London. Mandeville's Anglo-Dutch vision of a conspicuously consumerist society unfolded much less in Spain than on the shores of the North Sea. But knowledge of British culture and fashion came to Spain anyway, if not through the presence of hardy travellers, then via French tastes which dominated Spanish elite culture by the late eighteenth century. British fashion, which tended towards the elegant and comfortable, reached Spanish consumers, as did knowledge of English landscape gardening.[44]

Britain's invasive commerce with Latin America was further complicated by the fact that Spain herself remained a large trading partner: in the 1780s, Spain had been Britain's fifth largest continental trading partner, and Britain was Spain's largest customer.[45] Other cultural exchanges followed the growth of trade, contraband and war. Illicit smuggling or prisoners of war became the face of Britain in Spain during the repeated wars of the eighteenth century.

Richard Croker was captured off Cape St Vincent in 1780 and paroled near Arcos de la Frontera. His Spanish hosts regarded him and his compatriots with wonder for their failure to observe the siesta: 'the English, addicted to their habits in every climate, eat beef and drink wine at three o'clock, to the astonishment of the Spaniards, who say proverbially, that no animal, except an Englishman or a mad dog, would expose themselves to the mid-day heat of such a sun'.[46] Travellers from northern Europe, like Richard Ford and Alexandre Dumas, attested to the scarcity and bad quality of Spanish food, as if nutrition were an extension of the Black Legend.[47] If the oily garlic fare did not unsettle British stomachs, then the experience of travel across uneven roads did. Spain's roads had been either neglected or merely repaired until Carlos III, in the 1760s, mandated the gradual creation of a radial network centred on Madrid.[48] When Arthur Young, agriculturalist and travel writer, ventured into France from the Catalan side of the Spanish frontier, the contrast for him was striking:

> When one crossed the sea from Dover to Calais, the preparation and circumstance of a naval passage, leave the mind by some gradation to a change:

but here, without going through a town, a barrier, or even a wall, you enter a new world. From the natural and miserable roads of Catalonia, you tread at once on a noble causeway, made with all the solidity and magnificence that distinguishes the highways of France. Instead of beds of torrents you have well-built bridges; and from a country wild, desert and poor, we found ourselves in the midst of cultivation and improvement.[49]

The frontier areas close to supposedly more advanced territories created first impressions to British visitors. Amidst the Castilian hegemony in most of Spain, some British travellers showed interest in the surviving autonomy of the Basque country. The juridical and political organization of Biscay attracted the attention of Edinburgh writer John Geddes, who in 1792 published a Baskophile account:

> The Biscayans have among them a constant tradition, that their Señores or Lords ... drew their origin, at least by the female side, from Scotland. ... So that there is not perhaps any part of Europe, where more true and genuine liberty, without licentiousness, is enjoyed, than in the *Lordship* of Biscay, the *Province* of Guipuzcoa and the *County* of Alava, which all three are united together, and go under the general name of Biscay. This people have a very ancient custom of holding their general meetings for treating of their public affairs in the open fields, under a large tree near to the town of *Guernica* ... Every Biscayan is declared to be an Hidalgo or Gentleman, and to have all the privileges belonging to such, not only at home, but even throughout all Spain. ... Whatever order comes from the King, is to be examined in a junta or meeting of the Biscayans, and if it shall appear to them to be contrary to their liberties or privileges, it is to be received, indeed with all due respect; but not to be put into execution.[50]

By contrast, Spanish travellers to Britain wondered at the modernity of London and large provincial cities. The comedic playwright, Leandro Fernández de Moratín (1760–1828), remarked the 'formidable British navy' in a port near London, whose sight made it impossible 'to ignore its mastery of the oceans and domination of trade ... quite apart from its fame in battle'. The capital city, Moratín remarked, was crowded with such comforts and objects of wealth that the contrasts were all the more striking. Scenes of public drunkenness, unthinkable as routine street culture in Spain, shocked Spanish visitors. Inevitably, London's swaggering eighteenth century bred an ugly side to the British character which Moratín recorded as 'pride, the original sin of the English, so stubborn and incorrigible', which was bred of their knowledge of their superiority over their neighbours.[51] British pride would be tested to its extremes from 1792, when a generation of conflict with France engendered a war effort of a sort that had not been seen in any of the fighting of the eighteenth century. Both the army and the navy had to be raised to a strength that was absolutely unequalled, and this in turn implied an unprecedented demand for arms and munitions.[52]

As relations deteriorated during the episodes of hostile neutrality and outright war between 1795 and 1808, Anglophobic texts gained wider circulation. Britain was generally blamed for breaking the Peace of Amiens (1802–3) and for the invidious position into which renewed Anglo-French hostilities placed Spanish interests. Pedro Estala, cleric and literary critic, in 1807 published his *Four Letters from a Spaniard to an Anglomaniac*, attacking the pernicious corruption of the British parliamentary system and its hoax claims to represent popular rather than just monied interests. For all Britain's industrial and commercial achievements, Estala indicted Britain for egging on the Habsburgs in 1700, thereby making Spain's devastating Succession War possible, sowing discord across Europe and for predatory views towards the Americas. Estala dedicated his invective to the 'noble and generous citizens of Buenos Aires', recently triumphant against two failed British amphibious invasions of the River Plate.[53]

Few in Spain could imagine that within a year Britain would become a vital ally against Napoleon's treachery. Carlos IV (reigned 1788–1808) still thought he had his own version of William Pitt in the form of Manuel de Godoy, Spain's all-powerful prime minister.[54] But Godoy, a scion of an impoverished but old Extremaduran noble line, made enemies easily, most ominously in the person of Prince Ferdinand, heir to the throne. The burden of war and armed neutrality sent inflation surging amidst rural disorder and natural disasters. The British Hispanist, Richard Ford, attributed Spain's nineteenth-century ills to this 'blasphemy of such a creature … a foul beast of prey (to whom) Spain owes the impoverishment of her hospitals and charitable institutions, whose funds he seized, giving them government securities, which proved worthless, and while none were benefitted save courtier sharks'.[55]

Britain's illicit inroads into the Spanish American economy during times of war and peace appalled Anglophobes like Estala. The situation was radicalized by Britain being the only power with the global reach and economic interest to affect the cause of Spanish American independence. Spanish American rebels like Francisco de Miranda (1750–1816) leveraged British hospitality and help by offering commercial treaties in return for formal military assistance.[56] Even without hostility towards Spain, the Latin American markets were permeated with British commerce. By the end of the eighteenth century, a quarter of all British exports went to the West Indies, primarily to Spanish America.[57] The re-export trade across southern Spain, combined with outright contraband, led to Spanish America receiving more than a fifth of all British exports. Britain thus enjoyed unrivalled access to Latin American markets even without independence. As one historian noted, 'Spain kept the cow and the rest of Europe drank the milk'.[58] In times of peace, Britain would not risk alienating a major European trading partner in order merely to formalize an American trade monopoly that it already possessed. Paradoxically, Britain's informal commercial domination served both imperial powers. British interest in Spanish America could be described as benign neglect, as long as powers other than Spain or Portugal did not show ambition in the same hemisphere.[59] Thus, as John Lynch argued, 'it would be an exaggeration to say that British trade undermined the Spanish empire'.[60] But in times of war, Spanish colonies – like their French counterparts – became targets for the world's most formidable navy. Britain and Spain were more often at war with each other over the course of 1795–1808 than they were at peace. The difference this time was the emergence of a Spanish-American autonomy movement which was eager to enlist outside help against the overbearing rule of Bourbon Spain.

Pitt's death in 1806 and Miranda's escape to London on board a Royal Navy vessel augured a more muscular British intervention against Spain's empire in the Americas. Miranda persuaded Arthur Wellesley, later Duke of Wellington, to assemble a force in Ireland tasked with sailing to liberate Venezuela. But the main British efforts lay in the South Atlantic, and even the Ireland force ended up being diverted – ironically to Iberia to support Spanish Patriots in the wake of the surprising events of 1808. In 1810 Spanish Americans revolted anyway, even without British support. But Spain failed to secure from the British anything more than an offer of mediation in the post-1810 Spanish American revolt. This 'Perfidious Albion' posture led to enduring Spanish mistrust of Britain, even when the Anglo-Spanish alliance forced the French out of Spain in 1814. The Spanish liberal politician, Álvaro Flórez Estrada, combined a mean-spirited view towards the Spanish American revolutionaries with a suspicious attitude towards his British allies. He criticized the Spanish Americans for letting down the peninsular motherland by supporting ambitious despots and defended the racist exclusion of Blacks and Indians from new voting rights which Spanish Patriots granted the empire in 1812. The British, for their part, were to blame for their obvious financial interests in Spanish American independence and for the utterances of much of their press.[61] The question of America would be a new barb in Anglo-Hispanic relations at the start and close of the new century.

4

The Peninsular War and its aftermath

The Peninsular War (1808–14) opened a 'short' nineteenth century for Spain. Bounded by two foreign wars, the first causing devastation at home and, indirectly, in Spanish America, and the second (1898) stripping Spain of its remaining pretensions to world empire, the nineteenth century was marked by war, revolution and counter-revolution. It was spawned by the impact of the French Revolution and the rise of Napoleon, a period of trauma which robbed Spain of its eighteenth-century Bourbon alliance and made its own progressives more progressive and its much larger number of traditionalists reactionary. The Peninsular War (known in Spain from the 1830s as the 'War of Independence') snatched away Spain's world-power status whilst also guaranteeing her conflicted future. These six years etched indelible marks in French and especially British political and cultural identity. In Spain, these years bequeathed the fault lines of 170 years of subsequent history: from the national and international image of guerrilla warfare to the founding myths of incompatible Left *versus* Right claims to national identity, from the origin of the stereotypical 'Two Spains' to the decades of military interventionism in modern politics which would culminate in the civil war of 1936–9.

From a British point of view, the Peninsular War might seem merely a footnote (albeit a large one) in over a century of Anglo-French struggle. But this bird's eye view would miss a more profound entanglement arising from a generation of young men who served in the only protracted British land campaign during the French Wars of 1792–1815. Over the past four decades, a wealth of studies has placed the experience of the British soldier in his late-Georgian context, as well as his privations and adventures on campaign in Iberia.[1]

The fact that the acclaimed Spanish irregulars had to do so much of the fighting from the outset was due to the fact that the war lacked an opening front line. Rather, Napoleon's troops had peacefully occupied Spanish roads, cities and fortresses as part of the Franco-Spanish alliance against Portugal in 1807.

Thus, these armed men were in an excellent position to turn treacherous once Napoleon made the decision to overthrow the Spanish royal family. Amidst simmering Francophobia in the spring of 1808, the first major clash against occupation came in Madrid on 2 May. The uprising of the Dos de Mayo (1808) ensued after rumours flew around the capital, a crowd congregated outside the palace and panicked French troops opened fire on a crowd that threatened to outnumber them. Forced by the French into violence, ordinary people spontaneously took to arms against the 30,000 French troops stationed in Madrid. This uprising would cost the lives of 413 civilians in combat, including about 100 killed by Murat's draconian practice of executions after his troops re-established control.

The Second of May ushered in what one historian called an 'exaltation of Spanish identity', cherishing its possibilities in the manner of Romantic poetry rather than being a single-minded xenophobic rage against the French.[2] Even though the Madrid rising was bloodily crushed, further risings (mostly targeting real and imagined Spanish traitors) took place over the summer. Soon the Spanish 'Patriots' claimed provisional authority, the allegiance of what remained of the Spanish Army establishment and a crucial alliance with Britain. The Peninsular War produced a generation of British involvement with Iberian affairs. Apart from the commitment of Britain's only available field army, London also bankrolled its Portuguese and Spanish patriot allies. Britain in 1810 paid for 25 per cent of all of Portugal's expenses, along with such other supplies as food, camp equipment, uniforms, weapons, artillery and forage besides.[3]

The Spanish insurrection of 1808 presented itself both as a model and as an opportunity for British progressives and Romantics. On the one hand, the Patriot resistance to Napoleonic imperialism inspired a generation of Hispanophile writers and travellers. On the other hand, the war in Spain attracted Britain's only major army fighting on the European continent. Britain's peninsular campaign was the classic example of what Basil Liddel Hart called the 'British way of warfare', namely the reliance on naval superiority and the despatch of regular troops or mercenaries as a form of 'indirect approach' (basically choosing far-flung theatres of operations that promised to offer less resistance).[4] But the Peninsular War also opened a generation of veteran experiences of war in a campaign which was gruelling and protracted by British standards. This Napoleonic invasion contrasted the Romantic and imagined Spain of Anglophone culture with the grim realities of battle, privation and campaign. The war left behind a legacy of Anglo-Hispanic protagonists and veterans, including such transnational figures as Lord Holland, Xavier Mina, John Downie and Blanco White.

The Peninsular War was Britain's first great literary conflict. The number of books published in Britain about Spain grew from only forty-two between 1801 and 1808 to almost three hundred during the reign of Ferdinand VII (1808–33), the vast majority of which dealt with the Peninsular War.[5] Its story was told not just through campaign memoirs but also through a rich afterlife of novels, including those by the prolific Victorian writer, G. A. Henty. The author of a long series of historical novels that attained great popularity, Henty first turned his attention to the Peninsular War with the publication of *The Young Buglers*, a tale of how two young British schoolboys enlist in the army as buglers and are eventually promoted to the rank of ensign, and then charged with a mission of liaising with the Spanish guerrillas.[6] For almost a century after Henty's heyday, most British histories of the conflict tended to be Anglo-centric homages to Wellington, with a cursory or even dismissive attitude towards the Spanish Patriots. As recently as 1975, one historian could justify focusing entirely on the French and British participation with such a disclaimer as: 'It is important to remember that behind all the maneuvers and battles lies the Spanish contribution to victory, its all-pervasiveness and fragmentation making it impractical to describe it in detail.' Wellingtonia (adulation of the British commander-in-chief in Iberia) and Hispanophobia sometimes overlapped. As recently as 2008, one popular British author of Wellington's campaigns lauded the British, respected the French and either excoriated the Spaniards or damned them with faint praise.[7]

Spanish war memoirs, by contrast, did not experience the boom of their British or even French counterparts. But where they existed, Spanish memoirs were as likely to be written by irregular *guerrilla* veterans as regulars, and Patriot accounts of all kinds were careful to justify the politics of their authors in the context of Spain's political tumult of the first half of the nineteenth century as well as awkward questions of collaboration with the enemy.[8]

The pull of a Romantic Spain and its attraction to a generation of British literary icons remains a source of fascination for historians. The trope of a brave but poorly governed Spanish population persisted amidst nineteenth-century British writers. An 1830s historian of the War of Succession (1700–14) asserted that Spaniards in the early eighteenth century were 'a brave people with a wretched government … the same observation holds good with respect to the last Peninsular War'.[9] Romantics and political progressives saw in Spain a whole people rising up in defence of liberty and seeking, in the process, to overhaul ossified institutions. Some well-heeled intellects visited the Patriot capital of Cádiz, and some Britons went further still. About forty men of British nationality were so inspired by the example and opportunities of the Patriot cause as to obtain commissions in the Spanish Army.[10] But probably about a thousand times this number of volunteers died in action in the British Army fighting in the peninsula. The common soldiers of Wellington's army were different volunteers, motivated by hunger, unemployment or repression rather than the idealism and opportunism of a handful of social elites. Nonetheless, the dual reality of a Romanticized and idealized Spain played out in the minds of literati and Whig debating societies, and another brutalized and agonizing Spain, experienced by the 160,000 British soldiers on campaign, speaks to a new reality in Anglo-Hispanic interactions. The aristocratic gaze of eighteenth-century travel literature was now joined by a plebeian narrative of blood and suffering, some of which found its way into letters and autobiographies.

One of the first British officers to enter Patriot Spain was Charles Leslie, who passed through the south-western town of Ayamonte when his brigade was en route from Gibraltar to Lisbon in June 1808. The euphoria of the new Anglo-Spanish alliance was remarkable: 'the Spanish officers, both of the army and navy, almost crushed us in their fraternal embraces and insisted on carrying us from house to house and introducing us to all the pretty ladies in the place'.[11] Soon afterwards, the elegant port city of Cádiz became the safest port of entry for British dignitaries assessing the prowess of their sudden ally against Napoleon. The city had become prosperous and outward looking ever since 1717, when it gained the monopoly for all Spanish trade with the New World. The learned Member of Parliament, William Jacob, on a visit in September 1809 was impressed at the beauty and prosperity of the capital of Anti-Napoleonic Europe:

> The splendour of the scene of the bay of Cádiz filled with the vessels of different nations displaying their various colours against a forest of masts. The whiteness of the houses, their size and apparent cleanliness, the magnificence of the public edifices and the neat and regular fortifications form together a striking assemblage of objects.[12]

Cádiz became the focus of British Hispanophilia. Spain's War of Independence impacted the British literary imagination like no other. As historian, Henry Kamen, has observed, 'military intervention, together with sympathy for Spanish exiles ... stimulated appreciation for Peninsular civilization and gave a push to English creativity'.[13] For the Irish Whig playwright, Richard Brinsley Sheridan, the Spanish Patriots were wielding as a weapon the principles of the French Revolution against the dictator who betrayed them. William Jacob thought that Spanish indolence, once roused to anger, could not be vanquished: '(despite) the indolence which a warm climate and the consequently luxurious habits produce ... The Spaniards are brave, acute, patient and faithful, but all their characteristics are insulated, all their exertions ... individual'.[14] Romantic poets such as Robert Southey and Lord Byron would soon praise the exploits of the guerrillas. They did so from the safety of the Patriot capital of Cádiz which, apart from occasional long-range bombardment from French forces entrenched across the bay, retained a lively carnival and politicized atmosphere, far removed from the privations of the Spanish mainland.[15] Particularly captivating was Agustina Zaragoza y Domènech (nicknamed Agustina de Aragón), a kind of Patriot Joan of Arc celebrity whose decisive moment of local heroism during the Napoleonic siege of Zaragoza helped prolong resistance in the doomed city. The poet, Lord Byron, dedicated a verse to Agustina replete with notions of women transgressing their roles into the military sphere, embodying a people's war:

> Is it for this the Spanish maid, aroused,
> Hangs on the willow her unstrung guitar,
> And, all unsexed, the anlace hath espoused,
> Sung the loud song, and dared the deed of war?
> And she, whom once the semblance of a scar
> Appalled, an owlet's 'larum chilled with dread,
> Now views the column-scattering bayonet jar,
> The falchion flash, and o'er the yet warm dead
> Stalks with Minerva's step where Mars might quake to tread.[16]

Patriot Spain attracted the attention and sometimes the visits of a generation of young writers. The leading Whig politician, Henry Vassal Fox, Lord Holland, toured Spain with his wife during the chaos of 1808. Lord and Lady Holland incredibly chose to travel through the country amidst the upheaval of French invasion. They remained a few weeks in Seville, at the time the headquarters of the Patriot Junta Central, where they met the greatest Patriot intellectual (and from January 1810, leading member of the Patriot Council of Regency), Gaspar Melchor de Jovellanos, and the emerging circle of young liberals who were keen to use the war to reform Spain. The couple saw in the torment a chance for a liberal and free Spain to emerge from the ruins and became confirmed Hispanophiles for the rest of their lives.[17] Visitors to wartime Spain blended their ascendant Romantic style with a vision of a forthright, ungovernable and valiant Spanish people which influenced literate opinion in Britain and exalted Spain and things Spanish in post-war British Romanticism.[18] The spread of Patriot guerrilla warfare unleashed a militant variant in the Anglo imagination. Many liberals in both Spain and Britain, such as the poet Robert Southey, romanticized the partisans.[19] English society ladies wore small lockets adorned with the pictures of prominent guerrilla commanders.[20] Stirring posters and flyers, which dominated the public sphere in Patriot Cádiz, found their way into the British press and further afield.

The war opened up opportunities for renewed appreciation of Spanish arts. The works of the seventeenth-century painter, Diego Velázquez, were largely undiscovered by British aristocrats performing the French and Italian 'Grand Tour'. Yet the looting and smuggling caused by the passage of European armies across Spain during 1807–14 affected the works of masters like Velázquez along with minor works.[21] Their baroque otherworldliness compounded the Romantic view of Spain which had already gripped Britain in the wake of the Patriot guerrilla phenomenon. Friedrich Schiller's play, *Don Karlos* (1783–7), perpetuated the Black Legend in Europe and inspired a nineteenth-century opera version by Verdi. Spanish guerrillas were pleased to exaggerate their heroic exploits, or to see them exaggerated by British admirers in art and press form, especially when constant references to the ill-preparedness and ill-trained nature of the Spaniards served only to magnify their achievements.[22] The theme of Spain as a frontier of civilization reasserted itself as British officers on campaign bemoaned the lack of accurate maps and as the precious supply waterways offered by the rivers Duero and Tagus had to be dredged for the first time. A British artist enlisted as an ensign in Spain in 1813 marvelled at the country's landscape and architecture, 'making military surveys trigonometrically of such portions of the country as were accessible; and also in taking sketches of the most remarkable scenery'.[23]

The war in Spain also provided opportunities for self-interested men to flourish as front lines shifted, and Patriot authorities were willing to believe tall stories in the hope of victory. John Downie was born in 1777, the third son of a modest Scottish landowning family. After making his fortune in the West Indies, he ingratiated himself with Francisco Miranda and joined an ill-fated attempt to liberate Venezuela. Following Miranda into exile in Britain, Downie rebuilt his fortunes serving in a humble position in the British Army. But the advent of the Peninsular War gave him renewed chances to escape humdrum commissary duties by engaging in valuable reconnaissance duties along the Luso-Spanish border. He acquired great fame and public recognition after hyping up a single act of suicidal heroism, and he managed to gain the begrudging recognition of Wellington and eventually even a commission. His grandiloquently titled 'Loyal Extremaduran Legion' ('Leal Legión Extremeña') ended up behaving like

Downie's private army.²⁴ Snubbed by Wellington and running out of options once most of the Spain was liberated in 1813, Downie made a visit to Britain in 1813 where he declared himself depressed with regard to the obsession with the Allied triumph at the Battle of Leipzig. The Britons, he complained to the Cádiz press, now judged the Russians rather than the Spaniards to be the true victors of Napoleon, an attitude which ignored Spain's poor preparedness for war in 1808 and Britain's inadequate help since then.²⁵

But the real impact was not made by such opportunistic Britons as John Downie nor by the artists, but by hard-pressed soldiers. The original British intervention came from Portugal in the form of an army led by General John Moore. But Moore's outnumbered force was pushed back into Galicia, where survivors were evacuated from the port of La Coruña. Reinforcement of the Anglo-Hispanic effort was difficult. The year 1809 was that of a crisis for the state of the British Army, not just because of the retreat from Spain of General Moore's army, but also in the wake of the defeat in the Walcheren Expedition and the deleterious effect of malaria from the Dutch marshes upon Britain's manpower. After the disasters of the Spanish and Walcheren campaigns of 1809, many of the first battalions were incapacitated, and so second battalions were sent to reinforce Britain's stronghold in Portugal. The British Army tradition of sending one regiment battalion overseas whilst feeding it drafts from a second battalion at home could not be maintained. The continual supply of drafts made many of the second battalions small and inefficient, a situation that worsened when first battalions were campaigning for any length of time. This structural challenge was compounded by the absence in Britain of conscription for overseas service. The situation would have been impossible if the Spanish Patriots had not continued the fight, if a viable Portuguese Army had not been forged on the British model and if the British reinforcements sent to the peninsula had not been assigned to the command of a defensive military genius, Arthur Wellesley, later Duke of Wellington.²⁶

The only reliable link in the Anglo-Hispanic effort lay at sea. Cádiz remained secure with seaborne supplies and Lisbon became the main supply port for Allied armies.²⁷ But British domination of the seas did little to overcome the same problem experienced during the Succession War a century earlier. Overland logistics foundered on the poor physical and social geography, made worse in wartime as civilians starved amidst the pillage and requisitioning of Napoleonic armies and foraged lumbering baggage trains. George Simmons, a rifleman in Wellington's army, noted how 'our Spanish friends infested every road for miles and robbed the peasantry who were bringing bread and vegetables to us for sale'.²⁸ British soldiers suffered almost constant starvation rations, averaging just over 2,000 calories, a quantity inadequate for constant marching and fighting. The only advantage in the constant war for food was that the Napoleonic forces were starving even more. The logistical quandary affected not just food, but also artillery trains. Wellington's army made a virtue out of a necessity of being able to field only modest artillery and soon developed innovations (such as shrapnel shells and rockets) as well as the defensive use of topography in order to maximize firepower. But some requirements were immune to innovation. Wellington's siege train remained weak, making Allied sieges of fortified cities even longer and bloodier than they might otherwise have been.²⁹

The apocalyptic nature of war-torn Spain hardly commended itself to cordial relations between British and Spanish allies. A British unit marching through a war-torn mountain village witnessed the reduction of local women to prostitution. As an officer in the King's German Legion recalled, the place was 'Sodom and Gomorrah, where the girls and women of the higher as well as the lower classes were practically all disreputable. Pure virgins were rare.'³⁰ British military or civilian followers were often barred from hospitals and the dead excluded from burial in hallowed ground because they were assumed to be heretical Protestants. As more than a third of the British Army was recruited in Ireland, a common and plausible ruse was to claim that the casualty in question was Catholic.³¹ Soldiers and civilians alike were caught in a hellish trial of survival. Spain beyond the hubbub of Cádiz became a tortured and starved wasteland, riven with prowling armies, Patriot guerrilla bands who behaved little better and civilians subjected to brutal Napoleonic reprisals.

The Gothic suffering of Britain's major ally made profound impressions on literate soldiers. For the first time, large numbers of British visitors arrived as 'soldier-tourists'. As Gavin Daly has shown, several Britons identified with the plight of brutalized civilian populations and identified with the vengeful motives of guerrilla chiefs citing murdered family members.³² But many other British diarists of the Peninsular campaign thought Spanish atrocities were a product of an inbred Catholic intolerance rather than an understandable response to Napoleonic reprisals. The strains of alliance warfare and 'Black Legend' prejudice echoed in British memoirs speaking of 'ungrateful' Spaniards, and of a nation that was 'barbaric', priest-ridden and picturesque.³³ Traditional alliance with neighbouring Portugal did not spare Lisbon from equally barbed British campaign memoirs. Private Wheeler, a soldier in Wellington's army, regarded the Portuguese as 'an ignorant, superstitious, priest ridden, dirty, lousy set of poor devils' and Lisbon as akin to a 'pig-sty'.[34] Cultural bigotry breathed through first-hand sources, whether from Spanish nuns barring admittance to hospitals to heretical Protestant soldiers, or British commentators venting on Spanish propensity for barbarity.

The intimate nature of violence and suffering was a focus for the gory imagination. The level of atrocity both experienced and exacted by the civilian population in Spain dominates memoirs from the period. The constant reference to summary executions, murder and rape speaks of a general phenomenon. In common with other 'dirty wars' in places like the Vendée, violence extended to the parading of tortured bodies, including in the wake of castration. As Alan Forrest has observed, these practices conformed to a common ritualistic practice of subverting the masculinity of captured enemies.[35] It marked a horrific breakdown of the traditionally held notions of civilian neutrality experienced in the 'cabinet wars' of the previous century. Much of the horror was embellished. In the words of the British Hispanist, Raymond Carr, atrocity stories are the 'pornography of revolution'.[36] But so much was real that eyewitnesses found in the theatre of suffering more proof of the Black Legend.

The Spanish term 'guerrilla' reached the English language because of the famous irregular warfare that swept Spain during the Peninsular War (1808–14). This huge struggle came amidst smaller-scale guerrilla struggles elsewhere during the Napoleonic Wars. In this sense, it is possible to argue that the Napoleonic Wars formalized the concept of 'asymmetrical warfare', because earlier episodes of insurgent warfare in European and global history (e.g. Spanish War of Succession) lacked the temporal, geographical and quantitative intensity of the early nineteenth century.[37] The conventional side of the Peninsular War was increasingly dominated by the British in terms of command and supplies. Almost nine-and-a-half million pounds in subsidies were given by the British government to the Spanish Patriots between 1808 and 1814, with about a quarter of this sum being paid out in 1808 alone.[38]

The Spanish guerrilla became the indelible symbol of the Allied war effort. For most of 1809, the guerrillas shared the field with regular Allied forces, both the Spanish Army as well as two consecutive British expeditionary forces, the ill-fated army of Sir John Moore and the more tenacious army of Arthur Wellesley (later Lord Wellington). But despite a tactical Anglo-Spanish victory at Talavera (New Castile) in July 1809, Wellington's forces were obliged to retreat into the safety of Portugal. Renewed efforts towards the end of 1809 exhausted the Allies, sending the Spanish reeling after their defeat at Ocaña and the British back towards Portugal. Thus, for two years until Wellington had summoned up enough strength to take advantage of Napoleon's ill-fated attack on Russia, almost all of Spain lay in enemy hands, leaving resistance to be carried out by scattered Spanish armies and the guerrilla. But the guerrilla phenomenon, as revisionist research by Charles Esdaile and other historians has shown, was at best a double-edged sword. Not only did the Patriot guerrilla bands fail to spark off popular resistance in Napoleonic Spain, there was also a popular apathy towards the Patriot war effort in areas under Patriot control, as evidenced by draft riots, hoarding and desertion.[39] The exception to this general rule was upland Navarra and the neighbouring Basque provinces, where religiosity, popular landownership inheritable by primogeniture, the pressures of overpopulation and wartime sales of common lands, and a local tradition of armed mobilization, all combined to create the very sort of 'people's war' beloved of Patriot propaganda. The fight against the French occupier also tended to bring out the worst in people, involving a wide array of banditry, adventure, opportunism and desertion from the appalling conditions of the regular army.[40]

The Allied victory in Spain in 1814 was thus borne of a very unprepossessing range of factors. Chief of all was the unlikely alliance between century-long rivals, and the supreme command of Spanish forces being invested in a foreigner, Wellington, in 1812. Wellington had a difficult relationship with the Spanish Patriots, especially the reformist *liberales* who dominated politics from 1810. He acknowledged the utility of the guerrillas and at the same time scorned all the romantic and politicized praise heaped upon them by foreign admirers and Patriot journalists. He also, with few exceptions, mistrusted the Spanish Army. Regular Spanish forces in the peninsula remained so decrepit that they were relegated to secondary status in their country's own liberation. Thomas Sydenham, a diplomat charged with easing Anglo-Spanish relations, complained that 'Lord Wellington declares that he has not yet met with any Spanish officer who can be made to comprehend the nature of a military operation.'[41] British overlordship understandably rankled with the Patriots, too. General Ballesteros, whose career was propelled by the Patriot revolution of 1808 and his limited military success in fighting the French occupier, became a focus for Anglophobic sentiment once Wellington became supreme commander-in-chief in September 1812.[42] Patriot Spanish resentment peaked during the British-led liberation of 1812–14. The atrocities following the Allied storming of San Sebastián in September 1813 led to an Anglophobic press campaign. Generalísimo Wellington grew worried at the hothouse press atmosphere of Cádiz and Madrid. In January 1814, he was subjected to character assassination in *El Duende* newspaper.⁴³ Radical elements amongst the Patriot *liberales* feared Wellington's designs on Spain's fledgling constitution and British plans more generally to penetrate Spain's restive American territories.⁴⁴

Very soon, the Patriot liberals would have a greater fear than their British allies. As Generalísimo Wellington led the liberation of Spain over the course of 1813, the constitutional future of the Patriot cause came to a head. Towards the end of 1813, Napoleon tried to cut his losses in Iberia by releasing Ferdinand from captivity and back into Spain, in the hope that the lionized symbol of the Patriots would cancel his alliance with the British and return to the French fold. Once defeat overwhelmed Napoleon the following year, there remained three options for the Spanish constitution: a liberal monarchy designed by the Cádiz Cortes, a moderate monarchy similar to the 1814 *Chartre* in post-Napoleonic France or a return to absolutism. The first path was a credible possibility in 1814, accepted by a portion of British diplomacy and Whig Hispanophiles, and the second sort was favoured by Wellington and several other Tory commentators. One proponent of the British bicameral system was a Spanish Anglican of Anglo-Irish ancestry who had fled Spain ahead of the popular violence of summer 1808. Dampening the Romantic admiration of his friend, Samuel Coleridge, José María Blanco White (1775–1841) judged Spain to be 'incurable', and in thrall to a revolution in the name of the people which did not ask what the interests of the people were.⁴⁵ When the newspaper he edited published a defence of the Spanish American revolution in Caracas, Venezuela, the Cádiz press railed against Blanco White for selling out his country's interests and inciting the Americans to do the same.⁴⁶ The self-exiled Spaniard read the final draft of the Constitution of 1812 with a sense of despair. Remarking the charter's intolerant Catholicism, Blanco White remarked, 'the Spanish people must be free in all but in their consciences'.⁴⁷

Ironically, King Ferdinand was as incapable of political nuance as the Cádiz liberals who had condemned Blanco White in absentia. The king possessed considerable popularity as well as the support of most of the Patriot army and wanted the last option. In May 1814, the army imposed a 'pronunciamento' (a soft coup d'état) in the name of the king, rendering null and void all constitutional changes since 1808.⁴⁸ Ferdinand's first mission was to punish 'traitors', who in his mind were both collaborators with the Napoleonic regime (*afrancesados*) and the Patriots who had usurped his God-given rights to rule as an absolute monarch (*liberales*).

Anglo-Hispania in the wake of the Peninsular War

For all the favourable views in Britain of Patriot liberalism, the ecstatic behaviour of the Spanish crowds greeting King Ferdinand's triumphant return to Spain belied their faith. Wellington's confidante, Samuel Ford Whittingham, was a cavalry commander long transferred to the Spanish service. In 1814, he had the commission of escorting Ferdinand VII on his triumphant tour of Spain via Valencia and Madrid. Channelling the Allied Supreme Commander's preference for a sanitized version of absolutism, Whittingham became intimate enough with the king to be addressed as 'Santiago', and to be invited to share his views of the Constitution of 1812. Santiago disappointed Ferdinand with his opinion that the Cortes should continue but with moderate deputies. The king was determined to re-impose absolutism regardless.[49] British attitudes, both from contemporaries like Whittingham and later historians, tended to divide along political lines. Whereas most liberals embraced the reformism of the constitution, most Tories desired an evolution from absolutism to constitutionalism. Charles Oman, conservative historian who in the early twentieth century wrote an exhaustive multi-volume study of the Peninsular War, commented that 'One would have felt inclined to sympathize with the Liberals when one reads of Ferdinand's first acts of foolish malevolence, but when they came to power they proved themselves quite as intolerant and unwise as the Serviles.'[50]

It was no accident that the Tory Generalísimo, Lord Wellington, by all accounts, favoured the authority of a pseudo-dictator, probably in the form of a Bourbon Regent, with executive power to overawe the legislative mayhem of the Patriot Cortes.[51] But liberal opinion in Britain was outraged. After 1814, the Whig *Edinburgh Review* turned against Spain for having submitted to absolutism.[52] Much of this condescending disappointment had been present since the start of the war, such as when British officers' hopes were dashed that the Patriot victory at Bailén (Andalucía) in July 1808 would lead to a regroup and effective organization of the provisional government (Junta Central).[53] As Gavin Daly has explained, Anglo-Spanish relations gradually unravelled over the course of the Peninsular War, with faults on both sides. The widespread Hispanophilia, which gripped Britain in 1808, had lapsed into indifference or outright Hispanophobia by 1814.[54]

Spain's regression into absolutism became the subject of disdain at the dinners of London's Whig club. William Napier, a British veteran of the Peninsular War published his account in 1828, and his unfavourable preconceptions of Spain's central authority were evident in his work. 'The successive juntas, apprehensive of offending the people, were inert of civil administration, corrupt and incapable of using the English succours justly or wisely.'[55] Amidst the invidious praise of Napoleon which had long gripped a section of progressive opinion in Britain, Ferdinand's absolutist power-grab was held up as further proof of how the former emperor's vision had foundered on the Spanish rock of ignorance and backwardness.[56] Charles Leslie, a British officer who had spent protracted time in Cádiz, remarked the plebeian nature of the counter-revolution in 1814, noting that 'all the rich and decent are either now state prisoners or left'.[57] Robert Southey, later conservative and British poet laureate, voiced the despair of Romantics who observed how King Ferdinand suppressed Spanish liberties to popular applause[58]:

> The soil that now with trembling steps you tread,
> Heroes have trod, when foes, when tyrants, fled.
> On you they call, from their dishonor'd graves:
> Awake! Arise! or be for ever slaves;
> Awake, ye sons of Spain! your fathers call,
> Arise to conquer, or, like them, to fall!

Whereas most Whigs were resigned to Spanish despotism, Lord and Lady Holland continued to agitate for liberty in their *segunda patria*. After their return to Britain, Holland House in London became a centre of liberal dissidence, largely focused on support for a more British form of liberty for Spain. The patrician view of liberty kept the Spanish cause at the forefront of Whig debates and set the climate for uprooted Spanish émigrés received at Holland House in London. In the wake of Ferdinand VII's coup d'état in May 1814, Holland House became famous as a refuge for political exiles. In August 1814, Espoz y Mina, the most accomplished guerrilla veteran, rebelled in Pamplona. Failing to raise the Spanish Army for the cause of the Constitution of 1812, Espoz and his adoptive nephew, Martín Xavier Mina y Larrea, fled to France, already familiar soil to younger Xavier Mina owing to his experience in French custody as a prisoner of war during the recent Peninsular War. The turmoil of the Hundred Days gave the guerrilleros a chance to leave France. Xavier Mina arrived in Bristol in April 1815, asking the British government for help. The Tory government, reluctant to encourage radicals like Xavier Mina or his adoptive uncle, Espoz y Mina, awarded the famous guerrilleros a pension but also detailed a spy (a certain Gordon) to watch their movements and meetings.[59]

Some merchants and financiers from the city of London chartered a textile ship to take Xavier Mina to Mexico. Xavier Mina, beloved of his British hosts, was a political example of a wider phenomenon of British veterans and volunteers fighting for the cause of independence in the Spanish Americas.⁶⁰ Hundreds of unemployed British veterans on hard times made their way to fight for liberty in Spanish America. Despite Spanish government protestations, Britain refused to turn its stated neutrality in Madrid's favour, instead making appeals for negotiations and even that British officers should be hired in the Spanish service so that they could be prevented from travelling across the Atlantic.⁶¹ Allegedly, the passage of Xavier Mina via the United States to New Spain made him the focus in 1816 of an elaborate attempt to create a new Bonapartist monarchy. Xavier Mina was mooted as the head of an independence group which was to have offered José Bonaparte, now in North American exile in New Jersey, the hypothetical imperial crown of Mexico. A prospect bordering on the ridiculous made greater sense in the minds of adventurers uprooted by exile.⁶² During that voyage, the expeditionaries suffered both Atlantic storms and headwinds, reaching Baltimore on 30 June 1816. Soon, Xavier Mina and other adventurers reached the soil of New Spain, where they joined independence fighters looking to turn their old viceroyalty into an independent Mexico. But the royalist counter-revolution was in full sway. Xavier Mina was captured and executed for treason, aged twenty-eight, in November 1817.⁶³

The French Wars of 1792–1815 exalted Britain and benighted Spain, despite both powers having fought together for six years on the winning side. The Allied victory ended a century-and-a-half of French attempts to establish hegemonic power in the west of Europe, and left Britain as the only global power. But the wars also shattered the grip of Spain and Portugal on Central and South America whilst leaving Spain, unlike large parts of Germany and Italy, unreformed to prosper in the new era. Spain's decline was clear to contemporary statesmen. Spain's post-imperial nineteenth century and demotion to second-class status placed the old universal monarchy on par with the Netherlands, another demised power past its prime. Klemens von Metternich, Habsburg chancellor and architect of the peace process of 1814–15, was condescending towards Spain's defence of legitimacy in the Americas: 'Spain defends her rights with much zeal, often even with a haughtiness, which little agrees with her extreme feebleness.'⁶⁴ A century later, a leading British historian wrote that 'Spain, with her colonies in open revolt, and impotent outside the Peninsula, was too proud to admit her weakness.'⁶⁵ The Spanish delegate to the Vienna congress, Marquess Labrador, personified the decline and otherness of post-war Spain. In an international congress whose success depended as much on networks of sociability as foreign policy, Labrador was short of funds and acquired an unwelcome reputation of being a prickly Catholic. Both qualities made him a poor host.[66] Spanish diplomatic machinations with the defeated French on the question of Bourbon rights and Italy alienated Ferdinand's erstwhile British allies.

The British Whig press, which was already disaffected by the ease with which Ferdinand had overthrown Spain's constitutional experiment, turned on its comrades in arms: 'no country ever did so little for itself under circumstances of such excitement and encouragement. It has been liberated entirely by British valour and British enterprise.'[67] Ferdinand, who had been lionized by wartime Patriot opinion, had his own plans not only to eradicate liberalism but also to modernize his absolute power in the face of old-fashioned corporations and liberties.[68] Only his war-torn kingdom teetering on the edge of bankruptcy and the anti-colonial revolt in the Americas thwarted Ferdinand's will.

And as in the recent Spanish War, the American trauma invested British attention. While the British empire had long overcome the loss of its North American colonies thanks to penetrating markets in India and establishing an almost undisputed naval hegemony, the imperial foundations of the Spanish state had been undermined without hope of recovery. The insurgency in Spanish America, under way since 1810, focused British attention even as royalists gained the upper hand between 1815 and 1819. Some seven thousand Napoleonic war veterans from across the British Isles volunteered their services in Simón Bolívar's revolutionary army, seeking glory, fortune and a better life.[69]

Post-war Spain, humbled by second-rate status at the Vienna Peace Congress, and stuck with a moribund alliance with the world's only surviving global power, undertook soul-searching about restoring strategic power. King Ferdinand hoped to restore Spain to the status of one of a concert of great powers under the absolutist Holy Alliance. A surge in navalist writings analysed the reasons for Britain's supremacy on the seas. The naval officer, Ceferino Ferret, and naval minister, Luis María de Salazar, published books analysing the reasons for British success. Three factors stood out in their minds: neglect of naval power by the Spanish Habsburgs in the sixteenth and seventeenth centuries, British piracy as a school of warfare and naval expansion, and poor recruitment and rampant desertion by Spanish naval hands stationed in the Americas.[70] In 1817, in an act of desperation, the Spanish government policy of reinforcing the royalist effort in the Americas led to the purchase of a number of Russian naval vessels, which turned out to be unseaworthy.[71] But the Spanish navy was secondary to the army charged with suppressing insurrection in the Americas.

Late in 1819, King Ferdinand ordered ten army battalions to the province of Cádiz to await transport on festering hulks to Spanish America. The atmosphere of enforced delay and concentration on restless conscripts eased the efforts of liberal conspirators. So dire were the conditions amongst the troops and so disgruntled were their commanders that this reinforcement, meant for America, in fact turned north towards Madrid. Under the command of the liberal officer soon to be promoted to general, Rafael de Riego, the army of America forced the king to swear allegiance to the Constitution of 1812, ushering in over three years of liberal rule known as the *trienio constitucional*.

Exile and the Trienio generation

The *Trienio Liberal* was the first time in Spanish history when a liberal government took the power from its absolute monarch after an uprising of the military. The coup leader, Rafael del Riego (1784–1823), was a tragic figure lacking in statesmanship. But the radicalism his army bequeathed outshone his personal frailties.[72] Certainly, the years 1820–3 witnessed the effects of all the reforms that the liberals of the Peninsular War would have wished to have implemented. The constitution, with all its overhaul of local government, opening of a citizens' vigilante force called the National Militia and curtailment of the corporate power of the Catholic Church, was applied in earnest.

But the advanced nature of these reforms along with the insistence on a cash economy alienated the Spanish countryside. Funds were sorely needed by the liberal regime, which was expanding administration at a time when the traditional remittances from the Americas were dwindling to nothing amidst a general wave of irrevocable independence throughout that continent. Liberal attempts to modernize Spain's economy, for example by scrapping half of the tithe paid by villagers to the church but mandating that the surviving half be paid in cash (at a time of low agricultural prices), alienated the rural population and made it receptive to the appeals of embittered priests and royalist guerrillas. From 1822, an armed counter-revolution raged, especially in the more conservative north of Spain. The liberals were now irrevocably divided between the more conservative 'men of 1812' (the future *moderado* party), who were willing to curtail the excesses of liberalism and seek accommodation with the king, and the 'men of 1820' (*exaltado* party and future *progresistas*), who demanded the full radicalism of the constitution and who, from July 1822, governed the country.[73]

British views of the left-ward shift in Spanish liberalism were filtered in many ways by the ongoing presence of Spanish exiles in Britain. Exiles operated at a European and transatlantic context, cultivating ideas alongside plans for action. The different spatial and linguistic choices of emigration of these men and women that belonged to the Spanish intelligentsia resulted in the creation of new ideological models through debates. Anglo-Hispanic exiles and their friends were divided on the means and ends of the re-imposition of the Constitution of 1812. For Blanco White, the situation in 1820 was even worse than 1812, for now the Spanish Army had imposed the constitution by force, and also entrenched a tyrannical position in politics by insisting that no amendments should be made to the charter for seven years.[74] His friend, the philosopher Jeremy Bentham, celebrated the means but disputed the ends. In 1820, he welcomed the revolution with an ode to 'magnanimous Spaniards', who cast off their own slavery as an example of liberty to the rest of Europe, including to Britain's own corrupted and degraded liberties.[75] But like Blanco White, Bentham regretted the absence of a revising and moderating upper chamber in the Spanish constitution.

Very soon, Anglo-Hispanic liberals would have to ponder the collapse of a second Spanish reform project because of military force. The Holy Alliance of conservative great powers in Europe grew alarmed at what appeared to be Jacobinism south of the Pyrenees, and the Congress of Verona in October 1822 authorized France to intervene in Spain in order to restore Ferdinand VII to his full powers. In 1823, an army comprising French and exiled Spanish royalist troops invaded Spain to overthrow the liberal regime. There was little resistance. But there were isolated acts of active and passive opposition in major cities, especially in Cádiz (which held out for months under French siege), and other port cities like Almería where liberalism had been popular. The absolutist invasion of Spain in 1823 was condemned in British and other European liberal circles as an act of aggression. It inspired activism in politics, the arts and even in volunteering.[76] Lord Holland, the veteran Hispanophile, quoted a Dryden poem in consternation at Britain's mere rhetorical defence of the beleaguered liberal regime: 'War, he sung, is toil and trouble: honour but an empty bubble'. His fellow lords then heard his real charge: 'The very nation which, but a few years ago, had made so many sacrifices in support of the independence of Spain, now saw, unmoved, an aggression made upon that country, the most wanton and the most unjust that history could record'.[77]

But from a global perspective, the ensuing French occupation of Spain until 1828 was a small price to pay for British hegemony. George Canning (foreign secretary, 1822–7) knew that the French were tightening their grip over southern

Europe and thus compensated by pivoting British influence towards the Americas in late 1822, even before the French invasion of Spain had occurred. Britain's commercial inroads had already run deep, amounting to a de facto commercial free hand in Iberian America, to the effect that, according to a French agent in 1823, 'the power of England is without a rival in America … no fleets but hers to be seen; her merchandises are bought almost exclusively; her commercial agents are everywhere'.[78] In February 1824, King Ferdinand, recognizing the reality of blatant British penetration of Spanish American markets and hoping against the odds that his goodwill gesture might yet leverage London to withhold diplomatic recognition of the revolutionaries, issued a decree permitting foreigners to trade directly with Latin American ports.[79]

The period between the two liberal constitutions of Spain from 1812 to 1837 was intimately associated with political exile. It encompassed, apart from Spain, the rest of the places where the émigrés found refuge, such as London, Paris and Buenos Aires. A sort of global micro history, carried by print culture and disseminated in debate, made Spain's revolution a symbol in the British empire, too.[80] In 1820, a new edition of the Constitution of 1812 was dedicated by the Spanish liberals to the great Bengali political and religious reformer in British India, Ram Mohan Roy.[81] Spain's revolution existed not just in its exile but also amidst foreign interlocutors used to moving in the borderless world of ideas and refuge. Britain retained its status as the refuge for Spanish liberty. Juan Álvarez Mendizábal, the radical prime minister struggling in 1836 against both the Carlists and sectarianism on his own liberal side, recalled his exile in London fondly, because in Britain 'fair play reigned in politics'.[82] Britain enjoyed esteem amongst exiles on account of its perceived respectability in contrast to the violent pendulum swings of politics in France.[83]

When absolutism was re-imposed in Spain in 1823, tens of thousands of liberals were imprisoned, persecuted and some were executed. Some compromised individuals were rescued by powerful friends. General Miguel Ricardo de Álava (1770–1843), Wellington's comrade and confidante from both the Peninsular War and the battle of Waterloo, was accommodated at the Duke's Hampshire estate.[84] Thousands more fled into exile, especially to Gibraltar, the British enclave on the southern tip of Spain. Gibraltar became an early base for dissidents who launched invasions of their native land, either overland via the Serranía de Ronda or via amphibious landings along the Mediterranean coast. The Bay of Gibraltar in 1824 hosted more than 650 Spanish émigrés, most of whom lived aboard boats at anchor in British waters. Spanish coastguards watched from close quarters, charged with intercepting smugglers as much as revolutionaries.

There were dozens of invasions in total during the absolutist period known as the 'Ominous Decade' (1823–33) and they were all failures, usually because conspiracy networks inside Spain were not robust and because King Ferdinand operated a powerful police state. The August 1824 uprising of Los Coloraos was typical of these phenomena.[85] The exiles after 1823 set up two juntas, in London and Paris apiece. Of these, the former was in the ascendant until the Wellington administration scrapped its subsidy in July 1829, whereupon the latter took over and was in consequence well placed to monopolize all operations in the wake of the July 1830 revolution. Irene Castells divides the insurrectionary 'utopia' into two phases: the 1823–6 period of 'spontaneous agitation'; and the 1826–31 period of 'organised agitation'.[86] In fact, the most impressive popular mobilization against the absolutist order came not from the *exaltados*, but from the traditionalists (the 1827 *apostólico* rising in Catalonia known as the War of the Aggrieved, or *Guerra de los Agraviados*).

Spanish liberal exiles in London had mixed feelings. On the one hand, they appreciated the climate of liberty in the press, religion and politics.[87] But the climate and cost of living imposed cold penury. Ramón Alesón arrived in London from Lisbon in October 1823. Even though as a constitutional judge in Valladolid he had come from a relatively sophisticated background, he confided to his wife with mixed emotions that he had arrived in a country like El Dorado. His letters revealed the extremes of life in London, where everything cost money:

> Such a city! Such buildings! Such streets! Such stores! Such riches! Such lighting! What activity and movements! The weather couldn't be worse but the men can't seem to do more. I have seen, among other things, a vine between crystals with 2,200 bunches of grapes of a pound one with the other, which produces 50 thousand reais a year. How about one strain producing so much? Would you believe it if someone else said it? It is a matter of having ten or twelve thousand ships and small boats. 40 thousand carriages, an infinity of carriages and horses as gifts; In short, compared to what I have seen, everything is very despicable. What street lighting? What factories? What beautiful shops and how many? It seems impossible that anyone can buy and consume so much. Nobody rides a horse here unless it's for a walk, because I see everyone traveling by carriage. ... What pretty squares? What little gardens in front of many doors? ... I like everything. There are so many things that you would crave, that I don't know how many millions a craving woman would need to satisfy her cravings.[88]

Culturally, the presence of so many distinguished liberal exiles after 1823 boosted British interest in Spanish literature.[89] Some of this was already rehearsed. In 1822, José María Blanco White published his book *Letters from Spain* using the pseudonym Leucadio Doblado, purporting to be written by an inhabitant of Seville to friends abroad. Blanco White's theme was progress frustrated by obscurantist tradition. Thus, a walking tour of Cádiz is ruined when the correspondent has the misfortune to hear

> the sound of a hand-bell which made me instantly aware, unless pretending not to hear it, I could retrace my steps, and turn another corner, I shall be obliged to kneel in the mud until a priest, who was carrying the consecrated wafer to a dying person, had moved slowly in his sedan-chair from the farthest end of the street to the place where I began to hear the bell.[90]

Blanco White had cornered the market of catering to Anglo prejudices about backward and fanatical Catholic culture. But British political responses were rational, including those from the Tories in power (who had disapproved of the excesses of the last radical Spanish government of 1822–3). The Whigs, who had always defended the liberal cause in Spain, had even greater reasons to welcome the exiles.[91] But Fernandine absolutism grew its tentacles in British political life. The absolutist regime kept both British and French embassies in Madrid informed of successes in suppressing revolution.[92] After the last French garrisons left Spain in 1828, the Wellington administration in 1829 bowed to Madrid's pressure by cutting off the subsidy being awarded since 1823 to liberal refugees.[93] Certainly, the Duke of Wellington's experiences in Spain had given him a pronounced distaste for revolutionaries. But if the *exaltados* were hoping for more solidarity from the liberal July Monarchy in France, they were to be disabused. For the following year showed how the 1830 revolution – though hailed by Pyrenean exiles as evidence of the progressive march of liberty – ultimately proved no bar to relations with Spain. The new Orleanist regime supported the Spanish liberals as a mere bargaining counter to be exchanged for Madrid's recognition of the dynasty. Once diplomatic relations were normalized, the exiles were cut off.[94]

British travellers to Spain during the anti-liberal backlash of the 'Ominous Decade' found their *costumbrista* views of the country reinforced by a cultural xenophobia. Those sectors of the elites and the middle classes who adopted foreign fashions and manners were also labelled 'black' and pro-French (afrancesados). Certain clothes and attire considered by the elites as symbols of cosmopolitism and civilization were despised by the common people who defended traditional Spanish attire against foreign fashions and dandyism. As a result, any elegant person could be potentially labelled as a black (liberal) to the point that a decent suit was enough to denounce the wearers as political suspects. During the first (1814) and second (1823) absolutist restorations, well-to-do people were harassed for wearing certain types of hats, ribbons and garments, while some businesses (such as elegant coffee houses in the European manner) were attacked because their owners and clients were supposed to be blacks (liberals).[95] Scottish traveller, Henry David Inglis, noted the humbling of the educated classes amidst a climate of philistinism:

> Among the *estudiantes* (students) there were many paupers, who go regularly every day to one or other of the convents to get a basin of soup; and when vacation arrives, they beg their way home. One of these passed me on the road between San Felipe and Valencia; he had perhaps not heard the royal order for the closing of the universities; and having travelled to Valencia, and found the university shut, he was no doubt returning home. His dress was scarcely removed from rags; he had a patched brown cloak thrown over his shoulder; a cocked hat; and a sack, – probably containing his books, and some provisions, – slung across his back.[96]

The young novelist and later Tory statesman, Benjamin Disraeli, made Spain the highlight of his Mediterranean tour on the eve of the Carlist War. Inspired by a fascination for Iberia's Moorish heritage, Disraeli waved aside warnings of the bandits plaguing Andalucía and enjoyed the 'calm voluptuousness' of Spanish life which 'wonderfully accords with my disposition'. Travelling from Gibraltar to Cádiz and up the river Guadalquivir to Sevilla on board a new steamer, the sudden modernity jarred with Disraeli's romantic vision: '(the steamer) is the only evidence I have met of the vaunted regeneration of Spain'.[97] The dual accounts of progressive and traditional aspects of life in nineteenth-century Spain fascinated travel writers, and these features were at their most dynamic when placed in contradiction with each other. During the 1830s, Disraeli's political career switched from Radical to Tory, and he became one of the leading lights of the *Young England* movement which, among other things, celebrated Spanish Carlism.[98]

Class snobbery combined with Romanticism and an Anglo superiority complex in colouring British travel narratives. Writers dwelt upon two extremes of perceived Spanish character: the humble and the transgressive. John Kemble, a Cambridge 'Apostle' adventuring in Spain in 1831, objectified the sexuality of Andalucían women:

> A Spanish girl is a volcano; whether it be in her love or her anger. It is not hard to see that they bear with more impatience than the other women of the

continent that neglect which all men are made to suffer. The attentions of an Englishman in general therefore raise them in their own eyes; hence they take for us, and the comparative ease with which we seduce them ... Girls even of the lowest class will refuse even the smallest present from their lovers. And this, gentlemen moralists, is why a Spanish girl can be a man's mistress without being his whore.[99]

Water carriers in the cities drew admiration for their heavy work in the heat and their deafening cries of ¡agua fresca!, whilst in the countryside muleteers and draughtsmen fascinated British travellers unused to such poor roads and the unflappable labour of their charges.[100] Spanish travel offered wealthy Britons the prospect of edgy experiences off the map of traditional European tours in a manner which indulged their imagination without threatening their sense of propriety.

The Fernandine contempt for any sort of learning associated with liberalism rankled all the more with intellectual Spanish exiles and their equally learned British supporters. British progressives around 1830 cherished the success of peaceful popular movements for change in Britain and Ireland – movements seeking 'Catholic Emancipation' and 'Parliamentary Reform' – and they inspired volunteers like the Cambridge University 'apostles' for the cause of liberty in Spain. José María Torrijos, after 1827, dominated the London exiles' agenda, aided by his well-connected apostle friends at the University of Cambridge. But he could not offset the frustration and despair felt by underground *exaltado* networks within Spain. In fact, it appears that the inconsiderate disclosure made by expeditionaries of the names of *exaltado* agents was beginning to drive a wedge between London and the Peninsula.[101] Torrijos and his fellow adventurers from Cambridge made a fight for freedom on their own terms. Sailing to Gibraltar, they at first made an attempt to liberate Algeciras, which lay barely 17 miles across the bay. Meanwhile, young British Romantics, including the future poet laureate, Alfred Lord Tennyson, ventured to the Pyrenean border in the wake of the liberal revolution in France in 1830. But the Algeciras raid was frustrated, and Torrijos, in December 1831, led a desperate operation manned by exiled Spaniards, Apostles and Gibraltarians in a raid further east towards Málaga. Loyalist troops rounded up the adventurers upon landfall, and Torrijos and his fifty-two comrades were executed on the beach.[102] There is hardly a more liminal scenario imaginable than a multinational band of intellectuals landing on a beach. But Torrijos was celebrated during liberal episodes in power as a national and decidedly Spanish martyr.[103]

If the Anglo-Hispanic entanglements of Torrijos's expedition were not immediately clear, the pull of London would become obvious to all of liberal opinion within Spain in 1833. Ferdinand VII died in September 1833, leaving a throne disputed between his wife, regenting their young daughter, and his brother Carlos, styled by his eponymous supporters as 'Carlos V'. Spain was plunged into dynastic civil war from 1833, and Britain's economic, diplomatic and military involvement would prove decisive.

5

Anglo-Hispania and the first Carlist War (1833–40)

The first Carlist War (1833–40) was a confrontation between the Cristinos (supporters of the widowed queen mother, María Cristina, and of the throne that her daughter Isabel was to occupy), and the Carlists (who understood that the true monarch had to be the brother of the late Ferdinand VII, Carlos María Isidro). Carlists and Cristinos fought for dynastic reasons as well as for religious, regional and socio-economic reasons. The war can be divided into three parts: the first, the Basque phase, which took place between 1833 and 1835 and was dominated by the personality of the Basque veteran of the Peninsular and Triennium wars, Tomás de Zumalacárregui; the second, a period between 1835 and 1837 that caused political radicalization and revolution in Cristino Spain and the third, the failure of the Carlists in their attempt to win the war and their decline until the final defeat, a process which was complete in 1840. The final victory of the Cristinos, in the two main areas of armed Carlism, both in the main front of the north of Spain in 1839 – pacified by the famous Embrace of Vergara – and in the east in 1840, was due in large part to its greater military, demographic and economic capacity, along with decisive aid from Britain. Even though the Carlist War of 1833–40 rivalled that of the 1930s conflict in terms of its political decisiveness, it has continued to be largely ignored by foreigners. Out of the 217 writers of this conflict between the years 2006–2018, 206 were Spaniards.[1]

The brutality of the Carlist War (1833–40) had both centrifugal and nationalizing effects. While the experience of mobilization, violence and caudillos tied Spaniards into a national awareness more than ever before, especially in the context of politics, the same experiences also mobilized the peripheries to assert provincial rights.[2] The Basque country, especially upland Navarra and bordering rural areas, were as devoted to the cause of 'Carlos V' as they had been against Napoleonic occupation a generation earlier. The

Basque country in general became an object of interest north of the Pyrenees for more than just its usual philological reasons: now it was represented as a rural idyll of Catholic peasants and even a blueprint for a separate nation. The Cristino government's revolutionary response to the Carlist threat included the confiscation of Spain's vast clerical properties, including several leading art works, which were suddenly placed onto an eager European market. The number of Spanish paintings imported into Britain increased five times between 1833 and 1838.[3] Travel writer, Richard Ford, noted that the vast market of significant Spanish pieces due to the Carlist War should serve as a caution for interest buyers:

> Our readers are most earnestly cautioned against buying pictures in Spain; they will indeed be offered, warranted originals, by Murillo, Velazquez and so forth, more plentiful than blackberries; but caveat emptor. The Peninsula has been so plundered of its best specimens ... in war, and so stripped in peace by the gold of purchasers, that nothing but the varied dregs remain for sale.[4]

But major works of architecture were impossible to fake. Scottish Romantic artist, David Roberts (1794–1864), painted the Alhambra and other Moorish legacies in Andalucía. European Romanticism was switched on to Spain, with Hispanism in its diverse senses being all the rage amongst such writers as Chateaubriand, Schlegel and Hugo.[5]

The dynastic civil war which would devastate Spain and inflame European opinion in the 1830s arrived at a moment when British foreign policy was empowered. The foreign office, under Lord Palmerston's stewardship, expanded from a staff of 210 in 1829 to over 1,500 in 1832.[6] First in word, and then in deed, Palmerston's Britain led the way in providing diplomatic, financial and (from 1835) military support for the Cristino cause. For a long time, Spanish historians, especially those writing under the Franco dictatorship, saw self-interested motives in Britain's intervention.[7] To a large degree, the dynastic crisis of 1833 did allow Britain an opportunity to unwind the French diplomatic dominance in place since 1823. But more recent scholarship has also emphasized idealistic motives behind Lord Palmerston's advocacy of a 'liberal international' in western Europe.[8] Britain's role as the prime backer of the constitutional ('Cristino') side in the 1830s civil war paid off after seven gruelling years, making Anglo-Hispania a vector for the uneasy political settlement of mid-century Spain.

The British press condescended towards the Spanish struggle. A British *Times* correspondent reporting on the elevation of the guerrilla veteran, Espoz y Mina, to the command of the Cristino army of the north, noted that 'the regular army

… is highly discontented with the idea of being placed under a guerrilla chief'.[9] The Anglo-Spanish polemicist, José María Blanco White, retreated increasingly into private life, but continued to be horrified by the fanatical violence of the country from which he had exiled himself. His sectarian tirades, which had once entertained Protestant Britain, thus passed to newer commentators. *The Edinburgh Review*, reviewing a travel account published by the British pro-Carlist, Burke Honan, commented that 'the Spaniards' braggart disposition is exemplified by a reference to the gross exaggerations, so habitually practised by both sides in the war, which deprives of credit whichever news comes under the title of a Spanish despatch'.[10] The enlightened magazine might have done better to divine the motives of the travel author himself rather than the nature of thirteen-and-a-half-million Spaniards. Burke Honan was such a notorious figure as a frequent visitor to Carlist areas of control and as correspondent to the reactionary *Morning Herald* that the Cristino government kept a police file on him. After ambassador Villiers refused him diplomatic protection, Burke Honan was expelled from Spain.[11]

The phenomenon of some British support for the Carlist side only confused the picture further unless Spain's war between liberals and absolutists can be taken as a wider European struggle regardless of national borders. Zumalacárregui, as early as 1834, assembled a squadron of foreign volunteers entitled the *Defensores de la Legitimidad*, comprising Spanish and foreign officers who served as simple soldiers, and they increased in number and distinction.[12] It became fashionable for European aristocrats to 'slum it' in the Basque countryside fighting for Don Carlos. José Álvarez de Toledo, Carlist envoy to Naples, tried to sustain his own expenses and donations to the insurgent cause via marriage to the English dowager, Lady Drummond. The elderly lady promised to become a high-profile cash cow for Carlism and a vector for legitimist sympathizers in Britain. But the match was frustrated when a British official advised Drummond to turn finance back on Toledo by asking for money.[13]

Travel literature and the Carlist War

The most enduring images in Britain of Spain's fratricidal struggle during 1833–40 were human. Ramón Cabrera inspired one of Victorian Britain's greatest novelists, William Makepeace Thackeray, who in the late 1830s serialized a novella based on his contacts with confidantes of the 'Tiger of Maestrazgo'. Thackeray's *Tremendous Adventures of Major Gahagan* imagined a visit from

British Indian officers to Cabrera's headquarters.[14] But Cabrera's fame paled compared to the eventual victor of the war, Baldomero Espartero. Espartero proved particularly beloved in Britain and second only to Garibaldi in terms of his Romantic appeal. He outshone the tragic execution of the fifty-three-year-old mother of the Carlist warlord, Ramón Cabrera, a high-profile victim of the law of hostage operated by both sides, caused a scandal in both Spain and Britain. The Cristino commander of the eastern zone, the famous Espoz y Mina, was forced to resign, and the British ambassador threatened to withdraw support for Madrid if such scandals reoccurred.[15]

Spain remained a destination for British travellers even in wartime. By far, the most famous and successful British travel writer was the Bible Society missionary and devotee of Spain's gypsy culture, George Borrow. Borrow visited Spain in 1835 and then remained there three-and-a-half years, during which he had audiences with such distinguished figures as Mendizábal and Alcalá Galiano. His proselytization of Protestantism caused friction with clerics and officials, including with the Carlist forces which at times loomed very close to Borrow's journey.[16] So prepossessed was Borrow of Spain's intrinsically Catholic identity that he wrote of his amazement at his free preaching amidst the liberal revolution in Madrid in 1836:

> The authority of the Pope in this country is in so very feeble and precarious a situation, that little more than a breath is required to destroy it, and I am almost confident that in less than a year it will be disowned. I am doing whatever I can in Madrid to prepare the way for an event so desirable. I mix with the people, and inform them who and what the Pope is, and how disastrous to Spain his influence has been. I tell them that the indulgences, which they are in the habit of purchasing, are of no more intrinsic value than so many pieces of paper, and were merely invented with the view of plundering them. I frequently ask: 'Is it possible that God, who is good, would sanction the sale of sin?' and, 'Supposing certain things are sinful, do you think that God, for the sake of your money, would permit you to perform them?' In many instances my hearers have been satisfied with this simple reasoning, and have said that they would buy no more indulgences. Moreover, the newspapers have, in two or three instances, taken up the subject of Rome upon national and political grounds. The Pope is an avowed friend of Carlos, and an enemy of the present Government, and in every instance has refused to acknowledge the Bishops who have been nominated to vacant sees by the Queen.[17]

After traversing northern Spain during 1836, where nobody could be sure whether a person beyond immediate neighbours was Carlist or Liberal, Borrow learned to be circumspect with his interlocutors. Repeatedly asked 'who lives?' ('who goes there?') by armed men on his route, Borrow replied 'Long Live Spain!'[18]

For British travellers in Iberia, the new civil war was taking place in familiar ground, even amidst familiar faces, given the surge of veteran literature published from the Peninsular War. The veteran's account by Edward Costello reveals how, even though the peace of 1814 was at first welcome, many old veterans soon yearned for military action once more.[19] Lovell Benjamin Badcock was a Peninsular War veteran despatched on a military mission to the Spanish-Portuguese frontier in 1832. During his attempts to discern the intentions of the Spanish Army screening the frontier with Spain's neighbour during the Portuguese Civil War (1828–34), Lovell recognized old muleteers who had served the Anglo-Portuguese a generation earlier, along with peasants in receipt of British pensions and women who had served officers in Wellington's army.[20]

At the other extreme, bandits scintillated and anguished travellers. When the Bible preacher, George Borrow, traversed the Despeñaperros pass in the Sierra Morena, he was glad to have risked it in the depths of a freezing winter and with the help of an outlaw for hire:

> From Cordova I have ridden to Madrid in the company of a CONTRABANDISTA, or smuggler, whose horses I insured, and to whom I am to give a gratuity of 42 dollars. We passed through the horrible pass of Despeñaperros in the Sierra Morena. Providence here manifested itself; the day before, the banditti of the pass committed a dreadful robbery and murder by which they sacked 40,000 REALS; they were probably content with their booty and did not interrupt me and my guide. We entered La Mancha, where I expected to fall into the hands of Palillos and Orejita. Providence again showed itself. It had been delicious weather; suddenly the Lord breathed forth a frozen blast, the severity of which was almost intolerable; no human being but ourselves ventured forth; we traversed snow-covered plains and passed through villages and towns without seeing an individual; the robbers kept close in their caves and hovels, but the cold nearly killed me.[21]

As the war dragged, British journalists dared traverse a country riven by irregular war. The journalist writing under the pseudonym 'Poco Mas', who visited between 1835 and 1840, reported on the invasion of Carlist bands who terrified Cristino officials as well as the lawlessness caused by opportunities for smuggling from unwatched coastlines and cumbersome military logistics. Even in war-torn Old Castile, Poco Mas could not resist his Romantic imagination when he witnessed the passage of a chain gang:

> A chain of presidarios, or convicts, arrived at Villarcayo in the evening. They were lodged in the church. These presidarios reminded me of the adventure of the galley-slaves liberated by the chivalrous Don Quixote, who received such rough and ungrateful treatment in return. The presidarios were on their way to work on the canal of Castille. Their jackets and trousers were of coarse brown cloth; they were chained two together and fettered, and a strong chain ran along the centre of the line when they were travelling. I happened to be present early in the morning when they were about to commence their day's march; the majority were athletic.[22]

The ongoing interest in travel narratives of Andalucía contrasted with the main location of British military campaigns in the north of Spain. The focus of British attention towards lawlessness in Andalucía was too alluring. The index of a major work on British travel narratives cited the Andalucían cities of Seville, Cádiz, Granada and Córdoba several times more than comparably sized cities in the centre and north – and this despite the fact that the Pyrenees remained the main point of entry for British travellers.[23] Certainly, Andalucía was 'othered' by the rest of Spain. The Spanish anthropologist, Julio Caro Baroja, thought that the Castilian nation-builders of the modern era looked south with a mixture of disdain and fascination.[24] Generations of Castilian writers, some even as far back as the late medieval era, developed the trope of hardy and honest northerners and shifty southerners.[25] But foreign travellers also played a role. The infamous image of Andalucia was largely born abroad in foreign travel writings, and then recycled by Spanish elites.[26] Certainly, Andalucía appealed to British travellers. George Dennis, a young archaeologist visiting Andalucía in 1836, felt obliged to attend that most picturesque of Spanish traditions, a bullfight, for 'a book of travels in Spain, without a description of a bull-fight, would be an imperfect production'.[27]

The upper-class gaze towards Spaniards was interrupted whenever wars brought thousands of British soldiers to Spain, some of whom left testimonies of suffering. The end of the civil war in Portugal in 1834 and the terms of the Quadruple Alliance enabled Britain to intervene in Spain's conflict. Lord Palmerston shepherded parliamentary legislation allowing volunteers (known as the British Auxiliary Legion) to be recruited in the service of Queen-Regent María Cristina of Spain. The Spanish ambassador and Wellington's protégé, General Álava, persuaded the Napoleonic Wars veteran George de Lacy-Evans to serve as commander, in spite of opposition from Tories under the sway of non-interventionism. More than thirty literary works, including memoirs and other testimonies, were published by the members of the British Auxiliary Legion. It was still a Romantic event for many British travellers. But the sense of distance inherent in travel narratives, as during the Peninsular War, was removed from campaign memoirs detailing violence, suffering and everyday interactions. The Auxiliary Legion were, in the words of one historian, a 'forgotten army'.[28] Their relative oblivion lay in part by the polarization caused to British politics by the Legion's presence in Spain and in part by the refusal of nineteenth-century Spanish historians to acknowledge their role. Excoriated in Carlist propaganda, the auxiliaries did not fare radically better in the hands of historians sympathetic to the Liberal-Cristino cause. Antonio Pirala, for example, complained of the financial burden of the British Legion. Their cost of 200 million reales might have been better spent equipping larger Spanish forces and without incurring the diplomatic awkwardness and personal rivalries of allies at war.[29]

The British government promoted the recruitment to the British Legion to fight overseas, but made sure not to interfere formally in the war. The *London Gazette* on 10 June printed the exact details of the composition of the army of 10,000 men – 8,488 infantry, 552 rifles, 700 cavalry and 300 artillery.[30] The British Auxiliary Legion was composed entirely of volunteers, almost all of whom came from the poorest sections of the populace. It was a divisional-sized force composed of two regiments of cavalry and nine regiments of infantry. Having been assembled at ports in Britain, the recruits were sent to Spain late in 1835 and trained and equipped there (British law did not permit the presence in the country of armed bodies of men who were not part of the army).

As in earlier and later Spanish civil wars, the vast majority of British volunteers came from humble backgrounds. William Turner was a Kentish down-and-out who boarded the British Legion ship at Gravesend near London in July 1835. After a gruelling voyage in which his leg was broken and had to be reset on board, Turner reached northern Spain via Santander. Unlike well-off British war tourists who marvelled at the poverty and despair of Spain, Turner was impressed by the pitiful state of his comrades: 'I was struck with surprise to see the wretched condition of so many of my fellow countrymen, who were in a most degraded condition and half-starved'. Conditions worsened as winter approached on the march to Vitoria where 'we suffered greatly from frost and snow, and were quite unacquainted with military regulations. The captain in charge of our party was very severe, and some of us were punished, some only for complaining of being sick, others for not keeping up.'[31]

The cultural and strategic context of volunteering to fight in someone else's civil war was irrelevant for most British auxiliaries. Not only were they driven by extreme hardship to find such a dire prospect attractive, but their travails in Spain rivalled those of their Peninsular War forbears in their savagery. William Turner testified to the scourge of cold, hunger, disease and lack of pay:

> The Legion's sufferings were very great, so harassed from marching to and fro, and our provisions were scarce, and very bad, and many of our men dying in the hospitals, numbers of them owing to having been frost-bitten in the mountains. We could not receive neither back rations no pay, which caused a number of our men to desert. A sort of plague seemed to increase amongst our troops, that five or six of our men was buried in one grave. This continued for several months, when it was estimated there were about four thousand died, which was proved to have been through our Spanish bakers poisoning the bread.[32]

The British auxiliaries needed more time than the seasoned French legionaries to get used to campaigning in Spain. For several months, Spanish troops outpaced their foreign allies with a rapid march (*paso de Luchana*) as well as their superiority in mountain warfare, but the British Legion grew experienced in localized fighting in the environs of San Sebastián and Vitoria and in fortification work at Treviño and Peñacerrada.[33] In early 1836, the beleaguered Cristino commander-in-chief, Fernández de Córdova, was finally convinced that the advantages of using foreign troops to suppress Spanish insurgents outweighed the disadvantages. He asked the queen-regent to prevail upon London and Paris to spare more troops.[34]

The two chief bases were San Sebastián and Santander, and the legion was eventually concentrated at Vitoria. Later, it was shifted back to the San Sebastián area, where it participated in a series of actions against the encroaching Carlist forces in the course of 1836–7, including, most notably, the battle of Oriamendi. Casualties were very heavy, both on the field of battle against the Carlists and because of disease. The legion commander, George de Lacy Evans (1787–1870), was an experienced soldier and also a politician who favoured radical reforms and the liberal movements in the world. He was elected Member of Parliament for Rye constituency in 1830 and from 1831 to 1832, and then for Westminster, a radical bastion, from 1833 to 1841. Evans wrote that the Carlist movement aimed to preserve unimpaired the ancient customs of the country – 'Religion and Don Carlos' – but 'the distinct topic of the Basque privileges (without which the rebellion would have long since terminated) was an after consideration'.[35] Agents received a bounty of £2 for each man they enlisted (in total about 10,000 recruits). But the Spanish government did not pay salaries on time, and the legion was finally disbanded in 1837.

In addition, France sent its newly constituted Foreign Legion to Spain to fight for the Cristinos. In total, 18,000 additional troops were sent at a crucial time when the armies of the Carlists were gaining significant numbers in the north. Britain also lent María Cristina's government substantial sums for the purchase of arms, largely from state arsenals. During the war, Britain lent the Cristinos £616,000, without interest.[36]

The British Legion's French allies faced a more suspicious political environment than the one presided over by the Radical Member of Parliament for Westminster. The French government feared that its soldiers could get infected with Spanish radicalism. So, billets were vetted for the presence of likely exaltado agitators, and the French Foreign Legion deployed to forward positions wherever possible.[37] Feelings ran even higher because of the fear of falling into the hands of the Carlists. The humanitarian intervention of Lord Eliot, a British agent sent by the Duke of Wellington, achieved the feat of getting both war sides to reach an agreement respecting the lives of regular soldiers captured on the main northern front. The resulting agreement, the 'Eliot Treaty', signed by Carlists and Cristinos in April 1835, excluded from its humanitarian provisions both foreign auxiliaries and Carlist guerrillas, militiamen and Cristino soldiers fighting the war on the most asymmetrical fronts in Aragon and other areas. British volunteers could expect no mercy if they were captured in the heat of battle. Conditions became so bad that several auxiliaries defected to the Carlist side, thereby circumventing the draconian 'Durango decree' that exposed foreign volunteers to being executed upon capture. The Carlists offered defectors 1 real for a private soldier and as many as 10 reales to those crossing the lines with a weapon and a horse. A British Carlist Legion was formed by a former legion captain. But the fact that its Spanish commanders on one occasion ordered the execution of twenty British defectors in reprisal for the re-desertion of eight of their comrades would suggest that conditions with Don Carlos were even worse than with Lacy Evans.[38]

The lack of a unified command and poor logistics constantly soured Anglo-Spanish relations. During 1836, General Lacy Evans accused Commander-in-Chief Córdoba of conspiring against the radical government in Madrid instead of focusing on the deteriorating northern front. Córdoba, for his part, was underwhelmed by the poor discipline and mediocre performance of the British auxiliaries.[39] British government pleas for Madrid to reinforce the northern front fell on deaf ears as the Cristino army was overwhelmed by the growing insurgency in the east of the country as well as revolutionary movement of the juntas in the cities. Inter-allied relations eased once the performance of the British auxiliaries improved and when in some instances they were joined in amphibious actions by elite Royal Marines units.

At the strategic level, the Cristino regime was relieved that the British were deploying their regular forces, in one instance several miles inland, in circumstances which proved that London's stated policy of non-intervention in Spain's war was largely semantic. But at the ground level, auxiliaries resented the peripatetic appearance of the much-lauded 'real soldiers', even though they were their countrymen. The auxiliaries knew that the Carlists has exempted British regular troops from the draconian terms of the Durango decree. The Royal Marines, for their part, disliked being lumped together with auxiliaries whom the Tory press was depicting as criminals and deserters. The legion in return resented the preferential treatment shown towards their comrades. Once the Royal Marines expressed their disgust at being ordered to fight alongside the auxiliaries, a compromise was reached which automatically promoted Marines officers to the next rank whenever they were called upon to command the Auxiliary Legion.[40]

As the Carlists had gained the upper hand in the north from 1835, with destabilizing effects on liberal politics in Cristino cities, original sceptics of British intervention now actively supported it. Despite Prime Minister Martínez de la Rosa's constant reluctance to see foreign intervention, the government now sought it, citing relevant clauses in the Quadruple Alliance, which had been signed the previous April. It was desperately hoped in liberal circles that even the symbolic showing of the Royal Navy flag off the northern coast would cow the rebels, whilst the French, it was hoped, would send in a proper army instead of its fledgling Foreign Legion.[41] But Britain would not move. The London government knew that greater intervention in Spain would need another act of Parliament and that this would be rejected in both chambers. Spanish historians tended to attribute personal animus regarding British prime ministers' support for Cristino Spain. The elderly Wellington has traditionally been credited with neutral, if not pro-Carlist, attitudes, whereas the Whig ministry of Peel has been viewed as radically anti-Carlist.[42] Great hopes were cherished by the rebels that the Duke of Wellington, hero of the Peninsular War, would declare his support for the Carlists, and both Liberal and Carlist historians since have held that he was pro-Carlist in thought if not in deed.[43] Tory opinion, best expressed through the *Morning Post*, usually came out in favour of the Carlists. But much of this sentiment came from a peculiarly personal antipathy to Lacy

Evans and his radical politicking, rather than consistent aversion to Spanish constitutionalism. Wellington's humanitarian intervention via the Eliot Treaty amounted to something of a moral victory for the Carlists. The right of quarter recognized them as equal combatants. But Wellington remained persistently non-interventionist and exasperated at the improvident Spanish and their war.[44]

British ambassador Villiers was condescending towards the liberals' wartime reforms in the 1830s. He strongly advocated Britain's 1832 Act as a model for Spanish reform. Improvement, he wrote, 'begins from above and not from below – it is given and not taken'.[45] By mid-war, the diverging trends between *progresista* Anglophiles and *moderado* Francophiles had become clear. Two eminent examples, a literary icon and a journalist respectively, both turned to politics, show the bi-national divide. The dramatist Francisco Martínez de la Rosa (1787–1862) spent most of the Ominous Decade in Paris where he became friends with François Guizot, at the time professor at the Sorbonne and later architect of the moderate liberalism (*juste milieu*) in France's July Monarchy. Guizot remembered Martínez de la Rosa's rise to power fondly as 'the first step towards constitutional government'.[46] On the Anglophile side, the editor of the left-liberal *Eco del Comercio*, Fermín Caballero, had been exiled in Britain after 1823 and was elected as the representative for Madrid and Cuenca in the elections of 1834. His Anglophile line dominated the editorial section of the *Eco*, which served as the semi-official voice of the *progresista* party. When *moderado* finance minister, Alejandro Mon, tried to repair the Spanish treasury in the wake of the Carlist War, he spent time in Paris consulting on tax reforms and options for a French loan. The *progresista* press punned him as a pawn of French interests: 'mon Alejandro'.[47]

The summer of 1835 witnessed a radical movement in liberal politics seizing localized power via the militia and juntas. The vanishing power of the central government saw local juntas take power into their own hands. Imports from Britain worth £500,000 came tariff-free through Mediterranean ports, leading to thousands becoming unemployed in Catalonia.[48] Meanwhile, Britain was using diplomatic pressure to strongarm Madrid, with ambassador Villiers virtually chairing discussion about who should be in the new cabinet and how it should come about in order to meet the revolutionary challenge.[49] When the August–September 1835 revolution of the juntas threatened to sweep Toreno from power, Britain wasted no time in pressing for a more radical-liberal Mendizábal to come to power.[50] But Mendizábal – suffering the pleas for supplies of the Cristino commander of the Army of the North, Córdova, and a resurgent Carlist leadership – could not work miracles.

As the Carlist insurgency spread during 1835 in rural Catalonia, Barcelona's formidable Ciudadela fort became a prison for captured Carlists. City authorities, aware of how the Ciudadela was now doubly hated as a badge of Bourbon oppression and a concentration of deadly reactionaries, interceded with their British allies to evacuate the captives. The civil governor asked the British consul, Sir James Anesley, to accept Carlist leader O'Donnell's transfer as a prisoner of war on a Royal Navy ship. All of this was to no avail. Meanwhile, radical politics were overtaking Barcelona.[51] Britain, in the wake of brokering the Eliot Treaty, was recognized as a humanitarian intermediary in the Carlist War. This role was scorned by the Carlists. It also grated on several liberals on the Cristino side. Agustín de Argüelles, author of the Constitution of 1812, resented the preachy approach of the British ambassador, as if Spaniards were devoid of any notion of humanitarianism.[52]

Tensions in Barcelona reached such a level that the Ciudadela was stormed anyway. The Barcelona mob fraternized with sympathetic militiamen and descended on 4 January 1836 on the lightly defended Ciudadela.[53] Despite last-minute, desperate mediation from Governor Pastors (who at one point, judging the catastrophic risk of explosion, only just persuaded the mob not to invade powder stores), all Carlist inmates were brutally murdered. Espoz y Mina of Peninsular War fame and captain-general of Catalonia arrived to take charge in Barcelona. One of his first actions was to stamp out the proclamations of the Constitution of 1812 (which had buoyed up the assailants) and to round up and deport to the Canaries known and suspected troublemakers. But as with several similar incidents, the Cristinos boarded British vessels to take outlaws into their own custody. Aviraneta, a leading conspirator, and others were transferred from Royal Navy ships onto a Spanish ship bound for the Canaries.[54]

During Carlist General Eguía's early-1836 campaign to break the Cristino ring around the Basque provinces, he made good on his word, much reported in Carlist and liberal press alike, to chastise the foreign auxiliaries fighting on the liberal side, promising to 'exterminate all Englishmen at least as far as London'.[55] Some British legionaries, captured during February 1836 on the heights at Arlabán, were taken to Heredia to be shot. The French Foreign legion, meanwhile, was so incensed by Carlist atrocities that its Spanish allies even handed over some unfortunate Carlist prisoners to be executed at their ally's hands.[56] Even though martial law was meant to suppress disorders, by summer the revolutionaries seized the centre of power. In August 1836, amidst the onward march of a Carlist expedition, rebellious sergeants at the royal summer palace of La Granja forced the queen-regent to swear allegiance to the Constitution of 1812. The dizzying march of revolutionary and military events confounded British observers. George Borrow, writing to the British Bible Society from Madrid in May 1836, noted how 'there are so many changes and revolutions here that nothing is certain even for a day'.[57]

Bilbao and British Basqueophilia

The first half of the Carlist War found the British travel gaze still centred on Andalucía. In part, this reflected Gibraltar as a port of entry as well as the heady atmosphere of political exiles and spies on the rock from the Carlist War.[58] But British military engagements in the north and a growing awareness of the intractability of the Basque autonomy question underlying the Carlist War shifted the attention of writers, journalists and politicians northwards of the River Ebro. Most of the British military effort centred on the coasts and inland areas of the Basque country, the main theatre of the war and host to the most important port left in Cristino hands. During the 1836 rebel siege of San Sebastián, Cristino commander-in-chief General Córdova was confident that the city could not fall because British steamships could borrow reinforcements from Bilbao and get them safely to San Sebastián in a matter of hours.[59]

A few miles inland along a navigable river lay Bilbao, target of Carlist attention throughout the 1830s. Their first attempt to conquer Bilbao in 1835 was based on the desire to gain international recognition, as a large loan was pledged from supporters in Europe in the event of the city's fall. The second attempt stretched from the summer of 1836 until the winter (when the city would finally be delivered from siege). From summer 1836, rebel control of the Nervión estuary had cut off the British consul in the city. But relief was at hand owing to localized attacks launched by British auxiliaries along with the Royal Navy and their Cristino allies. Most decisively, over the Christmas holiday of 1836, General Espartero broke the siege. Espartero was hailed as a liberal hero, and he would thenceforth dominate Spanish politics until 1843. In the thanksgiving celebrations of early 1837, the British were explicitly thanked for the deliverance of Bilbao, along with the Cristino army and militia.[60] For the Carlists, their obsession with Bilbao turned out to be counterproductive. Their time-consuming efforts cost them the life of their best commander (Tomás de Zumalacárregui) and a draining of resources which could have been used more profitably in a general invasion of Castile.

Bilbao was certainly the centre of international liberal concerns. John Francis Bacon, a British diplomat resident in Spain between 1830 and 1837, spent five years of this time in Cristino Bilbao. Bacon became engrossed with the Cristino cause of liberation and left vivid accounts of the Carlist siege of the city.[61] But British commentary from the liberal atmospheres of Bilbao and San Sebastián was a poor measure of Basque attitudes as a whole. The outward-looking ports could only gain with a more liberal settlement, unlike the traditional regions of Álava and Navarra. Further inland towards Vitoria-Gasteiz (Álava) and Navarra, the serving British auxiliaries were clear about the difference. William Turner, a private in the British Legion, recalled a defensive action at Oriamendi near San Sebastián where 'the Spanish women were very attentive towards our wounded, doing everything they could towards their assistance; how different was these [sic] people to what we had seen in Vitoria, which detested the very sight of an Englishman'.[62]

Bilbao was not only a source of veteran pride. As it was the most important city in the region, it also focused British attention on the anomalous and inspiring position of Navarra and the Basque provinces of Guipúzcoa, Vizcaya and Álava. Some of this interest doubtless came from corners of anthropology and racialism, especially from Irish and Scottish writers who were keen on linking the mysterious linguistic and ethnic origins of the Basques in some way to the Celts on the fringes of the British Isles.[63] But most interest concerned the ancient liberties which had survived north of the river Ebro. Lord Carnarvon (1800–1849), a Tory nobleman and traveller, waxed lyrical about Basque traditional liberties[64]:

> Biscay retains its ancient laws, customs and tribunals, and is governed by its own national assemblies; it yields contributions to the sovereign as a free gift; it arranges its own taxation; it has no militia laws; it is exempt from the odious system of impressment for the navy; it furnishes its own contingent of soldiers and sailors; it appoints its own police in peace; it provides for its own defence in war; no monopoly, royal or private, can be established in Biscay ... The debates are public, and the measures submitted to their consideration are proposed in Spanish, but discussed in the Basque language. The Biscayan parliament possesses exclusively the right to legislate for Biscay ... no order of the Spanish government is directly received by the Basque parliament ... Their veto upon any resolution of the Spanish government is absolute, and the seemingly inconsistent, but not uncourteous formula of 'obedecida pero no cumplida' ('obeyed, but not carried into execution') is their peculiar but decisive mode of rejection.

Ongoing Tory opposition to British involvement in Spain, combined with Anglo-Hispanic war weariness amidst the revolutions and Carlist invasions over the 1835–7 period, provoked British parliamentarians to press for a compromise peace based upon respect for Basque autonomy. In practice, Palmerston's rhetorical support for Spanish liberalism always exceeded his material generosity. On the one hand, he encouraged Cristino recruitment of British auxiliaries, whilst on the other he rejected all Cristino pleas for British government aid or loans.[65] Discussions about a compromise peace seemed stark in the wake of General Lacy Evans's appeal (which had made him famous even amongst the Carlists) to declare Don Carlos 'an outlaw', in the same way that the British Parliament had done with Napoleon in 1815.[66] In 1836, Lord Londonderry reminded the House of Lords that the Spanish cause was not purely a matter of local succession but was equally 'an English and European cause', a struggle between 'freedom and absolutism, the great principle which divides the European nations'. And if Britain could not intervene, 'the legion must immediately dissolve' and he was in favour of 'preserv[ing] the conciliatory measures in the Basque Provinces'.[67]

The Tory opposition argued against military intervention because the war was a conflict between the Basques and the Spaniards. If the liberal Spanish government wanted to abolish the Basque laws, how could the British, with an age-old constitution, help the liberals to destroy Basque institutions, so similar to the English ones? Lord Carnarvon used the example of Scotland and Ireland to find similarities with the Basque country within the Spanish kingdom. He wrote, 'the Biscayan Parliament, thus elected, possesses exclusively the right to legislate for Biscay, to make new laws, to propose the budget … to adjust the taxation … '. Finally, he referred to the veto of the Biscayan Parliament on any resolution of the Spanish government as being absolutely conclusive.[68] But the Whig supremacy on Spanish matters proved unassailable. Lord Palmerston, architect of foreign intervention in Spain, made a speech in 1837 full of the circular logic of Cristino liberalism:

> It would be a greater advantage to the Basques to get rid of their privileges than to retain them. Those privileges were great and valuable so long as the rest of Spain was subject to arbitrary government and a despotic King. So long as neither justice nor law were to be had in Spain, then the exemptions of the Basques were an approach to constitutional freedom.[69]

This was an opinion similar to the Spanish and Basque radical liberal view on the continuity of the Basque representative assemblies, which was at odds with

Basque conservative liberal opinion and to the Carlists. The conservative liberals were in favour of the composite kingdom and the conservation of the Basque institutions inside the new liberal and constitutional kingdom of Spain. There was also a division within the liberals between conservatives and radicals from 1833 to 1837, which became a focus for a parliamentary speech by Palmerston:

> We have been told that it is a crime in us to have allied ourselves with parties who are endeavouring to rob the Basques of their privileges. We have been accused of assisting to oppress, to subjugate, to reduce to degrading servitude, a free and independent people, who are fighting for their liberties and privileges ... Now I say that this is not the question ... The poor Basques are made the victims of persons who have other ends in view than the welfare of Biscay ... The war which is carried on in the Basque provinces is not a war between the modern institutions of Spain, and the ancient institutions of Biscay ... The question is not simply what has happened, or may happen, in the Basque provinces ... The House has to decide to-night between two opposite systems of foreign policy ... One party is to support Carlos and despotism, the object of the other to uphold Isabella and the constitution.[70]

But from 1837 onwards, a new strategy was implemented to separate the question of the continuity of the Basque laws and Representative Assemblies from the Carlist cause, with the aim of finding an agreed solution that would end the civil war in the Basque country. In 1837, the pretender Carlos controlled the greater part of Basque territory, except the urban nuclei of Bilbao and San Sebastián. In Catalonia, his territorial control was smaller and limited to the mountainous interior. The new peace strategy developed the principles of 'Peace and *Fueros*', separating the continuity of the Representative Assemblies of the Basque country and self-government from the claim of the traditionalist Carlos to succeed to the Spanish throne. On 19 April 1837, the Tories tried and failed to bring down the Whig government over the question of Palmerston's Spanish policy.

British radical opinion generally supported the cause of the legion. But doubts were also raised on the British left about how the centralizing project of the Cristino liberals would affect the liberties of the Basque country.[71] The philosopher, John Stuart Mill, in 1837 published his *Essay on the Spanish Question* which tried to rally the British anti-Carlist left in two ways. First, it justified British military intervention as a counterbalance to recent invasions by absolutist powers in Poland and Italy. Second, it tried to neuter the Basque-Carlist rallying cry of defence of autonomy (fueros) by supporting the extension of similar autonomy across the whole of Spain after the war, giving the liberal victory a veneer of traditionalism.[72] But Mill's treatise was not widely read at the time, and for most Britons and Spaniards alike, the symbol of Anglo-Hispania remained General Lacy Evans. After rushing back to Britain in 1837 in order to contest his Westminster constituency as the radical candidate, Lacy Evans was returned in the general election that year despite the ongoing Tory press campaign targeting him and his legion.

Whilst Westminster debates over the Spanish issue waxed and waned, the British Legion became acclimatized to fighting the Carlists, if not to the ongoing lack of pay and logistics. The British Legion's success in victories at Hernani, Oyarzun, Irún and Fuenterrabia strengthened the Whig hand. The death of King William IV triggered an election in August 1837 in which the Whigs retained their majority. On 10 June 1837, the original legion was disbanded in accordance with the two years of contracted service. On 3 July 1837, part of the British Legion at Hernani mutinied over severe arrears of pay. As William Turner recalled,

> A short time, the 10th June (1837), was now drawing at hand, which was the expiration of the Legion, we now marched to our former quarters outside of San Sebastián, we delivered up our arms and accoutrements, and received our arrears of pay, with the exception of six months' gratuity, which they gave us notes to receive in England, as we expected, but they were of no more use than a piece of blank paper. It is well known to the country at large in what wretched condition we returned, after we were paid up, they opened Randearousses again for volunteers to different regiments, for twelve months longer. Our sorrows now being drowned with drink, many of us entered again, forgetting our past sufferings.[73]

A hard core held out and refused either to march or to defend their position against the surrounding Carlists until the personal intervention of Colonel Wylde (who was second only to Lord Eliot in foreign office terms), the Irish brigadier, O'Connell, and Spanish colonel Leopoldo O'Donnell and finally, the settlement of pay arrears. These were made politically acceptable in the face of the equal privations faced by Spanish troops only by winding down most of the legion and transferring its contingents from operations. In Carlist quarters, news of the name O'Connell led to some confusion that it was the famous radical, Daniel O'Connell. Even though this assumption was mistaken, it led to recriminations about why so many Catholic Irish troops were serving under British arms and the Cristino flag against the interests of the true faith.[74]

Hundreds of desperate volunteers agreed to serve longer in a replacement legion under the command of General O'Connell. Finally, after the new legion suffered a massacre at the hands of Carlists at Andoain, and amidst renewed Tory efforts to topple Palmerston's Spanish policy, on 10 June 1838 the Order in Council authorizing recruitment to the legion was allowed to expire.[75] By then, Carlist military efforts were exhausted, and it was only a matter of time before Cristino commander-in-chief Espartero forced them to sue for peace. But British political influence on the Cristino side continued. While in the Westminster Parliament Palmerston defended the position and vision of the radical liberals – a single nation in Spain with a single Parliament – in practice, however, he adapted his attitude towards a compromise peace just as the Spanish government changed its position in 1838. On 27 July 1839, at the meeting with the Carlist military commander Maroto and other Basque military leaders, Lord Hay set out the conditions of the British government: 'The British government ardently desires that the civil war of Spain should speedily and finally terminate, by an amicable arrangement between the chiefs of the insurrection in the Basque Provinces and the Spanish government.'[76] Within a month, the British government's desire was achieved over the heads of the Madrid government, when the opposite numbers commanding rival forces in the northern front agreed upon a conditional surrender of the Carlists.

Britain and the end of the Carlist war

Britain's role in the Cristino victory did not lend itself to a glowing legacy, either in Spain or Britain. The growth of Basque nationalism from late nineteenth century led some writers to consider the struggle of 1833–9 a first Basque war of independence from Castile.[77] The so-called English cemetery which inters British dead on a hillslope near San Sebastián has been neglected by local authorities and even targeted by ETA vandalism in the late twentieth century.[78] In Britain, a lot of the gradual resolution to Spain's trauma was read vicariously through the vainglorious figure of Lacy Evans. Some parts of the British press, such as Blackwood's *Edinburgh Magazine*, were pro-Carlist even without the provocation of Lacy Evans's grandstanding. But even ambassador Villiers detected in the Member of Parliament for Westminster delusions of grandeur normally associated with Napoleon or Wellington. The Westminster MP's cause was not helped by his curious physical resemblance to Baldomero Espartero, to the degree that the two men had often been mistaken for each other on campaign.

For the remaining four years that he held his constituency, he became a polarizing symbol of Britain's involvement in Spain's war. The Tory *Morning Post* scorned Lacy Evans's award of a knighthood, ignored his significant record of humanizing the conditions of service in the British Legion and failed to respond to veterans' repeated pleas for their back-pay. William Turner fell on hard times after following the legion back to England and was imprisoned for a scam which misfired. Turner recalled his post-war misery from Yarmouth gaol to a devout female prison visitor in May 1840, presumably flattered to have his experiences heard and written down.

Other veterans remained in Spain. The officer Alexander Ball stayed fighting until 1840, after the bulk of the legion had left for Britain. Thereafter, he remained in the Basque country, having shaved off his militaristic moustache and resolved 'that the remainder of my life would pass in peace and quietness, among a people in whom I had taken so very peculiar an interest'.[79] But some years afterwards, amidst the post-war chaos in the Basque country, Ball returned to Britain, where he published a defence of the British Legion's reputation in the recent war.

The men of the Spanish Army, who entered politics in the 1830s, perpetuated a new aristocracy of ability and wealth. The image of Napoleon fitted into this scheme and was associated with Baldomero Espartero who had risen from nothing to everything, knocking over structures on the way.[80] Physically brave, militarily competent and politically mediocre, Espartero's greatest travails would come with peace in 1840, when he would soon lose his wartime ability to outmanoeuvre political rivals and retain the support of his veterans. Like the greater man from Corsica, Espartero would face exile, along with a romanticized cult of personality, after the fact of his rule. His example inspired contemporaries, like the vain British Legion commander, Lacy Evans, whose own pretensions to greatness were modelled on Espartero.[81] After all, there was no home-grown great man for British veterans to admire apart from the now elderly Duke of Wellington. The legion veterans thus fashioned their own plebeian celebrations. John Brown was a rank-and-file soldier who was wounded and battle-hardened during two years of service in the Carlist War and also got married to the daughter of a San Sebastián flour merchant. The death of the Duke of Wellington in 1852 inspired Brown to publish an autobiography of his service in the Carlist War including an eight-stanza eulogy to the commander-in-chief of the Peninsular War.[82]

The Carlist War also bequeathed Britain a new variety of Anglo-Hispanic veterans and exiles. London became the centre of Spanish war veterans fallen on hard times. A landmark study of urban poverty chronicled during the 1840s included Spanish Legion veterans amongst the bustling precariat of the world's biggest megalopolis. The investigative journalist, Henry Mayhew, recorded how veterans acquired their own nicknames like other street-hawkers. Whereas 'Spuddy' was the nickname for a man who sold bad potatoes, and 'Cast-Iron Poll' for a woman who had been struck with a pot without suffering injury, 'Foreigner' was the name for an Auxiliary Legion man who made a living selling humble wares. But such was the notoriety of the veterans from Spain that other men tried their luck impersonating them. Mayhew recorded the presence of wounded veterans along the north Kentish coast: 'I met seven chaps out on *the Spanish lark* as they called it – that is, passing themselves off as wounded men of the Spanish Legion. Two *had been* out in Spain, and managed the business if questions were asked: the others were regular English beggars, who had never been out of the country' (emphasis in original).[83] Another man called Peter, from a proletarianized weaving background in Leicestershire, developed the knack of faking wounds and ailments in order to elicit charity: 'For years he went about showing wounds which he said had been inflicted fighting in the Spanish Legion – though, truth to say, he had never been nearer Spain than Liverpool is to New York'.[84]

The 1840s also witnessed the presence of hundreds of Carlist exiles in Britain. Many secured amnesty from the Spanish embassy to return home. But several others, who were either listless individuals or failed applicants for amnesty because of criminal investigation, were left down and out in London, cut adrift from the Carlist elites beloved of *Young England* circles.[85] The exile in Britain from 1850 of the Carlist warlord, Ramón Cabrera, appeared to have eased matters somewhat for exiles old and new in the wake of the failure of the second Carlist insurgency of 1846–8. Cabrera resided in Britain from 1849 until his death in 1877. His marriage in 1850 to the heiress and devout High Anglican, Marianne Richards, was widely thought to have 'civilised' him into the family life of a Surrey English gentleman. Certainly, pro-Carlist writers attributed the early years of Cabrera's exile with the low point in Carlist fortunes. Melchor Ferrer, Carlism's most prolific writer, attributed the influence of Marianne and Cabrera's own headstrong inability to distinguish the malign and the benign aspects of British culture to the decline of the traditionalist movement.[86] But the exile life was also a world unto itself. Much of the work of Cabrera's staff and that of his English wife, Marianne Richards, concerned the welfare of Carlist exiles in Britain. But hundreds of assorted exiles escaped the Anglo-Hispanic couple. In 1852, London's Metropolitan Police estimated the presence of some 1,970 refugees in the capital, of whom two-thirds were living in penury. Pedro

Vacheco was arrested in 1855 for stealing some bottled tomatoes. In court, he protested he 'either had to steal or die of hunger'. Vacheco could secure no help from the Society of Friends of Foreigners in Distress, a charity founded in the Napoleonic Wars, because of its policy of excluding refugees on British soil. In the end, Vacheco appears to have joined the French Foreign Legion.[87] The afflictions of exiled Carlists mirrored those of the veterans within Spain, from both sides of the conflict. The right-wing suppression of Spain's national militia in 1844 created an unwitting community of suffering with the British veterans. Around the mid-1840s, as failed harvests brought hungry faces onto the streets, the Spanish press reported on the presence of marauding militia veterans protesting their unredeemed service against the Carlists.

Lacy Evans, for his part, could never manage the right tone for his veterans, nor do much to expedite their back-pay. He often alienated audiences with his long-winded claims to have acted in Spain like Lafayette in America, and in the self-aggrandizing memoirs he published in 1840. His *Memoranda of the Contest in Spain* downplayed the role of the Royal Marines and brushed over the appalling conditions of the legion. By the time Lacy Evans lost his seat in Parliament in 1841, his fame had become intertwined with so many other historical Spanish figures, chief of whom was the generally popular but still divisive figure of Espartero himself.[88] Men on horseback like Lacy Evans and Espartero continued to colour British impressions of Spain, even as questions of commerce, empire and tourism opened up new Anglo-Hispanic entanglements in the second half of the century.

6

Anglo-Hispania and the world

The Cristino victory in 1840 established what would turn out to be a century of constitutional rule resting on a liberal property revolution. The army became the chief agent of Spanish politics during this period, producing a remarkable degree of social mobility in its ranks. While the civil war propelled generals into political power, even into a regency between 1841 and 1843, lower-ranking officers often shared the arrears and political views of their men, the result being a military occupation of politics right across the left–right spectrum. Both *exaltado* (from 1836 *progresista*) and *moderado* factions of the liberal movement looked to strongmen to champion their politics, while contemporaries lamented the weakness of the civil power. The post-war edginess of Spanish society and politics left much room for other Europeans to make Spain the focus of their Romantic imagination. As the popular travel author, Richard Ford, noted, 'despite the ravages of foreign and domestic Vandals, Spain is still extremely rich in Edifices, civil and religious, of the highest class'.[1]

At the war's end in 1840, war hero General Espartero's power was untrammelled. He was lauded during two weeks of political festivities celebrating the end of the Carlist War on the main front in August 1839, and the ending of the eastern insurgency the following summer turned the so-called Sword of Luchana into a symbol of national reunification and veteran political sensibility. He became the first modern political celebrity in Spanish history.[2] Beloved of the *progresista* wing of liberalism, at the war's end, Espartero championed a rally in defence of town hall autonomy which led to the exile of the queen regent and the raising of her ten-year-old daughter and symbol of the liberal struggle against the Carlists, Princess Isabella, by a group of palace *progresistas*. Espartero soon reigned as regent in his own right.

But the *moderado* opposition was not cowed. In September 1841 from exile in Paris, María Cristina launched a coup with the rallying cry of 'the queen is kidnapped' ('la reina está secuestrada'). But National Militia veterans blocked the military risings in major cities and formed defence councils with revolutionary elements. The pro-government *Gaceta de Madrid* syndicated news of the failure of *moderado* risings in the provinces. The newspaper reported from Almería how local national militia from Canjáyar 'view with utter indignation the scandalous incidents in Pamplona, Zaragoza, Vitoria and Madrid', and how the worst outrage was caused by the plot to seize the palace:

> Violating the sacred Palace where Majesty and Innocence slept calmly, these rebels are desperate in beholding a nation justly governed by an illustrious Cortes and a just Regent (Espartero), and possessing at last the benefits of peace and genuine liberty after so many years of suffering and bloodshed ... These diabolical actions are spawned from treacherous hearts that desire to start a second civil war.[3]

Foreign observers drew Romantic inspiration at the anachronistic raid on the palace launched by war hero Diego de León and his *moderado* conspirator, Manuel Concha. British Hispanophile, David Hannay, considered the attempt to kidnap Princess Isabella an uncivilized throwback to the days of Bothwell and Mary Queen of Scots.[4] The quixotic otherworldliness of Spain was confirmed in British minds when news arrived of the theatrical aftermath. Espartero tearfully rejected pleas for clemency on behalf of his fellow veteran in the Carlist War, and Diego de León reportedly donated his cigar to his firing squad and encouraged them to shoot straight. The execution of Diego de León turned him into the greatest Romantic figure since 1837, when the young power, José de Larra, had committed suicide in the first act of consummate Romanticism in Spanish intellectual history.[5] It also sullied Espartero's reputation, made worse when he ungratefully disbanded the defence councils which had risen in his name.

Espartero's cronyism and free-trade policies alienated his own side.[6] During Espartero's personal campaign against the juntas in the autumn of 1841, he was closely accompanied by two British military attachés who fed reports to London of the rise and fall of the regent's popularity. The Espartero regency marked the highest point in British influence in Spain before or since. Opposite the regent's residence in Madrid lay the British embassy. One morning, graffiti appeared saying 'The Regent lives here, but the man who governs lives across the street.'[7] Much of Anglo-Hispanic ministerial intimacy in the wake of the Carlist War concerned the temptation of free trade. For Britain the advantages of liberalized trade were obvious. But several men in Espartero's circle also thought free trade would solve Spain's endemic smuggling problem, benefit consumers outside of industrial Catalonia as well as solve lesser problems like the open border on the isthmus with Gibraltar. In 1842, amidst a growing press campaign against Espartero's willingness to sacrifice Catalonia's captive Spanish market, a secret republican society disseminated Anglophobic propaganda: 'the British want to turn Iberia into a new India, have no principles beyond their own egotism, and want to keep us poor and ignorant so that we might work for them as slaves'.[8]

Espartero's allies attracted opprobrium whenever the opposition invoked Romantic appeals to the innocence of the young princess. One incident which triggered the majority reign of Isabella in 1843 illustrates this. The *progresista* leader, Salustiano de Olózaga, tricked the young queen into signing the dissolution of the Cortes in a desperate ploy to keep the *moderados* from coming back to power in 1843. The legend ran that Olózaga physically forced the thirteen-year-old queen's hand in the signature, even though the likely scenario was that he buried the key document amongst a pile that the queen would routinely sign off. The image was set that the monarch was not above politics, but rather an abductable authority at the hands of whichever dynastic liberal faction was in the ascendancy.[9]

In 1843, a *moderado*-led army rising toppled Espartero from power. The downfall of Espartero's regime and imposition of a more centralized monarchy in 1844 began the process of stronger state building and draconian law and order via the creation of the paramilitary Civil Guard. Amidst this modernization, British travellers raced to capture a last glance at the old ways of Spain. The British traveller, Richard Ford, paid special attention to the vanishing customs and self-rule of the Basque region:

> A sense of separate weakness has kept these provinces together, and has taught the secret of union, the one thing wanting to unamalgamating sectional Spain. The binding ties are a common council of representatives, and a common alliance against all that is not Basque. This federal association is expressed in their national symbol of three hands joined together, with the motto 'Irurac Bat', which is equivalent to the tria juncta in uno of the Bath order of our united kingdoms.[10]

The Diego de León tragedy was the most captivating episode in the British Romantic imagination since the execution of Cabrera's mother in 1836. The tone was set for post-war British visitors to Spain to prioritize the Romantic caricature over the nuance of political reality. In part, this situation reflected the peculiar public sphere of nineteenth-century Spain. Press censorship remained in force, even under more left-leaning regimes, which made the caricature of controversial politicians and phenomena more attractive than print literature which risked attracting fines and censorship. Added to this, the general illiteracy of Spain and the pictorial satire became an accomplice in the country's exotification in foreign eyes. Particular motors of this phenomenon were the stereotyped national images inserted into cigarette packets from the 1860s. As British travellers also liked to smoke, a Spanish invention, they imbibed the images along with the tobacco.[11]

The Carlist War hastened the Madrid government's recognition of its liberated Latin American territories. Mendizábal rebuffed the British ambassador's interference in this process, rebuking Villiers that Spanish America was a 'family affair'. Once Madrid in December 1836 formally recognized the independence of most Latin American states, it did so using the language of 'the motherland recognising that her children had grown up'.[12] Spanish commentators, influenced by pan-Hispanic ideas, hoped that the definitive end of wasteful land campaigns in the Americas would yield a kind of voluntary empire based on the seas, trade and values. In 1839, the politician and later naval minister, Alejandro Oliván, argued that post-imperial Spain should focus on expanding mutually beneficial trade across the Hispanic Atlantic. The seas, Oliván believed, would avoid the territory trap which the British, despite their naval supremacy, were walking into via their expensive and ultimately self-defeating march through India, Australia and Canada.[13] It was a curious reading of British colonialism borne in part of frustration at London's inroads into Spanish America.

The Carlist War completed the Americanization of British economic interests, turning the Spanish-speaking world gradually into an informal empire and bestowing British diplomatic leverage at the same time when pan-Hispanism was gaining traction. The cane-sugar boom made Spain's continued imposition of plantation slavery all the more reprehensible in British eyes (Britain having abolished slavery outright in 1833). Yet, a Hispanophile strand of British opinion supported the institution of Spanish slavery and claimed, despite personal gains in the bondage, to have been motivated by more than just money. Captain William Woodville, a Catholic born in Liverpool around 1735 and died in La Havana, Cuba, in 1815, was one example of an Anglo-Hispanic profiteer from the slave trade. His story was told through his famous son, the Cuban poet and patriot, José Agustín Quintero y Woodville. Imprisoned for his Cuban independence activities, the younger Woodville followed in the pro-slavery footsteps of his father by working for the Confederacy in the American Civil War (as an agent for secessionist interests in Benito Juárez's Mexico).[14] John Downie, the adventurer of the Peninsular War, was an ardent defender of Spanish slavery. George Dawson Flinter, an Irishman and naturalized Spaniard, married into criollo society in Spanish Americas and profited from Puerto Rico slavery. Independence in Venezuela sent him relocating to Puerto Rico, from where he tried in vain to influence ardently abolitionist British public opinion by claiming a paternalism in Spanish bondage and the unpreparedness of Blacks for liberty.[15] In 1834, Flinter published a pamphlet arguing for the Spanish recognition of Latin American independence as part of a new and informal Spanish seaborne empire of commerce. True to the cause of his adopted homeland, Flinter ended up fighting on the side of liberty in the Spanish Cristino army during the Carlist War of 1833–40.

But such Anglo-Hispanic men were outliers with little influence over British public opinion. Henry Brougham, prominent Whig abolitionist, condemned Spanish and Portuguese slavery so vehemently that the Spanish consul in Bristol spent much of November 1838 managing his country's reputation in its most important ally against the Carlists.[16] The Cristino government grew more protective of its remaining colonies, especially sugar-rich Cuba, in the face of its dangerous British ally. Increasingly, aggressive British abolitionism provoked a growing Anglophobia in Spain, even amidst sympathetic liberals. As a result, some Spaniards felt prodded into defending their slavery system in Cuba as a sort of 'necessary evil'.[17] When the British missionary, George Borrow, secured an audience with Prime Minister Mendizábal in the hope of gaining permission to sell Bibles, he was taken aback by the tone of the meeting. Mendizábal, whom it was 'as difficult to get nigh as it is to approach the North Pole' spent most of the interview airing his suspicions of British designs on Cuba: '[he had] the preposterous idea, which by some means or other he has embraced, that we have been endeavouring to foment disturbances amongst the slaves of Cuba'.[18] Borrow's attempts to explain apparent acts of subversion as the likely work of missionaries from the United States failed to mollify the radical prime minister. Mendizábal, despite his close association with British ambassador Villiers and his profound anti-clericalism, refused Borrow permission to print the New Testament in Spain. British abolitionism appeared to Spaniards as a virtue-signalling variety of Perfidious Albion and as a type of moral superiority which, in the words of one recent historian, 'hardened into arrogance'.[19]

British observations from the Carlist War confirmed the belief that Spain was a backward country. After Espartero was received with much fanfare into British exile in 1843, his past soured attitudes even amongst his supporters. A dinner hosted in his honour by the City of London Corporation was almost cancelled once it became known that General Nogueras, the Cristino officer who had ordered the execution of Ramón Cabrera's mother, was to be one of the invited guests. After much recrimination, including letters from British Auxiliary Legion veterans published in *Times*, Nogueras was dropped from the list of invitees.[20] Even though Espartero in exile proved inactive in politics and poor in his command of English or French, he continued to attract the devotion of Whig circles. In 1847 Lady Palmerston noted that her famous husband said 'we are all *progresistas*, and Espartero is the head of that party'.[21]

The 1840s, even before the European Revolutions of 1848, made Britain the foremost refuge for political exiles. Count Montemolín, Carlist pretender in the wake of the abdication of 'Carlos V' in 1845, spent several months in London before launching an ill-fated insurrection in Catalonia during 1846–8. The Whig foreign secretary, Lord Palmerston, did not allow his pro-Cristino pedigree and cultivation of French support in the Quadruple Alliance (1834) to sacrifice British asylum to exiles of all political stripes. Replying to criticism from the French ambassador, Palmerston replied, 'Britain is a hospitable country for so many unfortunate exiles seeking the protection of our laws. I can neither extradite Count Montemolín nor subject him to surveillance.'[22] The souring of Anglo-French relations during 1846–8 was in part a product of Palmerston's interest in Montemolín as a potential ally against French ambitions in Spain.[23]

Inside Spain, the praetorian elites that had been victorious in the recent Carlist War were hostile to any notion of dynastic reconciliation. When Metternich pressed the marriage of Don Carlos's son with Isabella as the best solution, General Narváez quickly vetoed it, even though, arguably, the victorious liberals in so doing overestimated the dynastic threat to the victory of 1839.[24] Abroad, Britain and France, Europe's liberal superpowers, supported suitors in their own national interests. But in September of 1845 at Eu (France), an Anglo-French agreement was forged that neither of their preferred candidates should be proposed. Thus, Britain voiced protest when in August 1846, in the wake of a failed *progresista* rising in Galicia, it was announced that the pro-French candidate, Francisco de Asís, Duke of Cádiz, Isabella's cousin, was put forward as the match.[25] The diplomatic slight to Britain was a personal tragedy for young Isabella. Francisco's alleged feminine nature and his wife's sex drive made the royal couple a source of scandal and innuendo which was often fanned by dynastic politicians for partisan ends. Unlike Britain's Queen Victoria, Isabel II's overt sexual and political activities, and her patrimonial conception of the crown, exposed her to chauvinistic attacks whipped up even by dynastic politicians. As Isabel Burdiel has argued, the result was a 'captured' queen whose sex rendered her unable to divide the private and public spheres of her life at the head of a constitutional monarchy.[26]

British hopes of securing new markets in post-war Spain foundered in the protectionist backlash to Espartero's regime (1840–3). As early as 1835, Ambassador Villiers had pressed liberal governments either to abolish or reduce tariffs on British imports, arguing the virtuous cycle of reducing smuggling and aiding consumers. But, as Villiers himself confessed to Foreign Secretary Palmerston, 'Catalonia (centre of Spanish textile manufacture) would suffer, and that this province is divided between republican and Carlist forces, both looking for a cause to throw off the central government'.[27] After the war, William Cobden, Britain's most distinguished champion of free trade, was soon disabused of his hopes of promoting a virtuous cycle of free trade and anti-smuggling in the war-torn country. Crossing into the Basque country, he remarked the backwardness of his surroundings, including the women spinning textiles in villages by hand, and the poor logistics: 'ever since we crossed the frontier we find the wheels of the country carts made of solid wood about a yard in diameter no spokes – two bullocks always attached to carry as much as would be drawn in England by a pony or a donkey'.[28]

Cobden received a more encouraging reception at free-trade meetings held in cities with *progresista* sympathies. But General Narváez's instinctive protectionism, combined with the poor grain harvests and potato blight that swept Europe between 1846 and 1848 stalled Cobden's efforts.[29] Once General Narváez imposed a dictatorship in response to the revolutionary wave of 1848, prospects dimmed still further. The eponymous 'Cobdenism', coined to express the idea that free-trade internationalism would in turn promote peace, barely applied in a country of latent civil war. Food riots the previous year had taken on a xenophobic bent as imaginary 'Jews' and 'foreigners' were accused of profiteering from the hoarding of grain. Narváez's counter-revolutionary nationalism and rapprochement with the Vatican revived tropes of Perfidious Albion. British ambassador Henry Bulwer flagrantly supported the *progresista* opposition against the Narváez dictatorship by publishing a condemnation of the general's autocratic rule in the radical press. He also entertained hopes of Carlist reconciliation via the more compromising attitude of the pretender Montemolín. Spain issued a rare diplomatic rebuff by expelling the ambassador.[30] Anglo-Hispanic diplomatic relations cooled until the *progresistas* regained power in 1854.

Narváez's suppression of revolution had not relied solely on the army and the new Civil Guard. The state apparatus responded flexibly to reports of unrest, often by sponsoring public works schemes. When revolution finally reached Spain in 1854, it was caused more by domestic factionalism and the rise of a home-grown democratic movement than the internationalism evident across the West in 1848. The two years of *progresista* rule known as the Biennium (1854–6) opened up a freer and non-hegemonic political atmosphere which created new avenues for Anglo-Hispanic relations. A generation of Spanish radicals acquired their political education during these years, especially in Andalucía where activists gained support in small towns and villages. Once Spanish politics swung to the right in 1856, these networks became clandestine while others made links with exiles in Gibraltar. The rock would thus become an irritation to *moderados* during their times in power, not least because many leftist exiles converted to Protestantism, which was promoted by Spanish converts resident in Gibraltar.[31] On an international level, Spain remained neutral in the Crimean War of 1853–6, albeit not without anxieties that the concentration of British shipping in the Mediterranean and Black Sea might expose Cuba to American aggression. Britain remained uppermost in the minds of Spanish policymakers and writers keen to harness Albion's global pre-eminence to revive Spain's position in world affairs.

But the rock was still a minor affront to Spanish nationalism which, in mid-century, was inspired by the British example in other ways. Plans to revive Spain's shrunken empire had long been mooted, with influential writings positing British naval predominance as a model to emulate. In the 1840s, Fermín Gonzalo Morón published several articles condemning historical neglect for the navy in contrast to the British, whose powerful Royal Navy secured transoceanic bases and trade.[32] Newspapers of varying politics around mid-century favoured the expansion of Spanish navy and the emulation of British norms. British steamboat and ironclad designs were avidly studied in the learned press.[33] Press reports and Cortes debates increasingly featured complaints about the tribulations of Spanish residents caught up in civil wars in the former colonies, furthering support for naval expansion and British-style 'gunboat diplomacy'. The navalism and growing nationalism in foreign policy had a remarkable effect. From a historic low point in Spanish naval strength on the eve of the Carlist War in 1833, by the 1860s, Spain would possess the world's fourth-largest fleet.

The advent of the comparatively stable regime of the 'Liberal Union' (1858–63) under Prime Minister Leopoldo O'Donnell augured a new alliance with Britain and France. Spain joined Franco-British 'gunboat diplomacy' in the initial stages of the expedition to Mexico in 1861. In addition, O'Donnell's 'long government' sent a Spanish contingent with the French expedition to the

Kingdom of Annam (1858), occupied the island of Fernando Póo in the Gulf of Guinea (1858), defeated Morocco between 1859 and 1860, re-annexed Santo Domingo (1861–5) and, finally, fought a naval campaign in the Pacific in the Spanish-South American war (1862–6). But efforts to restore Spain to great-power status were frustrated by the preponderance of Anglo-French hegemony in the Mediterranean.[34] In 1860, the patriotic press protested British diplomatic pressure on Spain to curtail its ambitions in Morocco.[35]

The Cristino victory in the Carlist War relegated Spain once more to secondary interest in British foreign policy. The Espartero regency continued to stimulate British interest with regard to the free-trade controversy, the Hispano-Portuguese dispute over waterways and the considerable personal popularity in Britain of the regent, and then ex-regent, himself. But the spectre of the 1848 revolutions, rise of a new Bonapartism in France and the growing German question all shifted British foreign policy away from the Pyrenees. The Anglo-French economic dominance of Spain, along with Britain's political domination of neighbouring Portugal, acted to constrain several Iberian interests. The railways, built in a mania that ended in bust in 1866, prioritized trunk routes to France over branch lines within Spain. Support from several intellectuals in Spain and Portugal to create an Iberian union based on the historical example of 1580–1640 foundered in part because of fear of a British veto.[36] British foreign secretaries of both Whig and Tory stripes opposed pan-Iberianism out of fear of losing Portugal as an ally along with its strategic positions in the Atlantic and Africa.

Spain of the three decades since the Carlist War offered little direct inspiration to British politicians. But even though its clear second-rate status in European diplomacy did not occupy British politics, the country continued to inspire art and literature. Benjamin Disraeli, novelist and Tory prime minister, drew inspiration from Spanish discovery writings of the conquered Americas in a sonorous attack on the Whig government of 1872: 'you behold a range of exhausted volcanoes ... where flame flickers on a solitary pallid crest ... There are occasional earthquakes, and ever the rumbling of the sea.'[37] The Spanish artistic greats, especially Diego de Velázquez, continued to inspire British masters. The Scottish painter John Phillip (1817–1867) was so devoted to Spanish culture that he was dubbed 'Phillip of Spain'. His 1858 oil painting *The Dying Contrabandista* used a stereotyped subject as its muse to vivid effect. The painting in turn inspired Arthur Sullivan's first opera, *The Contrabandista* (1867).[38] The *Smuggler* opera appeared twenty-three years after the creation of the centralized Civil Guard had been busy suppressing bandits and smugglers for good. It also appeared a year before the downfall of the Isabelline monarchy and its replacement with a revolution committed to a political modernity far removed from the romantic image of the smuggler.

The Revolution of 1868

The Isabelline political settlement frayed amidst the collapse of the railway boom in the mid-1860s. Political divisions between the old dynastic parties and radical democrats did not stop a broad-based coalition for revolution being forged in exile in 1866. The immediate background to this revolution lay in the democrat failure at the San Gil barracks uprising in 1866. This failed pronunciamiento prevented the democrats from gaining a Madrid stronghold to counterbalance *progresista* General Prim's revolutionary leadership from exile and the harsh but ultimately ineffective government crackdown of 1866–8. Cádiz, like with the Riego rising half a century before, was the cradle once more of revolution. Spanish naval forces under the command of Admiral Juan Bautista mutinied, sparking off a wave of risings throughout September. The Revolutionary Sexennium (1868–74) was a multifaceted and internationalized political experience. Amidst the preceding decade of national and human emancipation throughout the Western world, British Hispanophiles had been relishing a sui generis Spain. Francisco de Goya's gruesome *Disasters of War* paintings made an international impact when they were finally published in 1863, thirty-five years after the artist's death. The hallmark image of the Christ-like insurgent facing the firing squad after the Second of May uprising focused British memory on the Peninsular War.

But the internationalized political climate of Spain was sweeping aside the old and embracing the new. Rafael de Labra, Cuban-born educator and activist, drew inspiration from Britain as 'the mother of public freedoms and laws' in his lengthy campaign to abolish slavery on his native island. Backed unlike earlier British abolitionists neither by the church nor by popular opinion, Labra managed to use universal principles of liberty in the free-thinking atmosphere of the Madrid *Ateneo* to succeed in his mission by 1886.[39] The Catalan philosopher, Pi y Margall, produced a blueprint for a confederal republic based on individual sovereignty. Anarchist delegates were warmly received by working-class audiences, and even the political theatre celebrating the 'people's war' of 1808 was changing. The Madrid section of the Socialist International in May 1869 issued an appeal to the working class not to celebrate the annual *Dos de Mayo* festivities because 'the idea of the fatherland ('patria') is petty, unworthy of the robust intelligence of the workers ... The worker's fatherland is his workshop, and the workshop of the sons of labour is our entire world.'[40]

Spain's foreign policy, meanwhile, continued to be dominated by Cuba and the question of a dynastic replacement for Isabella II. On 26 June 1870, Isabella, who was in Paris, finally abdicated her throne. The unionists (moderate revolutionaries) wanted Montpensier as her replacement, whereas the Iberian unionist commander of the revolutionary army, General Prim, wanted Fernando of Portugal. Ominously for Franco-Prussian relations, Leopold of Hohenzollern was also a candidate. This candidacy was the trigger for the Franco-Prussian War and Napoleon III's defeat, which led to the French Republic. The proclamation of a republic in France immediately won the Spanish federalists' support and even the promise to Gambetta of a Spanish legion to fight the Prussians.[41]

The fall of Isabella II thus triggered a diplomatic revolution in Europe, in provoking Franco-German tensions when Napoleon III protested Bismarck's candidate for the Spanish throne, Leopold, prince of Hohenzollern-Sigmaringen. But the global reach of Spain's '68' was not confined to Sedan and German unity. The Paris Commune; the German and the Italian national unification processes and the severe limitation of the civil power of the Roman Pope, all linked Spain to European affairs. The Carlists rose again and a revolutionary cantonal movement gripped the Mediterranean littoral. The beleaguered government in Madrid also faced a civil war in Cuba (Ten Years' War of 1868–78) which obliged the revolutionaries to break their promise to end conscription (a blood tax paid by the poor). The Madrid government mastered all three challenges, but only after a more authoritarian monarchy was restored in 1875 in the wake of a dizzying experimentation with the 'democratic' monarchy of Amadeo I (1870–3) and the First Spanish Republic (1873–4). Unlike during the 1830s, the Carlist challenge was not met with foreign fighters organized by allied governments. The culmination of most of Europe by 1871 into bordered nation states augured in a conservative trend in diplomacy which made Spain's cantonal radicalism look either like a throwback to Andalucían lawlessness or a harbinger of wider revolution. In 1873, Britain's Royal Navy seized Spanish vessels at Cartagena they suspected of acts of piracy, before ferrying them to Gibraltar and offloading their crews.[42]

During the revolutionary ascendancy of 1873–4, the Spanish republic excited European interest like at no other time since the 1830s. Its chronic insurgent and guerrilla tradition, now married to a constitution based on popular sovereignty, made itself felt in international diplomacy. In the Brussels Declaration of 1874 regulating violence in wars, Spain was one of a few countries insisting on the right of inhabitants in occupied territory to defend their country, therefore leading to compromise wording in the final agreement against countries with great armies like Russia.[43] The civil war in Spain itself also excited new Anglo-Hispanic entanglements. The newly founded International Red Cross sent a mission to the battlefronts of the Third Carlist War led by Vincent Kennett-Barrington to organize hospitals to care for the wounded.[44] And London, the global capital of political exile of all stripes, hummed with Carlist conspiracies. Edward Kirkpatrick de Closeburn led a Carlist Committee in London which collected donations for 'Carlos VII', distributed propaganda and reported on the visits of reactionary British sympathizers to rebel areas of control.[45]

In the end, Spain's Revolutionary Sexennium (1868–74) was ended by a pronunciamiento launched from the Sandhurst military academy in Britain. Crown Prince Alfonso was a cadet at Britain's elite officer school when, in December 1874, he proclaimed his 'Sandhurst Manifesto', a blueprint for a centralized but constitutional monarchy. In many ways, this restoration resembled the *moderado* system in place before the 1848 Revolution: a very restricted franchise along with a partially successful demilitarization of the public sphere. The Bourbon Restoration turned the prince into Alfonso XII, rallied the army to defeat cantonalists, Carlists and Cubans alike, and set in motion an oligarchic political stability which would persist until the revolutionary crisis of 1917. Despite the economic development of the 'Restoration' era, Anglo-Hispanic attitudes for two generations would be marked by pandering and condescension regarding Britain's imperial zenith and Spain's demise in the Philippines and Antilles.

7

Anglo-Hispania between disaster and civil war

The post-1830s persistence of Spain's imperial identity, including the rebound of the 1860s, explains why Spain's loss of vast territories in the early nineteenth century had so little domestic impact when compared to the loss of much smaller territories in 1898. Even though rising Spanish nationalism certainly played a role in this démarche, the fact was also that early-nineteenth-century Americans were 'family' making their own way, whereas in 1898 Cuba, the Philippines and Puerto Rico were snatched by an alien Anglo-Saxon power.[1] Throughout the nineteenth century, Spain's surviving colonies were referred to as 'ultramar', whereas the loss of mainland America was downplayed almost as a personal trauma for the king.[2] But at home, Spain's economy fell even more under the influence of British interests, to the extent that Iberia formed part of London's 'informal empire'. Foisting a 'free trade' ethos on Spanish liberal elites benefited Britain's textile and manufactured exports and undermined Spain's own industrialization, as the repeated flare-up of economic unrest in Barcelona showed. By the end of the century, Britain's import needs helped distort Spanish exports towards iron ore, copper and sulphur, tying Spain's fate to the interests of a global empire even more tightly than its railway and financial markets were bound up with French interests.[3]

By the late nineteenth century, the imperial question became a focus of Anglo-Hispanic cultural interaction. In 1889, London's Earl's Court hosted the Spanish exhibition. But this showcasing of Spanish modernity, industry and culture left the British press and visitors cold. The original Spanish expatriate plan to project a progressive image fell away as British investors took over the exhibition and orientalized it along lines familiar to readers of travel narratives of Andalucía. This Anglo-Hispanic dialogue of the deaf left the exhibition, in the words of one historian, with a 'pervading sense of failure, emptiness and inauthenticity'.[4] As the century drew to a close and Britain reached its imperial apogee, most commentators were convinced of Spanish decline. Once rebellion in Cuba broke out again in 1895, British analysis was baleful. Ironically, by the end of the nineteenth century, Spanish commentators shared British pessimism regarding the crisis of Hispanic power. 'Spain without Cuba', *La Época* commented in 1897, 'would be as little valued amongst the nations of Europe as Portugal'.[5] But the threat to Spain's position in Cuba came not at the hands of independence fighters, who militarily by 1898 were on the back foot. Rather US military intervention blew the Spanish Navy out of the ocean in Manila Bay and Santiago de Cuba, and eventually prevailed on land against tough Spanish defence.

Spain's defeat at the hands of the United States in 1898 provoked soul-searching amongst Spanish intellectuals and politicians. They hoped to 'regenerate' Spain amidst the apparent superiority of Anglo-Germanic models. France had been humiliated by Germany in 1871, Portugal by its British ally in 1890, Italy at the hands of the Abyssinians in 1896, and now Spain in Cuba and Manila Bay. This suggested a waning power of the Latin world, of which Spain formed an integral part, and fed all sorts of pseudo-scientific racial anxieties about the legacy of too much Arabic and African blood in the Iberian population.[6] British prime minister and imperialist, Lord Salisbury, in May 1898 gave a speech at London's Albert Hall on the subject of 'moribund nations'. Using tones of social Darwinism, the Tory argued that the march of industrialization and armaments had divided the globe into winners and losers, and that 'the living nations will gradually encroach on the territory of the dying'. Nobody present, nor the Spanish press which went into a flurry at his remarks, could mistake his reference to a living United States and dying Spain.[7] The example of Anglo-American power also emboldened Spain's growing regional nationalism. In 1895, Sabino Arana founded the Basque Nationalist Party (PNV), a racist and conservative movement, which gained traction in the wake of Spain's defeat in the war of 1898.[8] In a mental somersault of racist anti-colonialism, Basque nationalists in the early twentieth century pivoted a great deal of their demands to be freed from Castilian rule on the example of anti-colonialism in the British empire. Economic links between Bilbao and the British economy made most Basque nationalists Anglophiles who praised the supposedly gentler colonialism of a superior civilization in contrast to what they believed to be racially inferior 'Spanish occupation' of Euzkadi.[9]

Attempts by 'Regenerationists' in the wake of the defeat in 1898 to bring Spain up to European norms were greeted with scepticism. In many ways, the so-called Generation of 1898 was part of the wider European cultural pessimism of fin-de-siècle literary culture. But the political context of Spain created unique opportunities for self-appointed Regenerationists to put their plans into action. Joaquín Costa, journalist and doyen of Regenerationism, scorned the liberal constitution in Spain which kept power in the hands of political bosses (known as *caciques*), who effectively manipulated elections at the behest of the Interior Ministry. Joaquín Costa wrote that 'suffrage is a farce, government is a farce, the country is a farce'.[10] Various Regenerationists, or figures who fancied themselves as such, attempted to learn from foreign models, particularly from France and from Britain. The young philosopher, José Ortega y Gasset, in 1909 expressed his frustration with the unforgiving condescension towering over his country by the rest of the continent north of the Pyrenees: 'Since I began writing for the public I have hardly written a page in which the word Europe does not appear with symbolic aggression. For me, all Spanish afflictions begin and end with this word.'[11]

The Regenerationalist mission was long nurtured by the Spanish military following its humiliations in the Caribbean and the Philippine Sea. Much of the new mood concerned the military. Defeat in the Spanish-American War provoked a period of intense intellectual activity within the Spanish officer corps as it sought a comprehensible explanation for its failure, prompting some to call for more comprehensive education of the Spanish conscript based around 'military morals'.[12] But other trends were cultural and scientific. King Alfonso XIII was married to a princess of the British royal family, and during his reign British sports became part of popular culture, sometimes controversially as in the case of an English boxing tour in 1911.[13] Plans to imitate best practice in terms of hydrography and irrigation were also controversial. The British Empire's Aswan Old Dam along the Nile in Egypt was the focus of investigation by a mission of Regenerationists who hoped to apply similar improvements to the Guadalquivir in Andalucía.[14]

Spanish governments influenced by positivism hoped that economic progress would satisfy material interests and displace the need for political mobilization. The impressive, if uneven, expansion of the Spanish economy and openness to British capital rendered the regenerationist mood ironic. The crisis felt by successive political and literary generations of the Spanish intelligentsia was spawned not so much by Spain's persistent backwardness, but rather by the acceleration of economic growth, urbanization and a more secular society during the period from 1898 to 1931.[15] Amidst the corruption that kept the Restoration system stable, British writers evinced an apolitical and timeless innocence on behalf of ordinary Spaniards. As Charles Petrie commented, 'the personal honesty of the ordinary Spaniard remained uncontaminated by the venality of his politicians'.[16] Britons working in Spain in this era saw themselves as vectors of modernity amidst a benighted population. In 1873, the Rio Tinto Company gained a licence to mine mineral wealth in Huelva province. Soon, this corner of Andalucía brimmed with Anglo-Hispanic entanglements. British nurses preached hygiene in the company hospital, British miners introduced locals to football and even English high tea became part of middle-class life.

And London resounded with the propaganda and networks of Spanish political exiles. The British capital was part of a 'feedback loop' comprising Barcelona and Paris, in which anarchists driven abroad by the repressive policing of Restoration Spain made contacts with British Independent Labour members and anti-colonial activists.[17] The Restoration government's execution of an innocent Catalan anarchist (Francisco Ferrer), in the wake of a revolution in Barcelona in 1909 called 'Tragic Week', attracted international condemnation of Spanish 'despotism' in large part because of the feedback loops of news, propaganda and solidarity campaigns.[18] The martyrdom of Ferrer and peripatetic repression by the Spanish state did not interrupt the growth of working-class education and culture. The concomitant expansion of the socialist and anarchist movements, both of whom embraced the socially transformative potential of education, ensured that these institutions became centres of a counter-hegemonic culture with new norms and practices becoming established through the circulation of affiliated newspapers, the delivery of lectures and the performance of plays addressing workers' daily concerns.[19] The result was, in the words of Ángel Herrerín López, 'a universe that disconcerted and in some cases provoked admiration among those who opposed it', with even police informants expressing wonderment at the liberated spirit of those who frequented these spaces.[20]

The modernity of anarcho-syndicalism, working-class education and mining colonies was all far removed from the pastoral vision of Spain which British travellers, eager to leave the smog and traffic of industrial Britain behind, wished to see. A popular turn-of-the-century travel guide promoted Barcelona as combining the modernity of British urban society with the curative appeal of the warm climate: 'Barcelona is now the largest city in Spain. It is most prosperous and improving, and although called the Manchester of Spanish Lancashire, it is free from the usual annoyances and appearances characteristic of manufacturing towns.' The Catalan capital shared the climate of health resorts further south in Valencia and Andalucía but boasted superior culture: 'mild in winter and agreeable at all seasons; the enlightened, kind, and bold-hearted, enterprising people who are seen in so thriving a condition, are all so many inducements for the invalid and general tourist to linger here'.[21]

The period between Spain's 'disaster' and the 1930s saw British interest bridge the nineteenth-century Romantic obsession and the advent of Republican modernity. Despite the ease of international travel to Barcelona, the romanticized spell cast by Andalucía had not broken, not least because the Spanish monarchy itself had begun using travel to the corners of Spain as a means of becoming popular and getting closer to the people. Like their European relatives, Alfonso XII and Alfonso XIII embraced their country's regional diversity and established political and symbolic relationships with each region. Their journeys, which in the case of Andalucía looked like a luxurious entourage for an anthropological expedition, were also mechanisms of nationalization and for the diffusion of what might be termed the 'welfare monarchy'.[22] The Spanish regions were no longer passive subjects where, in the words of Raymond Carr, 'politics ran, like an express train, through the desolate townships and villages of Spain, stopping only at election times'.[23] Spanishness, as Margarita Parral has shown, was becoming consolidated, and a variety of nationalist alternatives were emerging. Alfonso XIII's youth (aged sixteen when enthroned in 1902) and charisma came to symbolize a regenerated Spanish character: obstinate and impulsive, but also forthright, idealistic and brave.

Foreign travellers in Spain from the sixteenth to the nineteenth centuries tended to map their impressions of 'lazy' Andalucía onto the rest of Spain. Andalucía thus became associated with 'Spain'. The leading Spanish intellectual, Ortega y Gasset, in the 1940s even equated the 'theory of Andalucía' with the 'theory of laziness'.[24] Catalanists liked to contrast their supposed hard-working modernity and increasing integration with the rest of Europe with the supposed fecklessness of the south. Trade, travel and even foreign policy aligned to give the British the greatest share in what Kirsty Hooper has called a 'Spanish Obsession'. Britain replaced France as Spain's largest trade partner, the study of Spanish culture and language took off in British universities and a tourism boom from the Edwardian well-to-do gathered pace up to the First World War.[25] Local tourist agents played along with stereotyped Spanish images of flamenco and bullfighting in order to entice British custom. British visitors shared proximity with gypsy dancers whilst inhabiting a separate world. They relished the notion that Spain kept one foot in a mythical past and the other in a confused present. The celebration of sensual dance was all the more subversive as both conservative and liberal opinion in Restoration Spain opposed flamenco, as an assault on morality and rationality respectively.[26] By the turn of the century,

Prosper Mérimée's 1845 novella *Carmen* had been widely read in Britain and Georges Bizet's opera version enjoyed success. The opera reached its 1,000th gala performance by the turn of the century and became increasingly daring in its depiction of Carmen's transgressive sexual norms. Gypsies in the British imagination occupied the summit of the exotic within Spain, as being nomads apparently divorced from productive labour and as lazy products of hot climate and proximity to Africa which in vague ways influenced British impressions of Andalucía.[27]

Changes in travel, publishing and education meant that ordinary British people had unprecedented opportunities to tour the country, learn its language and even bring Spanish culture into their own homes in the shape of colourful books, prints and recordings. Postcards contrasted the timeless image of Romantic Spain with the modern means of efficient delivery. These changes, energized by the marriage in 1906 of Queen's Victoria's granddaughter Ena to King Alfonso XIII of Spain, allowed Spain's place in the British impressions of Spain to be informed by reality instead of the imagined black legend. As the anti-German Anglo-French alliance gathered pace after 1904, Spain adopted a subordinate role in British calculations. Earlier attempts in the 1880s to align Spain loosely with the Triple Alliance were long forgotten as Spain reverted to its abiding foreign policy mantra since 1834, or neutrality when Britain and France were at odds, and alliance with them when they were united.[28]

Britain promoted Spanish colonialism in Morocco in preference to creating a vacuum which might encourage a more formidable French or German presence in sight of Gibraltar. Spain's 'Disaster' of 1898 thus bolstered its diplomatic relations with Britain and France, global powers who posed no threat to the unprepossessing Spanish territories in northern Morocco, Western Sahara and Guinea. Whilst the Spanish army fostered an *africanista* wing intent on restoring an imperial dream over the heads of politicians, British diplomacy viewed Madrid's position benignly. The domestic backlash in the 1920s and 1930s caused by Spain's incessant wars with the restive Rif population was thus in part a by-product of Anglo-French 'informal empire'. Spain, like Portugal in 1890, had become a minor victim in the competition of great colonial powers.[29] As Anglo-German rivalry increased, Britain was relieved that Gibraltar remained secure and that Spain would be, at the very least, neutral in any confrontation with Berlin. British diplomacy viewed with relief that Spain by 1906 had abandoned the loose Germanophilia of the time of Alfonso XII and had rallied behind the French position in the Moroccan crisis.[30] The British military hold on Gibraltar grew ever tighter. But its guns and warships were planning a war with an expanded German fleet, not with a friendly neighbour across the 'Neutral Zone' which, by the early twentieth century, had become entangled in deep ties of royalty, tourism and culture.

Gibraltar became the nexus of Anglo-Spanish social interaction. For a long time, the British garrison at the rock had been a base for hardy travellers venturing into Romantic Andalucía. William Clark, author of a mid-nineteenth-century travel narrative called *Gazpacho*, anticipated the notorious culinary xenophobia of British tourists the following century when he recalled an English-owned hotel in Málaga, where 'you could have Harvey's sauce, pale ale, and Stilton cheese, for the asking'.[31]

Clark's travel base of Gibraltar was changing from the middle of the nineteenth century from being a liminal space of pickets, smugglers and labourers traversing the isthmus into a more traditional border. Neither the absence of a formal border (which in any case was ambiguous in the wording of the Treaty of Utrecht) nor its establishment predetermined the warmth of Anglo-Hispanic relations. Gibraltar's most Hispanophile governor, Sir Robert Gardiner, was appointed to command the rock in 1848 and saw the isthmus question as a way to deepen the colony's commercial ties with Spain. Spanish pride, he thought, was understandable, given 'the natural state of a nation fallen in greatness, and conscious of its material and moral weakness'.[32] The cholera outbreak of 1853–5 and changes in Spanish tariff policy led to the first appearance of a formal border, albeit in the form of a quarantine line in the neutral zone. In 1873, this embryonic border was tightened further in response to British insistence on residency checks amidst the cantonalist revolution in Spain. Finally, in 1908, a 9-feet-high border fence was established, annexing the old 'neutral zone'. In the interwar period, the British would establish an airfield there in timely preparation for world war.[33]

Despite the formalization of the border, Anglo-Hispanic relations thrived. British officers and aristocrats mingled with their elite counterparts in neighbouring Andalucía. Gibraltarians of some means spent Sundays picnicking in the open spaces of the Campo de Gibraltar, whereas elites went hunting. Monied and blue-blooded British tourists embodied a sort of informal empire, relying on local Spanish servants as if they were colonials in India, Egypt or Cyprus. Impoverished regions of Andalucía created a picturesque backdrop for visitors to appreciate without sacrificing their political or economic interests. The south-western corner of Andalucía became a focus for Anglo-Hispanic class interaction. From its origins at the end of the Peninsular War, the Calpe Hunt acquired royal status from 1906 when Alfonso XIII became its patron. Whereas

Gibraltar's ruling classes relished the open air and rocky ground of the Campo, Gibraltar working classes plied their own trade between the frontier town of La Línea and the rock. Off-duty soldiers and sailors frequented the brothels in the Spanish working-class town, and migrants passed over the border to work as cooks, cleaners and servants in Gibraltar.[34] Spanish women, with their different dresses and mantillas, were eroticized by young men looking forward to get away from the crowded garrison on Gibraltar. The hunting and picnicking idyll of the Campo stood at odds with the industrialized and internationalized conflicts mounting in Spain amidst the First World War. It was also a self-satisfying reminder to Edwardian imperialists of the asymmetric power relations that were played out on Spanish territory.

Amidst the Anglo-Hispanic idyll in the Campo, Spain's crisis of liberalism in the new century created a curious paradox of a modernizing economy alongside a reinvigorated monarchy keen to apply iron surgery to Spain's ossified and corrupted political elites. The crisis that liberalism and parliamentarism experienced at the turn of the twentieth century gave King Alfonso XIII a decisive role. The First World War gave Spain pre-eminence as Europe's most powerful neutral power. Unlike other neutrals closer to the scene of fighting, Spain did not mobilize its armed forces beyond peacetime levels. Even though British policy failed to move Spain away from a policy of strict neutrality, Anglo-Spanish relations grew increasingly close over the course of the war nevertheless. King Alfonso XIII sponsored humanitarian initiatives and the economy was geared towards supplying the Entente powers, in the face of considerable pro-Central Powers feeling. Spanish opinion was divided during the 'war of words' regarding Spanish neutrality in the First World War. The pro-Entente intellectuals and regionalists were accused by the pro-Central Powers *germánofilos* of choosing Europe over Spain.[35] A melancholy postscript to the war was the 'Spanish influenza' pandemic which broke out in 1918, so named because the absence of wartime press censorship in neutral Spain gave the international press its first high-profile survivor, King Alfonso XIII of Spain, but which in fact originated in the American Midwest. The king survived the flu, only to suffer a political death thirteen years later as a consequence of his reinvigorated rule. Amidst discussions before and during the First World War about models of monarchy for Spain, two examples stood out. The constitutional British system, heavily democratized upon peace in 1918, was less appealing than the authoritarian monarchy of Italy after 1922. Thus, between 1923 and 1930, the Spanish monarchy supported General Miguel Primo de Rivera (1870–1930) along with his military dictatorship.[36]

But hard-nosed British investments in Spain coloured attitudes amidst the revolutionary crisis unleashed by 1917. In February 1919, a conflict broke out in the Barcelona's Traction, Light and Power Company, an Anglo-Canadian hydro-electrical concern and main electricity supplier of the city (known as *La Canadiense*). The company's intransigence towards its staff's union membership became a protracted struggle of forty-four days between the employers, backed by the civilian and military authorities and the British embassy, and the workers whose cause had been taken up by the anarchist CNT. Despite initial promises made by the civil governor, the police led by the dreaded Inspector Francisco Martorell moved to evict those involved in the 'go-slow'. In turn, the English manager Fraser Lawton sacked all the striking workers. His uncompromising stance was backed by the British board and Captain General Milans del Bosch. Simultaneously, the British embassy was urging the government to take stern measures against the 'troublemakers'.[37] The class interests of Anglo-Hispania were a harbinger of the greatest international class conflict of the interwar period, the Spanish civil war as well as British concerns for the Spanish economy as the largest foreign investor. The rising protectionism and indebtedness in the world economy after the First World War anguished British investors. The United States emerged from the war as a huge net creditor, having lent £1.89 billion to all her allies. Britain, in her turn, had lent £1.74 billion to her European allies, having borrowed £842 million from the United States. The total debts of £166 million lent to Russia were irrecoverable. The problem was further complicated by the burden of reparations imposed on Germany. British capitalists feared a Red Spain as a reprisal of the chaos of wartime revolution. The power of the City of London and France's wealthy 'Two Hundred Families', with their respective interests in the vineyards of Jerez and the Río Tinto mines trumped the tragic activism of left-wing solidarity with the republic.

The revolutionary and counter-revolutionary upheaval in Spain underlined the contrast that British visitors glimpsed between the old and new. The military dictatorship of Miguel Primo de Rivera (1923–30) saw itself as an 'iron surgery' regenerating Spain. It sought to create a 'New Spaniard' through the spiritual and physical improvement of soldiers and civilians, resulting in programmes to combat illiteracy and the importation of European physical education regimens. But budgetary restrictions, lack of public interest and the increasing demands of the campaigns in Spanish Morocco limited the impact of such regenerationism on the Spanish population. British observers were unimpressed by the dictator's claim to solve the Moroccan problem once and for all. In the summer of 1921, a poorly supplied and badly led Spanish Army suffered a resounding defeat at Annual in which the victorious Moroccan rebels killed or massacred thousands of troops. The rebel leader, Abd El-Karim, sent his brother to London with an offer of peace as soon as the European powers recognized the independence of the Rif.[38]

The political crisis in Spain allowed the captain general of Barcelona, Primo de Rivera, to seize power in a military coup launched on 13 September 1923. The timing was a great help for the beleaguered King Alfonso XIII, whose personal role in the Annual catastrophe was being investigated by civilian politicians. Primo de Rivera pledged himself to the cause of *abandonismo*, or of retreating from Moroccan territory beyond Spain's historic enclaves along the coast. But army sectarianism dragged his military dictatorship back into the Rif cauldron. British consular reports of the Spanish effort were damning, claiming 'anarchy' in defeated troops in the wake of Annual. For all the inefficiencies of the Spanish order of battle, an implicit Hispanophobia laced the comments, suggesting a low opinion of Madrid's colonialism.[39] Primo de Rivera's eventual success did not alter British views greatly. The Spanish victory in the wake of the world's first modern amphibious landing using combined arms at Alhucemas Bay in September 1925 brought little credit from London. Rather, France's entry into the Rif War on the side of the Spaniards in 1925 was given as the main reason for the brutal 'pacification' of the Rif by 1926.

Military glory did not offset an economic downturn in the homeland. A structural trade deficit persisted despite an aggressively protectionist government policy. Foreign investors were frustrated by the oil monopoly, and the peseta, which was already weak in 1926, would lose almost half its value over the following five years, imperilling the living standards of workers and soldiers alike.[40] Soldiers remained apathetic, desiring only, in the words of one historian, 'to survive in barracks for eight months waiting for permission to return home.'[41] But the hard-bitten officer veterans of the Moroccan wars continued to nurture a desire to transform the military into a genuinely nationalizing institution, convinced of the latent potency of the Spanish 'race' and of the rural poor in particular. This proto-fascism could not carry the dictatorship through the economic crisis and reinvigorated opposition to Primo de Rivera's regime by the end of the 1920s.[42] But it did nurture a military opposition to the republic which followed the end of dictatorship in 1931. The radicalism of the 1930s would retrospectively endear the Primo dictatorship in the eyes of British conservatives who saw in the avuncular general from Andalucía the last tragic hope of defending Spain's monarchical order.

The Scottish artist Muirhead Bone, who spent a lengthy stay in Spain in 1929, recorded how 'disaffection to the monarchy was even then audible, and an impatience of backwardness and old fashions manifest in all parts of the country'. Bone noted that 'with the passing of old customs picturesque history also recedes; and it may be that even such recent scenes as are described in the present volumes have been witnessed for the last time by the Spaniard himself'.[43] The passing of old ways, inherent both in Muirhead Bone's book title (*Old Spain*) and in its publication in the fateful year of 1936, preoccupied British observers of Spain's decade of the 1930s.

The proclamation of the Second Republic in 1931 was a source of anxiety for British investors in Spain. The Primo de Rivera dictatorship had been sceptical, when not outright hostile, towards foreign investment in Spain. Britain as the largest investor faced the ire of finance minister, Calvo Sotelo, who thought that the Restoration model of encouraging foreign exploitation of Spanish resources placed Spain in a colonial relationship. He used a whistle-blower's report about shenanigans in the Rio Tinto mines designed to reduce the company tax bill to demand an increase in headline taxes for foreign companies.[44] But Primo de Rivera's regime also kept the anarchists jailed and the socialists neutered. The collapse of his authoritarianism preoccupied foreign investors in the country. Albert Holland, a Leicester businessman and the Barcelona director of the Boston Blacking Company since 1925, had long become inured to the radicalism of Spain's industrial capital. But from 1931, he recalled how the demands of the working classes became unbearable:

> They tried to force conditions until we could stand it no longer. One of the conditions was that extra workpeople should be set on despite the fact that, according to the business we were doing, we should have been on short time ... Eventually, there was a strike. I was threatened. Several times, I was shot at in the street but escaped and eventually, I got a fresh crowd of workmen who were really good fellows.[45]

Amidst the buoyed-up activism of the anarchists and unionized socialists, Spain's centre-left Republican government tried to implant a secular democracy with cultural improvement as a priority. Its first coalition government (1931-3) invested heavily in schools and launched cultural outreach programmes (involving theatre, travelling exhibitions and literacy classes) targeting the neglected countryside. Progressive cultural organizations, sponsored though rarely led by the state, came to play a key role in this undertaking. Republican propaganda tried to generate new bonds supporting a re-imagined political community in the face of political extremism. The conflict in Spain, which included a failed right-wing coup attempt in 1932 and a failed miners' revolution in 1934, attracted a trend of British literary sensibility which was stimulated by political turmoil. V. S. Pritchett toured Spain on foot and reported on a timeless nobility in the Spanish character: 'The Spanish live in castes, not classes. Their equality – the only real equality I have met anywhere in the world – is their sense of nobility, or rather, in the sense of the absolute quality of the person.'[46] Similarly, the novelist Laurie Lee walked around Spain living by his violin-playing and the generosity of local people. His journey began in 1935 and continued into the civil war.[47] The hopes and perils of the republic attracted British interest and residence, like the emigrant and retired zoologist to Málaga, Peter Chalmers Mitchell.[48]

But the timeless praise of Spanish nobility stood at odds with the consciously modernizing efforts of left-wing governments in power between 1931 and 1933 and again after the Popular Front election victory of February 1936. Within a week of taking office, the new leftist government banished General Francisco Franco to a command on the faraway Canary Islands, correctly identifying the war hero as a likely coup plotter. The separation of Franco from his elite Moroccan command became a focus of tension on the Atlantic archipelago. After a British sailor from the warship *HMS Hood* had taken ill and died in a hospital onshore, his funeral cortège was given police protection in order to 'guarantee the most perfect order in the neighbourhood surrounding the English Cemetery'.[49] The Canaries, like mainland Spain, were awash with strikes, lockouts and agents of law and order triggered by the mobilization of crowds. The presence of General Franco also fed anxieties about unregistered aircraft. In May, a 'most urgent' telegram from the Spanish air command ordered Las Palmas aerodrome to ban all unregistered civilian flights and to check the documentation of all aircraft performing stopovers.[50] The anxiety was well placed. Within two months, a British flyer would spirit General Franco back to his Moroccan command, making the right-wing revolt possible. Popular Front policies turned revolutionary from July 1936, when this military coup, which sought to arrest further reform and defend traditional hierarchies, escalated to full-scale civil war. The republic's ability to defend itself would now rest on its ability rapidly to secure mass support for its war effort and on reconstructing its army. But by the time hostilities commenced in July 1936, Spain would also depend on foreign fighters.

8

Anglo-Hispania during civil war and world war

Civil war began in July 1936 in the wake of the partial failure of a coup d'etat plotted by a group of officers led by General Mola. By the time war started in July 1936, the fear of revolutionary violence and expropriation suddenly dawned upon British residents. Peter Chalmers Mitchell recalled the unreality of the tension amongst his fellow expatriates: 'neither any of my friends, nor any of the English residents I knew, saw any reason to suppose that great troubles were about to come to Spain'.[1] The failure of the military revolt in major cities such as Madrid and Barcelona, where foreigners were disproportionately resident, led to anarchist workers seizing control of private property, production and even policing. Horrified British nationals sought refuge across the border in Gibraltar or in France, where they provided journalists with the kinds of exaggerated atrocity stories which confirmed the conservative bias of most British dailies.[2] Eye-witness accounts of war and revolution made up for the lack of accurate information on the political and military situation in Spain during the first days. Many resorted to stereotypes and hysteria which anguished Britons caught in the tumult. Some eight thousand British tourists and residents found themselves in a country in civil war, and the vast majority of these were in areas held by the Republican government, especially along the northern coast. Within a week of the military rising, Royal Navy vessels, operating in cooperation with other navies, had deployed to coastal waters to protect British residents and evacuate those who so wished.[3]

For British capitalists and propertied residents, the revolution in Barcelona and other towns in Republican hands seemed a rerun of the events of 1917 in Russia. The destruction, confiscation and street rallies seemed the work of an orgiastic mob, very much at odds with the coordinated and logical assault on capitalism which historians such as Chris Ealham have identified.[4] But not all British residents wanted to be rescued. Several British leftists who had gone to attend the anti-Nazi 'People's Olympiad' in Barcelona (cancelled due to civil war breaking out) remained in situ, and some were caught up in the street fighting. The most famous British Olympian was the poet and photogenic symbol of volunteering, John Cornford (1915–36), who joined a local libertarian leftist militia (the POUM) and later recruited several volunteers in Britain to serve in the International Brigades.[5] Other Britons were residents who refused to leave. Nancy Johnstone, a hotelier who had set up her business on the Costa Brava in 1934, witnessed the unreal atmosphere of hospitality in the revolutionary summer of 1936:

> We knew that probably these same charming young men who sat peacefully in the cafe or who came up to pay polite calls on us ... had killed perfectly innocent people in the excitement of the moment; that, although they scrupulously obeyed the rules of etiquette that insisted on all weapons being piled on the table when one was drinking with a friend, they were ready to snatch and use these same weapons lying among the glasses should the occasion demand it.[6]

As for British leftists at home, Spain's trauma offered more inspiration than dread. Byron, the first British Romantic volunteer for somebody else's war, left a legacy which was picked up by British intellectuals in the 1930s. The march of Britain's small but growing fascist movement placed the Spanish situation in sharp relief. At the Battle of Cable Street in London in October 1936, some three thousand 'Blackshirt' supporters of Oswald Mosley's British Union of Fascists were repelled by tens of thousands of local working-class protestors, including Jews, communists, trade unionists and anti-fascists more broadly. Present at the disturbances was Bill Alexander, a British communist of humble origins who was inspired by Cable Street to fight fascism in Spain.

The Spanish foreground in the background

Given the subordinate role played by Spain in British foreign policy anxieties, a paradox emerged in British debate which simultaneously emphasized and marginalized the civil war. Spain's war certainly injected in Britain a sudden energy which rippled across domestic and foreign policy fault lines. In the words of one expert, 'of all foreign conflicts in the twentieth century in which Britain was not directly involved, the war in Spain made by far the greatest impact on British political, social and cultural life'.[7] Mainstream British political attention did not dwell on Spain before July 1936. Even when news of the failed military coup reached London, the knee-jerk response of politicians was dismissive and even racist. Winston Churchill's son, Randolph Churchill, thought that the war amounted to little more than 'a bunch of bloody dagoes killing each other'.[8] The *Times* even complained that the Spanish atrocities of 1936 lacked the 'grandeur' of those of the 1830s.[9] A less obtuse but equally nonchalant view was expressed by the commercial pilot, Cecil Bebb (1905–2002), the Briton whose individual actions in July 1936 made the Spanish Army coup possible. Bebb accepted a contract to fly General Franco from his internal exile on the island of Tenerife to his previous command in Spanish Morocco. The flight of the *Dragon Rapide* acquired mythic status in Francoist Spain.[10] Before the actual rising began, and weeks before the Olympiad fighters and International Brigades had organized themselves, Cecil Bebb was the first, and by far most decisive, British volunteer in the Spanish civil war.

Ignorance of Spanish affairs was matched by a preoccupation with the strategic implications of one side or the other winning in terms of British economic interests and the balance of power in a climate of Appeasement. Thus an 'unknown diplomat' analysing the situation close to the end of the war stressed the internationalization of the conflict and its baleful implication for the Anglo-French alliance against German-Italian rearmament, taking aim at the objectively pro-Nationalist 'Non-Intervention' Agreement of October 1936 'which the British government imposed on the French government, under the pretext of preventing the so-called Spanish 'Civil War from degenerating into a European conflict'.[11] The appeasement-centric view of British diplomatic history has continued to consign Spain's war to secondary status in the crisis of the late 1930s.[12]

Once civil war was underway, Spanish affairs were viewed by the general public more through a domestic rather than a foreign policy lens. Consensus has rendered British foreign policy perverse in being objectively pro-Franco, the French as paralysed, the Fascist powers as evil and Soviet policy as pragmatic.[13] But the entangled nature of Anglo-Hispania in the Spanish civil war ranged beyond the Appeasement question and even the stated positions of political parties. The impact in 1928 of equal universal suffrage created a democratic civil society in Britain which viewed Spain's trauma through an apolitical lens in part aloof from support for or opposition to non-intervention. British women, influenced by their traditional role as housekeepers, organized donations to the Spanish Republic under such slogans as 'Milk for Spain' and mobilized outside of party political and trade union organs.[14] As Emily Mason has argued, 'the Spanish Civil War mobilised people across Britain because of the very fact that that individual projected onto "Spain" their own concerns about the crises perceived to be facing British society and the contemporary world order'.[15]

Much of Britain's projection onto Spain was rustic and pastoral in nature. Interwar Britain produced a rural idyll in culture and conservative politics which was expressed in popular paperback novels and invoked by politicians looking to soothe the barbs of industrial depression in northern cities and the horrific legacy of the First World War.[16] Conservative writers like J. R. R. Tolkien and fascist sympathizers like Henry Williamson produced idyllized works of rural life under threat. As a consequence, British views updated the Romantic view of nineteenth-century Spain, producing easy comparisons between the land conflict and earlier episodes in British history (such as the Peasants' Revolt and Cromwell) and showing particular interest in such ruralized explanations of the civil war (such as the documentary, *The Spanish Earth*). The Scottish resident in Andalucía, Chalmers Mitchell, insisted on rural inequalities driving revolution and adopted an Anglo-Hispanic gaze towards the surrounding poverty. He noted the contrast with Britain, where the rural poor enjoyed better diet and robustness than their urban counterparts. But in Andalucía, 'peasants and fishermen, although they may be burnt and brown, are as a class thinner, more worn and bent than those who work in the towns. I believe it to be a simple question of malnutrition'.[17]

Thus, the cultural cachet of Spain's democracy already caught the attention of British activists once civil war broke out. Harry Politt, British Communist leader, in the 1930s appealed to intellectuals to volunteer in Spain because his Communists 'needed a Byron in their movement'. In fact, most volunteers came from working-class backgrounds, not from the aristocratic class of early-nineteenth-century Romanticism. The outbreak of the divisive Second Republic and civil war produced an onrush of sententious interest in the burden of Spain's history. British Marxist literature condescendingly celebrated a 'backward' and 'feudal' Spain belatedly joining a modern fight against fascism. The Left Book Club published *Spain in Revolt*, whose authors at once Europeanized Spain while also deriding its separateness hitherto: a country 'isolated not only by the Pyrenees but also by the gulf of economic backwardness' was now 'exploded into the rapid and rising stream of European politics'.[18] The wealthy and conservative-leaning British expatriate community in neighbouring Portugal hosted Lisbon politicians to discuss the war in Spain in the summer of 1936. Both parties agreed that the real cause of Spain's trouble dated back to the insurgent tradition born on 2 May 1808.[19] To paraphrase Richard Kagan's analysis of the American 'Spanish craze', the 1930s gave Spain a 'sturdy' image, in contrast to the 'sunniness' of earlier vacations, travelogues and art forms.[20] The forthright and passionate Spain of Goya and Torquemada was reborn.

Communists and non-communist leftists found in the Spanish civil war a cause worth fighting for. Eric Blair (better known as George Orwell) found redemption volunteering in the Spanish civil war. After serving as an imperial officer in Burma, Orwell understood at first hand the humiliation and racism inherent in imperialism. His *Burmese Days* revealed his insight into the visceral and pseudo-pornographic environment of white imperialism. Orwell quit his post before he could get infected by those attitudes. He was thus absolved of being an accomplice and was to fight against fascism in Spain. Orwell's first impressions of revolutionary Barcelona were Romantic:

> Down the Ramblas, the wide central artery of the town where crowds of people streamed constantly to and fro, the loudspeakers were bellowing revolutionary songs all day and far into the night. ... Yet so far as one could judge, the people were contented and hopeful. ... Above all, there was a belief in the revolution and the future, a feeling of having suddenly emerged into an era of equality and freedom.[21]

The egalitarian ethos of the first weeks of the republic at war dazzled British intellectuals desiring new forms of political and social organization. Journalist John Langdon Davies observed that the Hotel Ritz was 'nowhere to be seen' and now existed as a 'popular kitchen' which served 'thousands of poor men and women daily'.[22] The feminist novelist and poet, Sylvia Townsend Warner, shared Orwell's sense of thrill but also imagined more possibilities for cultural and sexual liberation amidst the scenes of militiawomen and the confiscation of the property and symbols of the upper classes.[23] Even so, the image of emancipation was more apparent than the reality. Republican propaganda used women as a tool for the benefit of the war effort, rather than actively promoting the contribution of women.[24]

Very soon, thousands of armed British volunteers (a contingent of the Communist-organized International Brigades) would join the intellectuals. Ever since the first units of the International Brigades filed into Madrid in November 1936, the role of transnational volunteers from fifty-three countries in the Spanish civil war has inspired enormous literary interest. Many of the individuals who took up arms in defence of the Spanish Republic regarded the country's battlefields as just one front in a universal struggle between democratic progress and fascist barbarism. This grand narrative of international solidarity exalted the flawed Spanish democratic republic as an anti-fascist symbol, often at the cost of relegating the people, politics and culture of Spain to the sidelines. The exact number of International Brigade volunteers has been estimated between 45,000 and 50,000.[25] Exact details are hard to know because many volunteers travelled without passports, either because they were exiles from authoritarian regimes or because they surrendered them to recruiters. Even liberal democracies could not provide exact figures. At this point in history, a passport was not required for Britons with a three-day return train ticket to Paris.[26] Jason Gurney, a socialist sculptor from London, was one of many volunteers who allowed their return tickets to expire whilst they made their way clandestinely to the Spanish frontier.

Interest in the brigades waxed and waned with domestic politics: comparatively little research was conducted on them in the 1970s, for example. Towards the end of the decade, interest rebounded in sight of Spain's successful post-Francoist transition to democracy, along with the failure in leftist eyes of any viable parliamentary path to socialism in Britain. In 1979, Jack Jones, leader of the powerful Transport and General Workers' Union, offered a foreword to a new study of his own motivations for volunteering to fight in Spain:

> The awful realisation that black fascism was on the march right across Europe created a strong desire to act. The march had started with Mussolini and had gained terrible momentum with Hitler and was being carried forward by Franco. For most young people there was a feeling of frustration, but some determined to do anything that seemed possible, even if it meant death, to try to stop the spread of fascism … This was Fascist progression. It was real and it had to be stopped.[27]

With the coming of the Thatcher-era in Britain, interest in these heroes of the left was renewed. Mass youth unemployment alongside a reinvigorated anti-communism cast the volunteers of the 1930s in a fresh light, inspiring literary and academic works alike.[28] A coming-of-age novel, set in early 1980s Britain, recounts how a hardy gamekeeper from the Scottish Highlands met personal tragedy in his youth volunteering in the 'Spanish Civil War business'.[29] At least one major attempt at documenting the tales of brigadiers began in the mid-1980s. The march of social history also produced a shift in focus about international volunteers towards exploring their origins and levels of political engagement in such micro-histories as South Wales mining communities or the Glasgow dockyards.[30]

Most foreign volunteers were political exiles or the first generation of such hoping to fight for the brigades in Spain as a first step to reclaiming their homeland.[31] Esmond Romilly, who served with the German Thaelmann battalion, described the life of these exiles in sober terms: 'I remembered what I had heard from them of the exile's life, scraping an existence in Antwerp or Toulouse, pursued by immigration laws, pursued relentlessly – even in England – by the Nazi Secret Police. And they had staked everything on this war.'[32] Volunteers viewed Spain as the best, or maybe the final, opportunity to halt the spread of fascism in Europe. But in Britain the 'politics of diaspora' was indirect, for most volunteers came from rooted working-class backgrounds. It required a certain character to want to fight abroad, especially as most had never have even left their own country in a time of peace. In general volunteers were young, 80 per cent working class, 60 per cent communist or at least very highly politicized.[33] In total, more than 2,300 Britons volunteered, disproportionately from the urban and working-class areas of London, Liverpool, Manchester and Glasgow. Miners were heavily represented, given their traditions of radical politics and knowledge of the Spanish government's suppression of the Asturian miners' rebellion of 1934. While virtually all came from left-wing backgrounds, only slightly more than half were actually members of the British Communist Party (CPGB).[34]

The International Brigades enjoy much greater coverage than any British soldiers in previous wars in Spain. As James Hopkins has noted, 'the inarticulate and the silent have, at last, found their voices'.[35] Yet the Spanish civil war has continued to give the impression of being a 'poet's war'.[36] Much of the written accounts focus on the middle-class intellectuals such as Ralph Fox, John Cornford, Julian Bell and Christopher Caudwell who were all killed while in Spain. Though only a handful of the casualties, they have dominated the literature because they were newsworthy at the time.[37] Esmond Romilly, a socialist and nephew of Winston Churchill, published one of the most resounding literary accounts, *Boadilla*, before being killed in action (not in Spain, but in a bombing mission in the Second World War). Middle-class intellectuals were the most articulate, and most likely had easy access to publishers after the war had ended. The Spanish civil war as a source of literary inspiration remains peerless.[38] Home-grown literature within Spain and abroad ranged from supporting a Europeanizing, modernizing (the two were often used synonymously) project or, on the other hand, an anti-materialistic, Hispanic culture (the kind espoused, for example, by Miguel de Unamuno). The concept of 'Cainism', which posited that Spaniards were particularly prone to break out into irreconcilable and, above all, fratricidal conflict, convinced both Spanish writers like Antonio Machado and British readers of Spanish affairs.[39] The years 1936 to 1939 saw a vast mobilization of Spanish and foreign artists, writers and intellectuals in support of the Spanish Republic.

But in terms of mass audience, the Spanish civil war reached the British public not via novels, nor even always via editorials, but via images. Conflict photojournalism came of age in the Spanish civil war. It was a revolutionary medium because, in the words of Gisèle Freund, the image that would traditionally have been supporting the main body of the article itself became the story.[40] The images of the Spanish civil war dominated the British current affairs print media, and the wartime photographs were consumed as though they were official histories.[41] Photographs and posters from the period are remarkable in their ability to convey the ideological intensity of the conflict and the human damages that it wrought. The Spanish civil war widened the door for the correspondents of the Second World War to record history using images and to test the boundaries on what was deemed publishable in Britain.[42] It also transformed British journalists into participants in a way that written records could not. As Susan Sontag noted, 'there is something predatory in the act of taking a picture. To photograph people is to violate them, by seeing them as they never see themselves, by having knowledge of them that they can never have; it turns people into objects that can be symbolically possessed.'[43] Journalists almost always distanced themselves from the objects of their lens, raising the barrier between possessor and possessed.

Most publications were passionately committed to one side of the war or the other, and not just the Spanish war, but wars in general since the advent of modern telegraphy in the Crimean War.[44] A minority of the press coverage sympathized with Franco's nationalists, and tried to tie the gruesome images of Spain back into a morality tale about the danger of communism in Britain. The *Saturday Review of Politics, Literature, Science and Art* published an article entitled 'Clergy Tainted by the Red Virus', and lamented the links between Spanish Communists and the British clergy (the leftist dean of Canterbury, Hewlett Johnson, described the Popular Army as the 'finest in the world'[45]). The use of accompanying captions to enforce this theory was both emotionally effective and provided commentary to steer the readers' opinions. The first picture in the clergy showed two nuns being hurried along with their heads down by an unknown soldier. The caption did not permit any notion that the soldier was protecting them. Rather it read, 'Here are nuns being led from their burnt-out convent by Red soldiers in Spain. What was their fate?' The image was then linked to a quote from Hewlett Johnson, a cleric derided on the British right as the 'red' dean of Canterbury: 'Russia is not so irreligious as we might think'.[46] Images and editorials like these captured a conservative mood in Britain. Some three quarters of British exports to Spain during the first nine months of 1937 went to nationalist-held areas.[47] British capitalists, more fearful of the red republic and their own depressed industrial heartlands, had few qualms about

Franco. A number of Britons even volunteered for Franco's Nationalist Spanish Legion in the civil war (which included such literati as Peter Kemp and Jason Gurney).

British coverage of the events in Spain was generally far from static. The *Illustrated London News* in particular featured articles that appeared to promote both sides of the conflict, with no consistent loyalty to either side. But the abiding impact of the war in Spain was radical. British journalists in the Spanish civil war were less likely than in any war hitherto to claim to be impartial. They hoped not only to inform British readers but also to influence public opinion.[48] Given the severe restrictions imposed on foreign press in Franco's nationalist zone, journalists in any case had to develop their own impressions of the war and its meaning from one side of the firing line. David Deacon estimated that about 81 per cent of British media coverage focused on the republican side of the war.[49]

Tory Britain was a hard sell when images abounded of disinterred nuns, barricades and commandeered private vehicles adorned in anarchist liveries. British politics had avoided most of the revolution and counter-revolution of the European mainland, which bestowed even on radical leftist volunteers an esteem for moderation and order. Militia images were featured much more heavily in the French press than in the British, as the insurrectionary tradition north of the Pyrenees found a better reception than in law-and-order Britain. British readers needed to see the militias as controlled by the government in order to approve of them, and seeing such spontaneous action in these images challenged this view.[50] Photographic evidence of women fighters, even when many of these – unbeknownst to their readers – were staged, shocked traditional society. Equally, Britain's sensitive class ribs were prodded by images of armed working-class solidarity, especially when daringly furnished with such captions as 'civilian volunteers, including at least one woman'.[51] More impact was gained with the dissemination of images of victims. Some publications tried to provoke the government to abandon its policy of non-intervention. The famous photograph of a child killed in an air raid was captioned with the words (in English) 'if you tolerate this, your children will be next'.[52]

War and politics

As in previous Spanish wars, whatever ideological motivations and propaganda swarmed around the volunteers were given short shrift by the extremes of climate, privation and exhaustion of military service. Despite the fame of the Spanish Republic having the best-paid soldiers in the world, pay was often minimal and erratic. The International Brigades were actually paid less than Spaniards: in February 1938, a Spanish soldier in the 15th International Brigade was paid 100 pesetas, but a foreigner only 70 pesetas.[53] The volunteers also suffered from largely ad hoc administration due to a lack of military expertise in the brigade. As such, volunteers often found themselves subjected to treatment that was completely arbitrary, regardless of ideology. Many accounts exist of jobs being assigned on the basis of assumed military experience or simple personal connection. One famous account records brigadiers answering questions about what experience they possessed with 'private ambitions'.[54] Otherwise, the volunteers lived a life of static warfare amidst gradual retreats and a fear both of the opposing nationalists and their own political command. A brigade volunteer taken prisoner was even more deserving in the nationalist eyes of reprisal, even execution, than a Spanish 'Red' volunteer. A veil of silence over missing and wounded comrades compounded the fear. A letter from the International Brigade's headquarters at Albacete to London related the anxiety: 'We are not told when our men are sent to hospitals or when they are killed. Nor are we supposed to divulge information. Nobody knows.'[55]

The high casualty rate suffered by the International Brigades had multiple effects on nearly every level of the brigade structure. In some instances, the thrill of battle kept morale high despite losses, as new bonds of comradeship and reputations were forged. Bob Clarke, who joined after the Battle of Jarama (February 1937), in a discussion with some veteran friends mentioned that the stories of their engagement 'had a great effect on me and also on the rest of the lads who had gathered round to listen. We realised that we had a tradition to follow.'[56] But high casualties meant an increasing number of Spanish troops were incorporated into the brigades at most levels to replace prohibitive losses. One entire company of the British Battalion became Spanish after the battle of Jarama.[57] In total, around 23 per cent of all volunteers in Spain were killed outright, or taken prisoner, with a majority of survivors getting wounded at least once. The combat efficiency of the battalion was severely damaged by this rate of loss. During the Battle of Jarama, the battalion suffered nearly 60 per cent casualties, while at Brunete, of 331 men who composed the British Battalion at its start, only 42 remained at its end.[58] Walter Gregory recalled the brigadiers themselves asking such questions frequently, recalling that at Hill 481, 'we could not help but ask, "How much more have they got? How much more can we take?"'[ ] The influence of this palpable degradation of combat efficiency thus not only caused headaches for brigade command, but also in the ranks.[59]

As in earlier civil wars, volunteers stiffened their resilience with their own bonds of comradeship, ethics and leisure, strengthening what military historians term 'primary group cohesion'. The prevalence of spontaneous songs in the brigade as a means of keeping up morale warded off fear under shellfire. Javier Pérez-López has demonstrated that songs were used to bridge ideological and national gaps to strengthen the primary group and esprit de corps.[60] Singing bonded volunteers and strengthened morale amongst other nationalities, too, as Josie McLellan's work on the German volunteers of the Thaelmann battalion has demonstrated.[61] The bitter-sweet nature of the lyrics relating to the Jarama Valley revealed the intimidating and unifying power of collective singing.[62]

Morale and demoralization

There were protracted quiet times allowing for interactions with local Spanish troops and civilians. The volunteers, lodged in Spanish towns and villages, debated war and revolution in the rearguard, convalesced in Spanish hospitals and the luckier ones managed to take leave in Madrid and Barcelona. William Rust also noted numbers of men being 'invited … to the homes of the townsfolk', often confusing the battalion cooks since fewer men turned up at the mess hall.[63] Most volunteers recalled these meals fondly, despite the language barrier, mainly because of the food provided, fresh bread and roasted goat with peppers made a break from stew twice a day.[64] Close bonds were often formed between volunteers and families with which they were billeted. One volunteer married the daughter of his hosting family.[65] The British perceived Spanish innocence on account of neutrality in the cataclysmic Great War, which, combined with their love of the good life, led foreign volunteers to infantilize them. Scottish brigader John Londragon commented, 'We got on very well with the Spaniards. They were very child-like. I don't use the word in an insulting way … They had never been involved in war before and had known nothing about it at all.'[66] Elsewhere, however, condescension was replaced by a contempt that is all too redolent of the old 'black legend'. Jason Gurney complained that 'every Spanish unit I had [anything] to do with appeared to be devoid of any military sense'.[67]

British International Brigade volunteers, like their predecessors, found local food exotic. Everyday consumables such as cigarettes and food played a major role in governing the morale of all troops, but peculiar demands were made by men from northern European climes. Notably, the difference in cuisine often resulted in a significant culture shock to many Anglophone volunteers. Frank Thomas, a volunteer for the nationalist side, was scathing about chorizo sausage, as was George Orwell, famously commenting that it 'tasted of soap'. Fred Thomas commented that it was rare to meet anyone who enjoyed Spanish food at all.[68] British volunteers across the political spectrum took exception to the quality of provisions, especially when it was prepared at such a reassuring place as the 'English Cookhouse'. While the communist William Rust claimed that the cookhouse were popular among the men, other Britons sought culinary refuge in Spanish canteens.[69] Fred Thomas, a gunner in a British anti-tank battery, recalled the grim parade of the soup kitchen: 'Soup duly arrived by donkey cart from the village, but it was inedible as far as I was concerned. Beans in olive oil'. When hunger drove Thomas to eat the food, he regretted the 'bits of meat (donkey? mule?), rice and little scraps of potato … Nobody knew what nationality the cooks were, though we were quite clear that they had been born out of wedlock and were now fascist'.[70] Only in protracted battles did empty stomachs override British complaints. At the battle of Hill 481, the defence was aggravated by a lack of food and water, pushing the battalion to breaking point.[71]

Comforts and minor luxuries to distract troops also had a significant impact on the morale of the volunteers stationed on the front line. Simple items such as cigarettes and chocolate were in constant high demand throughout the war, and frequently supplies interrupted in the middle of combat produced much annoyance and grumbling throughout the brigade. Cigarettes became the perfect appendage to news from home. Frequent letters from home were welcomed not just for the obvious reasoning of homesickness, but often because cigarettes were sent with them.[72] Letters also gave brigade volunteers a curious liberation from the strains of communicating with Spanish and foreign comrades. The lack of a reliable *lingua franca* exasperated liaison officers and trainers. George Orwell recalled the limited utility of his French when training some Spanish volunteers and had to resort to his 'murderous Spanish' instead. The power of interpreters rose immensely, regardless of their ranks or backgrounds. British volunteers serving in the German Thälmann Brigade had to rely upon their German-speaking comrade, Arnold Jeans, in order to understand orders. Jeans thus became for all practical purposes their commanding officer.[73]

The reality of foreign language was a demoralizing reminder that the volunteers were far from home. The influence of news from home and post in general could be positive. Brigaders were frequently sent creature comforts in parcels and letters, and reading material was also provided; indeed, the post often became a lifeline for volunteers with little else to do in the boredom of trench life.[74] But letters could only do so much to stall homesickness. Complaints about food often related back to cuisine from home. British volunteers, like their Spanish Republican comrades, could rarely expect leave, with some units remaining unrelieved in the line for six months. They resented witnessing the young men of the republic's internal security forces (assault guards and *carabineros*) being lavished with new weapons while drawing an ample salary. An unfavourable comparison was noted after the war with the nationalist volunteers. Peter Kemp was easily able to acquire foreign leave for reasons such as family issues at least three times during his service in Spain. But foreign leave was a rare luxury for the International Brigades.[75] Disciplinary problems grew in the aftermath of the Battle of Jarama (February 1937) when repatriation was denied to foreign volunteers, and the impression was created that service in Spain would be for the duration of hostilities.[76]

Harsh conditions of service in the brigades frequently degraded morale, particularly in the front line. Morale also suffered from high numbers of wounded, and especially the significant issues of disease due in part to poor hygiene and living conditions on the front. Hardships at the front were often tolerated, but extended line service put severe strain on the morale, especially in the wake of the battle of Jarama (when the British Battalion stayed in the front line for nearly four months). Richard Baxell has noted how relative inexperience with frontline conditions combined with other issues such as poor hygiene and bad rations to create a crisis in discipline and morale.[77] Similar concerns appeared near the end of service around Gandesa in 1938, with William Gregory complaining about the poor conditions of foxholes, sanitation and summer heat.[78]

Prolonged service on the front lines and also medical logistics made disease the biggest scourge.[79] The defeat at Jarama was compounded by outbreaks of scabies, while dysentery, jaundice and other diseases filled entire wards. While some like Bob Clarke were 'whipped off to hospital', others such as Hugh MacKay who arrived in mid-1938 were not given appropriate medical attention. MacKay recalled, 'I lay out for three days in a ditch'.[80] Many volunteers noted how getting wounded often dispelled their initial idealism, replacing it with a cynicism. Nationalist volunteer Frank Thomas remembered the role played by convalescence in his decision to desert: 'in hospital my romantic fatalism became realism'.[81]

A great majority of international volunteers were either wounded or contracted disease. Poor pre-existing Spanish health infrastructure outside the cities meant that wounded soldiers faced a gamble as to the quality of their treatment, determined by logistics, the location of the front and the severity of the wound.[82] Some soldiers could be kept waiting at casualty clearing stations for such long periods of time that by the time they turned up at hospital, their wounds were infested with maggots and other larvae.[83] British casualties routinely faced evacuation times of several hours.[84] Treatment in hospital was by no means a pleasant experience either – long waiting times, again caused by an overstretched system and a lack of medical supplies, meant that casualties often spent hours waiting for wounds to be treated.[85] But even then, hospital stays could offer a welcome, if tedious, break from the front.

Another welcome break could be found in alcohol. British campaign memoirs from the 1700s abound with accounts of dissolute and violent troops alienating Spanish civilians with their inebriation, and the pattern repeated itself in the 1930s. Drunkenness featured prominently even in the most supportive of sources. The communist, William Rust, admitted that drunkenness was a major issue.[86] Vincent Brome noted the formation of patrols to visit the local town every night and round up all the drunks, including his own adjutant at one point.[87] In one instance, the Irish volunteer, Maurice Ryan, fired on his own troops while drunk.[88] Diary entries in turn revealed the demoralizing effect on others of a comrade's abuse of alcohol. As with the Spanish troops, foreign volunteers bonded with each other using tobacco, cannabis and the new pharmacological stimulants available in interwar Europe (cocaine, amphetamines and morphine).[89] The other problem facing commissars was prostitution. Prostitution was also alluded to in memoirs, with one by Bob Clarke recalling how battalion doctors would always try to provide men with medical treatment for sexually transmitted infections upon return from leave. Many volunteers succumbed to urges whilst in Spain, especially when in one city a hospital lay next door to a brothel.[90] The presence of lecherous and drunken foreign soldiers often caused a backlash from local communities. When attempting to receive billets in the town of Lécera the British Battalion found itself encountering a hostile mayor and population. In the middle of Albacete, home of International Brigade training, cultural misunderstandings abounded. The disturbing of crosses in a nearby graveyard angered the villagers again, and godless volunteers were automatically blamed. Interactions with the local population were an important part of the volunteers' experiences of Spain, despite attempts by the likes of communists like William Rust to frame them in the context of 'international-anti-fascist-unity'.[91]

Demoralization was the concern of political officers (commissars), who, in addition to political instruction, were also responsible for the volunteers' well-being. Communists were over-represented amongst these political officers.

The control exerted by the Comintern over the commissars and their methods of disciplining men have remained contentious.[92] Recent research by James Matthews has highlighted how commissars were interested in the physical welfare of the soldiers along with their strict orders to prevent mutiny and desertion.[93] Spontaneous efforts were made to keep up morale, such as VIP visits, theatre productions and more humorous aspects of brigade newspapers. British volunteers fondly recalled the morale-boosting presence of wine and field kitchens. Commissars also performed a pastoral function for brigadiers. The sculptor, Jason Gurney, thought they were like chaplains in the British Army.[94] But accounts abound of volunteers growing annoyed at the constant discourse involving politics.[95] Commissars did better in the eyes of volunteers if they came from the front. Dunlop, a defender of the Commissar system, recalled leaving 'in disgust' at one Spanish Commissar's speech about resistance, when in Dunlop's eyes the lecturing man looked as though he had never experienced any kind of fighting at all.[96]

The commissars were usually seen as the most ideologically committed of the Republican war effort. Certainly communists remembered their ideals and discipline. William Rust described commissars as a noble force using stirring speeches to educate and enliven the troops.[97] Others, by contrast, resented the austere high-handedness and inertia of the British Communist leadership in Spain. British writers seeking inspiration from the left-wing compatriots complained in a letter to Harry Pollitt that the British Communist leaders in Barcelona were 'cliquey, isolated and racist'.[98] More than the individuals in question, the orthodox communism represented was belied by the deterioration of the Spanish republic on their watch. To the disillusionment of campaign life was added political disenchantment at the counter-revolution underway in the republic at war. Old habits of military and political life returned, made worse by rampant corruption and shortages as the economy deteriorated. And the events of May 1937 left no group other than the communists to blame for the slide to defeat.

The ending of the Spanish revolution

At the peak of the International Brigade's fighting in the winter and spring of 1937, the revolutionary promise that had excited the likes of George Orwell had almost evaporated. The transformation achieved by revolutionary movements behind the lines had been impressive. But bourgeois Republican norms had long returned to civilian life and the government, under growing Communist influence, had militarized the ad hoc militias of the summer of 1936 and reconstituted a People's Army. The return of hierarchy, centralized authority and even a sanitized form of capitalism enraged revolutionaries on the left, especially anarchists, and soon a civil war within a civil war emerged.

The Barcelona 'May Days' of 1937, a shootout between communists and anarchists, accelerated the communist-dominated counter-revolution.[99] The May Days included some unlikely British actors. Ethel MacDonald, a working-class anarchist communications officer, was dubbed the 'Scots Scarlet Pimpernel' for her work in helping persecuted anarchists to escape the crackdown. The encroaching communist influence over the republic was obvious to the anguished British embassy. But the British Communist Party newspaper, *Daily Worker*, was unapologetic about the May Days, or as one columnist wrote 'the Communist Party and the United Front is the one true revolutionary programme', noting the importance of discipline and unity in winning the war. John Ross Campbell, a Scottish communist famous for a sedition trial in 1924 which helped bring down Britain's first Labour government, argued that the Trotskyists siding with the 'uncontrollable Anarchists' against the government was an act of counter-revolution. Campbell judged it a counter-revolutionary act to turn weapons against the government when it was fighting a life-and-death battle against fascism.[100]

As the International Brigades were disbanded or taken over by Spanish recruits, the majority of British volunteers suffered under the loss of comradeship. Spanish Republican authorities tended to indigenize the representations of foreign involvement in official propaganda.[101] Even though foreign volunteers from all parts of the world continued fighting for the Republic right up to the great Ebro Battle of 1938, the wider diplomatic climate doomed them. In September 1938, the Spanish Republican government, bowing to pressure from the nonintervention committee and hoping to set an example that Franco's backers would follow, decreed the disbandment of the International Brigades. Hundreds of British veterans left Spain, and many would fight another day. Veterans like George Orwell returned to Britain, confirmed more than ever in their anti-fascism (and also anti-communism in his case), marvelling at the superficially unchanged way of British life, of bottles of milk being delivered to homes, of the lack of bombing from the air and absence of malnutrition.[102] But Orwell, like the other Anglo-Hispanic warriors, would not have long to wait for bombs to fall.

Unlike supporters of the republic, British opinion which was either neutral or pro-Franco did not need to mobilize much propaganda or volunteering.

The Tory-led policy of 'Non-Intervention' already worked in favour of Franco's nationalists. Conservative personalities in any case were less inclined towards the sort of activism demonstrated by trade unionists, intellectuals and volunteers.[103] Republicans hoping in vain for British aid against Franco were amazed at the naïveté of conservatives who saw in the Generalísimo a lesser evil or even a more benevolent partner for British investments in Spain and security in the Mediterranean. As the Republican staff officer, José Martín Blázquez, explained in 1939, '(Spanish) reactionaries hate England. They hate her as the country of Liberalism, and even more because she defeated the invincible Armada and is the mistress of Gibraltar.'[104] The Anglophobic impulses of Franco's regime would soon disabuse British conservatives of much, but not all (thanks to subterfuge), of their fantasies. Mobilization was forced upon conservatives in Britain once it became clear by 1939 that the policy of appeasement (in which non-intervention in Spain and re-armament at home had played a central part) had run out of road. A general European war began in September 1939 in which Spanish civil war veterans, both British and Spanish, would play a significant role.

Second World War Spain

Following the defeat of the republic in 1939, the dominant view of the International Brigades was expressed by William Rust. *Britons in Spain* (1939) attempted to address the criticism that the war in Spain was an ideological battle between communism and fascism due to the fact that there were representatives of both ideologies during the conflict. The involvement of the Soviet Union in providing arms to Spain and the dominant role played by the Comintern in the formation of the Brigades undoubtedly gave the impression that the war was a pretext for Soviet expansionism. The blatant Nazi and Fascist expansionism in Spain was partly occluded by the alliance of Hitler's Germany and Stalin's USSR during the era of the Molotov–Ribbentrop Pact (1939–41). Historians have noted the contradictory legacy of the International Brigades. On the one hand they aided the republic and fought for democracy but on the other hand they boosted the credibility of Stalin.[105]

William Rust's image of the International Brigades was much influenced by the official doctrine of the Communist Party of Great Britain (CPGB) which in turn reflected the attitude of the Soviet Union: to abandon revolutionary tendencies so that a true Popular Front could be realized. Moreover, Rust acknowledged the presence of intellectuals, liberals and those he described as moderates. In essence, for Rust, the International Brigades were 'a mighty historical fact of our times … the spirit of internationalism, which welds men of different countries together'.[106] But his valediction was laced with ongoing communist sectarianism which seemed bizarre in the wake of the Nazi-Soviet Pact of August 1939. Fred Copeman, for example, was labelled a 'traitor' due to his critique of communist policies.[107]

The ideological representation of the Spanish civil war for a time faded amidst the upheaval of the Second World War in Europe. The baptism of fire ranked higher during the dark days of 1940 than the suspect political motives behind volunteering in Spain. Bill Alexander, communist commander of the British Battalion at the wintry battle of Teruel (1937–8), became the first communist cadet at Sandhurst Military Academy's officer training course. Until May 1940, the European war raged far from the British mainland, in ways which diluted the heady cocktail of ideology that had motivated the volunteers of 1936. Finland's Winter War (1939–40) against the Soviet Union distorted the ideological balance of foreign volunteerism. Most left-wing opinion outside of Moscow's orbit sided with the Finnish David against the Soviet Goliath, and even some International Brigade veterans went to fight amidst the frozen forests and lakes of Karelia. The fact that they were joined on the same side by volunteers from authoritarian and pro-Franco regimes, including some who recently fought on Franco's side, mattered as little as the fact that British and French volunteers in Finland rubbed shoulders with Germans against whom elsewhere in Europe they were conducting a 'phoney war'.[108]

Transnational soldiering did not end with the triumph of Franco in 1939. Almost four thousand Basque children had been evacuated from Spain by British charities in 1937 to start new lives in Britain. Despite pressure from right-wing activists and the victorious Franco regime to repatriate the children, almost all remained.[109] Several of them grew up to join the British armed forces towards the latter part of the Second World War.[110] Not only did British International Brigade veterans apply lessons from the Spanish civil war in the defence of Britain in 1940, but hundreds of Spanish Republican veterans would also join British ranks during the Second World War. Other Spanish Republican exiles worked with British covert operations, or languished in prisoner-of-war camps in England until their status could be established. Once Britain's Second World War switched from phoney to real, British defence planners drew on lessons from the Spanish civil war. An anonymous Republican refugee in Britain in 1940 in contact with Hugh O'Donnell, a photojournalist who had been in Barcelona and the front, offered sobering lessons about air raids to British readers who required no other introduction than the title 'I was in Spain':

I was there during all those years that Spain was at war with itself, and with Italy and with Germany. I know what a bomb looks like ... a bomb explosion ... and death ... I have seen people literally blown to nothing. I have seen men horribly maimed and torn by those people who used Spain as a field for experiment so as to guide them in this present war.[111]

The refugee counselled stoicism, reinforced air raid precautions in cities and the shooting of looters on sight, 'for a man vile enough to rob under such conditions is not fit to live in society under such conditions'.[112]

But the Nazi conquest of France in June made not air raids the immediate cause of anxiety, but invasion. In the invasion fear of 1940, British defence strategists borrowed ideas from a distinguished communist veteran of the International Brigades. The journalist, Tom Wintringham, found official support in 1940 for his writings on people's war. His best-selling *New Ways of War* argued for militia and guerrilla tactics in home defence in the event of a Nazi invasion of England. His recommendations for the hastily constituted 'Home Guard' drew heavily on his recent experiences in Spain.[113] Writing amidst the evacuation of Allied troops from Dunkirk in late May 1940, Wintringham argued: 'If the Germans land we should make it a people's war. ... We have soldiers. They will do most of the job. But in order to do the job quickly, completely, with as little loss as possible, we must become as far as possible – an aroused people, an angry people, an armed people!'[114] The Republican example synthesized a heterogenous set of veterans' motives and aspirations together, from communism to anarcho-syndicalism, and from statist liberalism to regional nationalism. In the desperate times of summer 1940 Wintringham's politics mattered as little as those of the communist Sandhurst cadet, Bill Alexander. Rather, Wintringham's Spanish expertise in tank and guerrilla warfare was highly prized. Osterley Park, a Georgian country estate in west London, became the training centre for Britain's new 'Local Defence Volunteers', soon indelibly known as the 'Home Guard'. Abandoned buildings were detonated and guerrilla fighters darted amidst the ruins.[115] The early training of the anti-invasion force was heavily Spanish, as Ricardo Sicre, a Catalan leftist and later Allied spy, had somehow managed to escape a French concentration camp housing Republican exiles and reach Britain to join Wintringham's training staff.[116]

But Nazi invasion plans, half-baked as they were, foundered upon the British aerial victory in the Battle of Britain in July–September 1940. As the immediate threat of Nazi invasion passed, Wintringham's central role training the Home Guards in Spanish tactics was diluted. The British Army started treating

Wintringham's trainees more like a reserve army. But the Spanish guerrilla ethos persisted in training. John Langdon Davies, veteran journalist of the Spanish civil war, worked as a trainer and manual writer in Britain's Home Guard in Sussex (a likely invasion zone). In a widely read instruction manual, Langdon Davies drew upon his Spanish experience of dive-bombing and Molotov cocktails to shape defence in depth.[117]

Furthermore, Britain from the summer of 1940 could count on not just Spanish lessons, but also Spanish manpower defecting from the French foreign legion to continue the fight against fascism. Allied retreats from France and Scandinavia brought hundreds of thousands of French troops to British soil, most of whom re-embarked to French ports in the hope of continuing the fight against Hitler. But as news of Marshal Pétain's armistice reached foreign legionaries on British soil, the response from its Spanish members was outrage. About half-a-million Republican soldiers and civilians had fled Franco's occupation of Catalonia early in 1939 and were interned in French concentration camps.[118] Thousands of men of fighting age joined the foreign legion, out of despair or conviction, and fought in French campaigns right up until the armistice of 22 June 1940. Their French officers accepted the legitimacy of Vichy France, and soon received orders to repatriate their men, including the Spaniards, to French territory. But Spanish legionaries launched a protest before they could be disembarked from British soil. They were doubly outraged in being both anti-fascist and largely anarchist in background (which made obeying any military authority, let alone a foreign defeatist one, a tall order). A stand-off ensued once the Pétainist officers received orders to use force on the mutineers. As the Spanish veterans of their own civil war and the Norwegian campaign were interned in prison, their cause was championed in the House of Commons. Osbert Peake, a government minister, spoke in their defence:

> They are interned in great numbers to-day in Stafford Gaol, and I suppose in other prisons. They were members of the French Foreign Legion. They fought at Narvik; they came back from Narvik and were sent to Brest; and they came back from Brest to England. At Narvik and Brest they saw the relations that exist between the British soldiers and British officers. They are now interned because they declined to remain under French officers who were Petainists. They are unable to fight for the cause which they love so well under British officers who would treat them as soldiers and not as criminals.[119]

Eventually, British officers brokered a compromise by offering the Spaniards service in British uniform. The men were thus initiated as 1 Spanish Company of the Royal Pioneer Corps. Logistical tasks gave the Spaniards greater opportunities to prove their loyalty in the eyes of their British officers, as well as to stay out of frontline areas (where the risk of capture could have seen them deported to Franco's Spain). Most gave themselves English *nomes de guerre*, both to cover their backs and to assist their British officers who lost syllables trying to pronounce Spanish names. Thus Francisco Jerónimo became 'Frank Williams'. An attempt by one of his comrades to adopt the name of one of the most famous British pirates in Spanish folk memory, 'Francis Drake', was vetoed.[120]

Over the remainder of 1940, other Spanish defectors from the French foreign legion would continue the fight in British uniform. About sixty Spaniards succeeded in a daredevil escape through the desert from Vichy-controlled Syria into British-held Palestine. They were accepted into British service and soon became known as the '50 Middle East Commando'. Some officers looked askance at these rough recruits of suspicious backgrounds. Evelyn Waugh, a British officer and author who had sympathized with Franco in the recent civil war, observed the men in training and called them 'a troop of denationalized Spanish socialists of very low quality'.[121]

But the 'denationalized' Spaniards' experience of the Spanish civil war and the legion commended itself to their British mentors. The renegades were soon deployed in the campaign to eject the Italians from Cyrenaica over the winter of 1940–1. During this time, 'Churchill's Spaniards', to borrow Daniel Arasa's term, were championed by their commanding officer, Lieutenant Colonel George Young. Later, as a prisoner of war in German hands, George Young would organize escape attempts from the infamous castle at Colditz.[122] After training, action in Cyrenaica and leave in Alexandria, the Spanish commando was shipped to defend the Greek island of Crete. Unfortunately, most of 50 Commando would be captured as prisoners of war during the German invasion of this last Allied foothold in Greek territory in May 1941. The Spaniards were part of the 5,000 troops who surrendered after the Battle of Sfakia, after successfully covering the evacuation by sea of a larger number of their comrades. But their Anglo-Hispanic identity shielded them from a fate worse than an Axis prisoner-of-war camp. A German capture of Spanish 'Reds' would normally have produced shock on the part of the captors, followed by routine deportation of the prisoners to Franco's Spain, where summary execution or hard labour would have awaited the men. But Captain Cochrane, the battalion medical officer who had served in the International Brigades, suggested a ruse. He instructed his men to call themselves Gibraltarians instead of Spaniards. The ruse worked. The Spaniards were treated comparatively humanely as British Commonwealth prisoners of war after being processed in Nazi-occupied Thessaloniki. They avoided a fate worse than death in Franco's Spain.[123]

Meanwhile, the real Gibraltar was the main focus of Anglo-Hispanic entanglements during the Second World War. The rock was fortified and its civilian population evacuated. Its terrible isolation was evident when a light air raid in July 1940 from an unidentified aircraft could realistically have come from any of four different sources (Francoist Spain, Nazi Germany, Fascist Italy or, the most likely candidate, Vichy France, as retaliation for the British attack at Mers-el-Kébir). Gibraltar, in the wake of the Nazi victory over France in 1940, sat in a maelstrom of hostile intent. Only the question of sovereignty stopped Franco from offering basing rights to the German Navy in the Canary Islands, and the Vichy French from facilitating the same in Morocco. Both scenarios would have imperilled Britain's control of the Mediterranean-Atlantic chokepoint.[124] When Evelyn Waugh was posted to Gibraltar in October 1940, his diary entry revealed 'a garrison of 10,000 men and a local defence corps. The women have been evacuated, all but six or seven; there was no beer in the town.'[125] By the following spring, another evacuation order was issued, according to the Reuters press agency 'list of over 1,000 people, including Spanish refugees'.[126] The importance of Mediterranean operations, and fears of a Spanish-aided Axis conquest of the rock (which would have tilted the naval balance in the Atlantic) focused British attention. As the Allies advanced in the North African theatre, Gibraltar's docks became essential not only for military supplies but also for Axis civilian refugees. In humanitarian exchanges of civilians captured in the war zone, Gibraltar was essential. In April 1942, ships carrying some eleven thousand Italian civilians captured in East Africa were refuelled and revictualled at the rock.[127]

Gibraltar was Britain's only outpost on the European mainland between the fall of Greece in 1941 and the invasion of Sicily in 1943. Its position controlling access to the Mediterranean made it a last redoubt of Britain's last gasp of 'informal empire' in Spain, most crucially by controlling the sea lanes carrying Franco's war-ravaged economy's desperately needed oil supplies.[128] Despite being subjected to frequent Axis air raids and submarine attacks, Gibraltar was never attacked with troops by land or sea. By 1943, lazy British attitudes towards this Anglo-Hispanic outpost had started to grate upon the garrison. A certain Reg Cudlipp, speaking 'on behalf of everyone on the Rock', published a protest in *Rock Magazine* against the Mediterranean luxuries his beleaguered men were reported by the London press as enjoying:

So, one more newspaper man has discovered Gibraltar! Not the Gibraltar that we who live here now know, the Gibraltar of hard work and confined spaces … but the Gibraltar where the shopping centre offers 'extraordinary variety', and where 'food is good and plentiful and even the best cuisine is spiced by exotic Spanish flavours' … Isn't it about time that home newspapers stopped printing this sort of tripe?[129]

The lack of any Francoist attempt to seize Gibraltar, or to allow German troops to perform the same feat from Spanish soil (the mooted 'Operation Felix'), was revealing. Franco's regime, even amidst the apparent collapse of the Allies in 1940 and Falangist ascendancy within the 'Movement', never risked a complete break with Britain, even when Spanish territory, natural resources and ports were made available to Hitler.

Gibraltar was prepared nonetheless as a base of defence and covert operations in the event of hostilities, as well as a launch pad for propaganda. Britain's Political Warfare Executive (PWE) knew that rumours flourished in contexts of ignorance and faulty information (like Francoist Spain). British agents made phone calls to influential Spaniards threatening them that 'our (British) time will come', while also offering bribes and patronage. The PWE also reported on Nazi efforts in Spain. In April 1942, British intelligence suggested a Nazi-Spanish attempt to annex Gibraltar. The British countered by disseminating propaganda in Spain explaining the Nazi threat to Catholicism. A particular rumour spread in November 1942 suggested that pro-Nazi Falangists in Barcelona wanted to confiscate clerical ornaments and melt them down for the German war effort. It seems unlikely that Nazi counter-propaganda was more effective than even Britain's flimsy efforts. Berlin's efforts to depict the Hitler regime as a 'defender' of neutrality in Spain (as well as in Eire), against the perfidious machinations of Albion, must have sounded hollow given the events of 1940 in Scandinavia and the Low Countries.[130]

Yet British propaganda had greater success at achieving wartime soft power via culture. The marketing of British music, and the efforts of the British Council, were more effective than flat-footed Nazi efforts, despite Francoism's affinity with the Axis.[131] British achievements were all the more remarkable for two reasons. First, British budgets for propaganda activities in Spain were limited, which meant that properly nuanced efforts were hard to implement. Economies of scale in wartime diluted the full potential of British propaganda.[132] Second, Nazi intelligence officers operated openly throughout Spain, often with the support of Spanish government agencies. Nazi agents, with the help of the

Spanish Post Office, managed to destroy about 50 per cent of printed Allied propaganda material distributed in Spain. Meanwhile, such freely circulating Axis propaganda as the German *Signal* magazine was available without impediment. Copies were frequently stolen in an information-starved country.[133]

Spain was also literally a starved country. British intelligence reports from Sevilla recorded how the cost of living for industrial workers had outstripped wages by four times between 1936 and 1940. The price of basic foodstuffs soared by 300 per cent in 1941.[134] The famine worsened and probably was at its most deadly in 1942. A British traveller who was passing through Spain reported that 'the poor live off acorns and chestnuts'. Food was scavenged from carob pods and dead draught animal flesh. The vanquished Republicans suffered worst, in large part because of ongoing political repression, but also because the left-leaning landless labourers and urban working classes were less able to secure food from source and were left to starve on insufficient rations. Unemployed and salaried workers without extra ration access to agriculture or distribution were especially penalized by hunger. Inflation and the black market ('estraperlo') dominated everyday life. Hunger exacerbated deaths from secondary diseases and infections. Typhus spread in 1941, the British ambassador Samuel Hoare noted, because of the absence of disinfectant products. As begging increased in the towns and tens of thousands fled to the countryside in search of food, Spain returned to a war-ravaged version of 'backwardness' which had obsessed early modern travel writers. The direness of Spain's war-torn economy eased British foreign policy goals of keeping Franco out of the Second World War. Britain donated wheat from Canadian storage which it had earmarked for domestic consumption, thereby augmenting the greater amounts of food arriving in Spain from the United States and Argentina.[135]

But British propaganda faced an uphill task, especially in the wake of the defeat of France and the installation of the collaborationist Vichy regime on the other sides of Pyrenees. In February 1941, four months before Britain allied itself with the 'anti-Christ' Soviet Union, the Spanish national daily *ABC* proclaimed 'fraternal solidarity with Italy and Germany' and that 'Europe's war of liberation, the first clash between new Europe and the old plutocratic democracies, had taken place in Spain'.[136] Equally, the Pétain regime lauded Spain's 'national' renewal under Franco as a model for France. Vichy-Spanish relations were close. The Francoist press dismissed the Free French forces headquartered in Britain as a ragtag of terrorists and communists. The regime cold-shouldered British diplomacy during the early 1940s and indulged Vichy attempts to foster a pan-Latin cultural bloc of Franco, Pétain and Salazar.[137] Spanish nationalistic propaganda about the Anglo-Saxon way of war found common ground with Vichy. Just as legends of British destruction of tobacco factories in Spain during the Peninsular War were recycled as evidence of mercantilist sabotage, the increasing British bombing of occupied France was countered by similar tones from the Vichy regime. French industry was targeted, according to Vichy, not to weaken the Axis war effort, but to please the City of London and, once the United States joined the campaign, the interests of Jewish American capitalists.[138] By May 1943, at a time when Allied bombing of western Europe had gathered pace but German bombing of Britain was almost negligible, Francoist propaganda leaned into Vichy protests by launching a 'humanitarian' initiative to limit the targeting from the air of cities. The Spanish Foreign Ministry proposal to split bombing targets into three zones (of military objectives, industry of some military value and civilian areas exempted from attack from the air) was not taken seriously in either London or Washington. The Allies knew that such a convention would only aid the Axis war effort.[139]

Meanwhile, the British made contingencies for responding to any formal alliance with the Axis powers. Propaganda campaigns planned to depict the Falange as making Spain a 'vassal' of the Nazi empire, and as loathed by the mass of Spanish people. Any Nazi-Spanish conquest of Gibraltar would have been answered by an Allied seizure of the Canary Islands, to be followed by anti-Franco propaganda accordingly.[140] In the end, none of these contingencies would have to be attempted. Wartime prime minister Churchill remarked that Britain's claim over Gibraltar should be left out of wider efforts to keep Franco out of the war. A British defeat would render any negotiations unnecessary whereas an Allied victory would rebuff Spanish claims. Churchill praised Franco for his non-interference during the Allied 'Torch' landings in North Africa in 1942, much to the dismay of several Labour members of his unity government. After the war, both Allied and Axis figures stressed the value of Franco's Gibraltar policy, or lack of policy. Goering, from his cell at Nuremberg, repeatedly claimed that Hitler's refusal to entertain an overland march across Spain to seize Gibraltar in 1940 doomed the Nazi war effort to defeat. President Eisenhower, veteran commander-in-chief of Allied forces in the European theatre, during military basing discussions in the early 1950s, thanked Franco for his helpful attitude regarding Gibraltar in the recent war.[141]

Franco kept his country out of the war, even when rhetorically and indirectly he continued to back the Axis until 1943. In some ways, the free movement of Axis agents throughout Spain was used to the British advantage. An elaborate intelligence plot to persuade the Axis that the Allied assault on Sicily would be a feint relied upon Spanish toleration of Nazi agents on their territory. A corpse disguised as a Royal Marine major was dropped into the sea off Spain in the knowledge that tides would wash it onto a Spanish beach. Faked documents suggesting a major Allied attack in the Greek islands had been planted on the corpse, in the hope that Nazi agents would get sight of the 'evidence'. Operation Mincemeat worked and appeared to have influenced an Axis decision to strengthen the Greek defences at the expense of Sicily. After the real invasion of Sicily, the war had shifted decisively in the Allies' favour, and Spain's long coastline would be more exposed than ever. In 1943, the British prevailed upon the neutral Portuguese to open the Azores to Allied airbases. British bribery of senior figures in the Franco regime was more effective than ever, and Spain switched from 'non-belligerent' status to 'neutral'. The corrupt Mallorcan financier, Juan March, the man whose wealth had enabled the military rising of 1936 to get underway, calculated early in the war that Britain would be triumphant. Captain Alan Hillgarth, naval attaché at the British embassy in Madrid and effective head of British intelligence operations in Spain, found a use in March's corruption. Hillgarth secured the approval of the British government to disburse some $14 million in Spain, shared between several Francoist generals. This bribery, along with the oil blockade and Franco's own growing doubts about the Axis cause, kept Spain out of the war.[142]

In fact, it is still hard to fathom whether British intelligence efforts in Francoist Spain were exaggerated. Most historians have argued that Franco was sincere in offering to take Spain into the Axis. Only the caudillo's exorbitant material requirements and demands for Vichy French territory in North Africa convinced Hitler against an alliance against the British Empire. But German military historians have argued that Franco in fact rebuffed Hitler and that Franco's compromise offer in summer 1941 to send Falangists to fight on the Eastern Front was rapidly accepted by the *Führer* in the hope of binding the Spaniards as early as possible into what Berlin thought would be a quick campaign. In the end, Franco sent a proper division, comprising volunteers amongst the conscript class who were by no means all Falangists.[143] Hitler appears to have cared little for the Blue Division's military potential. Rather, he appears to have hoped that the mere presence of Spanish frontline units would ease Franco into the next step of formally joining the Axis.[144]

But from 1943, Franco cooled his friendly relations with the Axis. The Falangist (Spanish fascist) ascendancy in the right-wing coalition of 'families' supporting the military dictatorship began to ebb in favour of National Catholicism as Franco astutely predicted an Allied victory.[145] By May 1944 he bowed to Allied pressure to release impounded pro-Allied Italian vessels, and to cut off wolfram exports to Nazi Germany to a mere trickle. 'The United Nations', a British Indian newspaper celebrated, 'have found the denial of petroleum supplies to Spain a most effective sanction'.[146] Unlike Spain, Britain's oil supplies were assured. The Allies won the Battle of the Atlantic in 1943, invaded Italy from the south and in June 1944 successfully launched the invasion of Normandy.

But Anglo-Hispanic in wartime entanglements were not yet over. As British forces liberated France in the wake of Operation Overlord in 1944, they encountered several dozen Spanish Republican exiles. Not all Spanish refugees joined the French Foreign Legion in 1939 or the wartime *maquis* resistance that was raging by 1944. Some took their chances returning to Franco's Spain and others still ended up working as indentured labourers for the Nazi 'Todt' organization. Once the western Allies spearheaded the liberation of France in 1944, many exiles who had been held prisoner or subjected to forced labour by the Nazis were liberated by Allied troops. As the Spaniards were wearing paramilitary uniforms, and as fears abounded that the Falangist 'Blue Division' might be operating in France, the Allied troops treated the captives with suspicion.

Fearing that the suspicious Spaniards might face reprisals at the hands of the Free French on French soil, the British shipped the captives to England where they joined Axis prisoners of war in a succession of camps. A diary written by the leftist Republican from Alcoi, José Ferri, a Todt captive who in 1941 had been sent to build fortifications on the German-occupied island of Jersey, detailed the strange circumstances in which he and 225 other comrades ended up being treated almost as enemies by non-plussed Allied troops. His diary entries speak of bitterness at the hypocrisy of his British captors who, having failed to defend the Spanish Republic, now compounded their immorality by treating the Spaniards as Axis suspects. As the notoriously cold winter of 1944–5 approached, Ferri grew miserable and Anglophobic at his prisoner-of-war status: 'so much miserable paperwork, so much hypocrisy used for the sole purpose of prolonging, with the appearance of legality, a detention that they know to be perfectly unfair, with the aggravation of the deadly conditions in which they have us here, are causing irritation in us that can drive us to a desperate act'.[147] His despair was compounded when he witnessed an opportunity of service in the British army offered to some Yugoslav men which was denied to his stateless comrades:

> There were two hundred and fifty, both soldiers and civilians, some Tito supporters, others Tito's adversaries, but all anti-fascists, or at least so they

say. There were old people, young people, and some who were children under fourteen years of age. Weird guys, many nice, of all shapes and sizes, both physically and morally. Most of them had been going through the same ordeal as us since we were captured by the Americans.[148]

Being held prisoner in the south-east of England exposed Ferri and his comrades to more than the cold. The Nazi flying-bomb (V1) and rocket (V2) offensive against London and its surroundings shattered the night-time chill with explosions nearby:

> We spent the night before yesterday suffering epileptic fits because of the V1 and V2 rockets hammering away at us for fifteen hours without interruption. The tents were shaking and the sky went purple from the effect of the explosions and fires. Last night was quieter. But just now the fireworks have started again. Not far from here a V2 has just fallen, which, in a gigantic spout of smoke and dust, has sent skywards a group of houses. When I think that there were children and women in those dwellings, however English they may be, my heart sinks and my gut rises to my throat! This continuous exercise of danger produces in us a hypersensitivity only comparable to what our ancestors in the caves must have suffered, when at every crossroads in the forest, in the thick of every thicket and behind every tree, they sensed the beast they had to contend with, and defend themselves under pain of being skinned alive.[149]

By February 1945, the plight of the Spanish Republicans had attracted the attention of leading British Hispanists, along with a Red Cross mission sent out from Geneva. Their treatment had worsened in Colchester and had drawn criticism of Geneva Red Cross. The leading left-liberal *Manchester Guardian* spoke in the Spaniards' defence, along with communists and such notable Hispanists as George Orwell and Gerald Brenan, both of whom were convinced of the captives' anti-fascist credentials. Their conditions improved, even though they remained prisoners of war. A two-day hunger strike in July 1945, two months after the end of the Second World War in Europe, brought matters to a head once more. Their conditions improved again, this time with day passes to secure outside labour and recreation, along with indulgences such as the emblazoning of the 'Allied' Spanish Republican flag over their quarters. Their final relocation to a camp in the north-west of England marked the end of their captivity in 1946. Their lengthy plight was in large part because the men were stateless: Republican exiles from a republic that no longer existed and whose Francoist successor was not a desired destination of return. In the end, several dozens remained in Britain, whereas others returned to France.[150]

9

Anglo-Hispania and Franco's Spain

The victory of the Allies in 1945 isolated Franco's regime and threw its diplomatic efforts into turmoil. To some degree, his regime was aided both by the continued dislocation of Republican exiles as well as the death in France in 1940 of the former president, Manuel Azaña. Azaña's posthumous *Causas de la Guerra de España* historicized the Franco repression, comparing it to the excess of the Carlist Wars the previous century. Even the old Carlist war cry 'Dios, Patria y Rey' was accepted as a shorthand for anti-Republican allegiance, even if the question of 'Rey' (king) was still ambiguous.[1] But public opinion in the victorious western powers, for perhaps the first time ever, was inclined to view Franco's regime as a product of the Axis as opposed to just another pitiful chapter in Spanish history. From the Western standpoint in 1945, the presence of one apparent fascist in power in Europe seemed like one fascist too many. As a British Indian servicemen's newspaper argued at the end of 1945, 'Spain today is the puzzle of Europe with its totalitarian Falange making desperate efforts to hide its totalitarianism and to acquire a semblance of democratic form.'[2] Until the onset of the cold war reset relations, the Allied powers saw the Spanish question as a European problem. A Dutch research project in the late 1940s cast Franco's regime as a product of Western democratic pusillanimity and, in a morality lesson to the new United Nations Organisation, of the irrelevance of the old League of Nations concerning internal atrocities.[3]

Franco was surprised and alarmed by the sweeping Labour Party election victory in Britain in 1945. News of the anti-militarist Potsdam declaration and the standoffishness of Ambassador Mallet (1945–6) unsettled the dictator amidst a growing diplomatic isolation.[4] Fears ran high that Britain's new 'Bolshevik government' would reinstate the vanquished Republicans with armed force. But in August, the new Labour foreign minister, Ernest Bevin, made a speech pledging Britain not to intervene in Spanish internal affairs.[5] But non-intervention still meant isolation. On 5 March 1946, the *Times* reported an anti-Franco statement by the Western victor powers of the Second World War, Britain, France and the United States: 'as long as General Franco continues in control of Spain the Spanish people cannot constitute a full and cordial association with those nations which have by common effort brought defeat to German Nazism and Italian Fascism'.[6] Anglo-Hispanic relations fell into a cold war, and remained so until the bigger cold war of the 1950s.

Frosty relations at diplomatic level were countered by clandestine interactions along the Gibraltar border. The Campo de Gibraltar, after 1945, resumed its role as a smuggling ground. No longer just the *mochileros* (backpackers) traversing the unmapped paths of the Serranía, Gibraltar's new generation of smugglers included desperate and hungry survivors of Franco's terror in Andalucía who otherwise had few opportunities to make a living in an impoverished economy run by an oppressive dictatorship.[7] Gerald Brenan, whose *Spanish Labyrinth* published in 1943 made him Britain's most famous Hispanist, did not re-enter his beloved second homeland until 1949. But at the end of 1945, he nonetheless offered a prescient analysis of the corruption and misery of Franco's Spain which amounted to a failed state held together only by the army and the mass prison system:

> Spain today is a totalitarian state, controlled by a single party. But it is totalitarianism broken down … As an illustration, let us take the rationing system. Today only one person in twenty is properly fed and about half the population is near the starvation level. The reason for this is that the Falange, through its syndicates and its provincial governors, controls both the official black market, known as the 'estraperlo', and the rationing system. Potatoes, for example, are sold for 1 peseta the kilo on a ration card and for 3 pesetas on the 'estraperlo'.[8]

British military attaché reports from Madrid were equally damning of the other powerful institution in Spain, the army. Despite its vast budget, Franco's army was too occupied with internal law and order, too starved of petrol and modern weaponry to undertake real training and manoeuvres and, above all, too obsessed with resting on the laurels of victory in the 'Crusade' (i.e. civil war), to pose any threat to post-war Gibraltar.[9]

But the Madrid regime was avowedly anti-communist, and events aided the Franco regime's diplomatic and propaganda efforts in London. Anticipating the later era of 'technocratic' Spain, the Franco regime had some success mitigating its isolation by infiltrating the discussions of the fledgling United Nations intergovernmental bodies with supposedly apolitical experts from fields of public health and social insurance.¹⁰ Humanitarian and technocratic activities offered great propaganda for a regime recently drenched in blood and collaboration. By the late 1940s, the British government had lost interest in supporting a non-communist alternative to Franco's regime. Foreign Secretary Bevin held inconclusive talks with such exiles as the moderate socialist, Indalecio Prieto, and the Catholic monarchist, Gil Robles. But Westminster anti-Francoism lapsed into protests from the Labour backbenches.¹¹ Britain's small and sectarian Communist Party refused to aid Ernest Bevin's efforts, knowing that any British-sponsored regime change would be anti-Stalinist in nature.¹² Conservative opinion noted how the UN boycott allowed Franco to rally patriotic support around his regime.¹³ Little rally could be expected from International Brigade veterans either. Many had been killed in the Second World War and George Orwell died a natural death in 1950. In any case, these communist-addled veterans increasingly fell foul of cold war politics, in the age of McCarthyism in the United States and anti-communist Christian democracy in western Europe.¹⁴

First tentatively, and then generally, new spaces were opened for an Anglo-Hispanic rapprochement with the victor of 1939. Britain's fascist movement, natural bedfellows with Spanish Falangism, had become a discredited and even more negligible force in the post-war era than it had been in the 1930s. Oswald Mosley, leader of the British Union of Fascists, had been imprisoned under emergency legislation during the Second World War, and his movements and meetings were watched by the intelligence service into the 1950s. In 1949, a year after Mosley founded the 'Union Movement' aimed at creating a neo-fascist European union, British intelligence reported the BUF leader's travel to Spain, via a 'Union' meeting in Lisbon and voyage to Gibraltar. Crossing into Spain on an ordinary visa, Mosley and his wife 'travelled by train to Madrid, ostensibly on a sightseeing tour. He was, however, very busy for four days in interviews with various people, including the Union Movement's representative in Spain, Robert Delfs.' The intelligence report concluded that Mosley met with leading members of the Falange, if not with Franco himself.¹⁵ Post-war Madrid was a haven for discredited and banished European fascists. Initially a ratline for Nazis on the run, Francoist Madrid turned into the capital of pan-European attempts of a fascist revival, or, in the words of one recent study, 'an almost obligatory destination' for former fascists.¹⁶ Mosley, knowing that his political career was over in Britain, used Spain as the first stop of a tour promoting his 'Europe as a Nation' ethos.

The negligible size of British fascism, combined with the fact that conservatives had been as strongly anti-Nazi in the Second World War as their left-wing counterparts, meant that any Francoist appeal to British fascism would have been ludicrous. Instead, the regime needed to appeal to anti-communism in order to win support in Britain. In 1950, the Anglo-Spanish League of Friendship was created in an attempt to revive supposedly 'apolitical' Anglo-Hispanic cultural exchanges. Membership comprised well-connected Spanish residents and British diplomatic veterans. In an unwitting nod to Britain's near-vanquished 'informal empire' in Latin America in the wake of two expensive world wars, the league concerned itself solely with bilateral relations in the Old World. First tendentiously, then openly, the league became a front for Francoist propaganda. During 1956–7, amidst Britain's humiliation in the Suez crisis and Spain's withdrawal from Morocco, the Scottish clinician and Catholic convert, Halliday Sutherland, gave lectures to league members which exonerated the Franco regime. Thus, Sutherland professed, Franco had not been pro-Nazi. The 'lovable and gullible' British public had been duped into believing that the *caudillo* had waged war on democracy, whereas in reality his fight had been with Russian communism. The didactic nature was too much for 'apolitical' league members, and amidst press controversy alleging that the Spanish ambassador had been the real author of the lectures, Sutherland resigned from the chairmanship of the organization.[17] The Franco regime took special care to cultivate British policymakers in the late 1950s. Entry into the new European Economic Community proved impossible in 1957, given its accession criteria requiring candidates to be capitalist democracies. But British plans to create a rival free-trade area, the European Free Trade Area (EFTA), seemed more attractive given EFTA's more modest political and economic ambitions. In the end, the frosty attitude of British governments, especially the Labour administration of Harold Wilson after 1964, along with the tension over Gibraltar and Britain's own application in 1961 to join the EEC, shifted Spanish policy towards the Franco-German axis.[18]

Sutherland's whitewashing of Francoism touched a nerve amongst post-war Anglo conservatives, especially Catholics. To some extent, opinion thawed towards Franco because of the unreflective behaviour of Spanish Republicans in exile. The bourgeois republican diaspora enjoyed a kind of privileged grievance bestowed by their artistic demonstration of 'revolutionary' credentials which, like all good intellectuals, placed them at odds not only with their own government in exile but also with host governments. Several thousand well-connected cultural and academic figures thrived in Mexico City. The friendly, seductive and cantankerous Spaniards of the Latin American literary imagination had some basis in reality.[19] Exiled Spanish Republicans conspired and campaigned, and in

1962 at a meeting in Munich even agreed a text to heal the division of the 'Two Spains'. But the sectarianism between communist and anti-communist exiles made the republicans increasingly divisive and irrelevant in the context of new working-class and student mobilization inside Franco's Spain.[20]

Anglo attitudes were also softened by the opinions of Catholic and anti-communist intellectuals. The Franco dictatorship's view that Spain was unsuited for democracy was partly shared by conservatives abroad. Charles Petrie, British historian and apologist for Franco, contrasted the Spaniards' love for forthright and masculine authoritarians with the British love of understatement:

> The Spaniard likes his leaders to be forceful characters, and if they come in this category much will be forgiven to them: with all his faults, (King) Ferdinand was '*muy hombre*', and on that score alone he was always sure of a considerable following. It is not easy for the modern Englishman to appreciate this, for he prefers those in authority over him, with the exception of Sir Winston Churchill, to be apologetic for the fact, and the more self-effacing they are the more popular they are likely to be.[21]

The American conservative and Hispanophile, William Buckley, in a 1966 debate concerning the Vietnam war, opined that some countries might never become democratic for lack of experience, and that some countries are 'too volatile for democracy … Spain cannot have complete democracy, even though it is an old civilisation'.[22] One of Buckley's friends, the British Catholic convert, Arnold Lunn (1888–1974), shared his anti-communist appraisal of Franco. After writing in favour of the nationalists during the civil war, Lunn became a post-war confidant of the aristocratic General Gonzalo de Aguilera Munro (Conde de Alba).[23] A few years after the civil war, Lunn attended a British embassy function in Madrid where the ambassador asked him to use his influence with the victorious nationalists to intercede on behalf of Spain's persecuted Protestant minority. But Foreign Minister Ramón Serrano Súñer rebuffed Lunn's entreaties: 'you're a Catholic and you're worried about a few administrative burdens facing the Protestants in Spain … yet when any Catholic priest found alive in the red zone was killed we do not remember any foreign Protestants coming to Spain to intercede on their behalf'.[24]

For the first two decades after Franco's victory, Anglo-Hispanic entanglements remained frozen in the ideological and political realm. Even though the Western economic boom benefited the former genocidal empires of Germany and Japan, Spain remained either closed or semi-detached in a manner that incriminated the regime's fascist origins and revived for a final time the Anglo Black Legend of Spanish difference.²⁵ But the opening up of the Spanish economy in the late 1950s and promotion of foreign tourism tilted these entanglements in a popular direction, as unprecedented movements of people experienced Spanish culture at first hand. More than at any time before in history, Anglo-Hispanic relations would be determined by mass consumer societies rather than poets or politicians.

Anglo-Hispania and the advent of mass tourism

For a long time in the 1950s, Spain continued to be marketed as an exotic and rustic outlier to more established foreign holiday destinations. In 1950, the travel agency Thomas Cook marketed Spain as anti-modern, as offering 'special charm in this old-world corner of Europe'.²⁶ In 1951, tourism acquired a ministry portfolio in its own right in the Spanish government, and the influx of foreign holidaymakers played a significant part in the so-called Stabilization Plan of 1959 which opened up the Spanish economy to foreign investment. In 1959–60, General Franco lifted the visa requirements which were required for UK tourists to visit Spain. This, coupled with the new perception of Spain, produced a huge boom in tourism. The Romantic vision abroad of the nineteenth century was promoted ironically amidst modern conveniences which defeated the heat, bad roads and oily food of British travel lore. As Nigel Townson has commented, 'the Romantic, pre-modern allure of the sun and sand of the Mediterranean was anchored in the very modern setting of international airports, motorways and air-conditioned hotels'.²⁷

In 1959, only 544 British tourists visited Málaga (Andalucía). But in 1962, that number rose substantially to 11,509, and by the mid-1960s, Spain had become the most popular tourist destination for Britons.²⁸ Benidorm, a sleepy fishing village of 3,000 inhabitants in 1957, expanded into a sprawling concrete resort within three years, attracting tens of thousands of Northern European tourists each summer. Between 1966 and 1971, the proportion of holidays taken abroad by British families more than doubled from 4 per cent to 8.4 per cent, and Spain was the most popular destination by a wide margin.²⁹ Spanish tourism agents, catering to disproportionately working-class visitors embarking on their sole, if not first ever, foreign visit, promoted a sanitized version of Spanish culture along with British beer and food. Posters abounded with stereotyped images of flamenco, beaches, bullfights and guitars. Spanish Romanticism had become accessible to Britons on modest incomes.³⁰ The package holiday was thus very different from the longer and ongoing tradition of elite travel narratives and wealthier expatriate communities. But even incomers, who often struggled with the Spanish language or ignored it altogether, found it hard to become part of the Spanish *pueblo*. Long-term British residents of the Spanish coast, from Peter Chalmers Mitchell in the 1930s right up to the retirement boom at the turn of the twenty-first century, have tended to adopt a socially distanced view of their Spanish surroundings. Despite deriving spiritual and health benefits from warmer surroundings, as well as inspiration from a simpler and slower pace of life, British immigrants continued to view their host communities from the outside in.

As Francoist Spain opened up to foreign tourism, interactions centred on catch-up in terms of economic development. As tourism drove Spanish prosperity during late Francoism, profit created new tensions between service providers and customers. Mallorca was transformed from an idyllic and relatively undiscovered destination in the 1950s and 1960s into the hard-nosed mass tourism of the 1970s. Local Mallorcan *senyores* had to limit their consumption of brandy amidst the rising prices in bars and restaurants, and were increasingly pressured by bar owners not to linger over their drinks. Higher-income foreign tourists were simply too profitable to be refused entry, and locals ended up being de facto second-class clients.[31] British package tourists, for their part, were subjected to condescension by their wealthier countrymen. The extrusion of working-class Britons on to Mediterranean beaches made Spain a proxy in Britain's notoriously parochial class system. Lobster-tanned Britons returning to new airports designed for mass tourism stood apart from the wealthier middle classes who took their foreign holidays skiing in Switzerland, touring Italy or on weekend trips to Le Touquet.

The tourism boom served Franco's regime in two major ways. Mass tourism offered a way for the Spanish regime to influence foreign opinion, whilst the income it generated to a large extent drove the process of economic modernization underway since 1959. The marketing of a 'different' and yet welcoming Spain also denied non-governmental organizations the chance to influence popular British opinion. Campaigns by human rights organizations to raise awareness of political prisoners gained the ear of British activists and politicians, but seldom of the new generation of annual tourists. In the early 1960s, the founder of the Amnesty International organization, Peter Beneson, met the Spanish socialist, Antonio Amat. Beneson was impressed how 'twenty-five years after the end of the Civil War, the atmosphere in Madrid has not really changed'.[32] But other Europeans, including even Amnesty itself, generally became less censorious towards Spain from the mid-1960s, as other repressive regimes, such as Greece after 1967, South Africa or Chile, attracted more attention. The *Economist* current affairs magazine in 1973 described those who attacked Franco's Spain as a 'militant and ideologically motivated minority' who still indulged in 'occasional day-dreams about the International Brigade'.[33]

Franco regime's ongoing repressiveness remained internal in nature, not least because Spain, unlike Portugal, had accepted the 'wind of change' of decolonization in Africa and had managed to cultivate good diplomatic links with such major non-aligned powers as India. Britain was prepared to vote directly against its old ally, Portugal, at the UN over its colonial policy on a total of nine occasions between 1969 and 1973. But when Labour MP John Golding asked the (Conservative) government if it would raise at the UN Commission on Human Rights the 'question of the continuing harassment of trade unionists in Spain', foreign office minister, Julian Amery, replied, 'No. We have no standing to raise this matter.'[34]

While elements of the establishment Left in Britain continued to rail against Franco's authoritarianism, the revolutionary Left took matters into its own hands. Exiled Spanish anarchists in the 'First of May' group launched bombing and machine-gun attacks against the Spanish embassy in London on two separate occasions in 1967. Small firebomb attacks during 1969–71 also targeted Spanish banks and the *Iberia* airline. The full nature of this anti-Franco urban guerrilla was disguised by the growth of political violence connected to Northern Ireland. But a number of British New Left revolutionaries from a group known as 'The Angry Brigade' were probably recruited by the Spanish exiles.[35] The post-1968 flurry of pan-European urban guerrilla sects was assisted in the case of Spain by a political crackdown during the last years of the dictator's life. The hard-line *búnker* politics kept the image alive in Europe of Spain as a repressive, pseudo-fascist, dictatorship. When ETA (a Basque armed separatist group) in 1973 assassinated Carrero Blanco, Franco's hand-picked successor committed to the hard-line policy of *continuismo*, the young British leftist intellectual, Christopher Hitchens, was impressed. He did not seek to criticize the racial and bigoted motivations of ETA, and instead chose to see this violence as resistance to Francoism rather than resistance to the Spanish state itself: 'if ETA's action is terrorism, then terrorism certainly has something to be said for it.'[36] Despite the presence of armed revolutionary movements and clandestine trade union networks, when Franco finally died in November 1975, the reaction of the British press was largely a mix of foreboding and earnest optimism. The consternation of civil war and the deluge of 1939 had largely vanished amidst almost three decades of post-war prosperity.

Francoist myths then, far from being deconstructed by the democratic state, were either inadvertently vindicated by it, or simply not debunked, and thus allowed to retain a certain degree of stock by default. Even the Socialist Party, in government from 1982 to 1996, continued to adhere to the unspoken precepts of the so-called pact of silence, abstaining, for example, from wielding the fiftieth anniversary of the outbreak of the civil war in 1986 as a partisan stick with which to beat the right, as it might well have done with some justification.[37] Young Spaniards' only connection to Francoism is likely to derive from relatives who lived through the 'miracle' of the 1960s and 1970s, which catapulted Spain, in the words of one historian, into the 'exclusive club of those countries with a per capita income of $2000 or more' and transformed the material living standards of the population.[38] The 'Spanish miracle' was – precisely as the regime had intended – a formula for widespread apathy, inducing many ordinary Spaniards to conclude that 'Franco's Peace' had indeed been a vehicle for prodigious national development and that any political dissatisfactions they might harbour were ultimately outweighed by unprecedented prosperity. Possession of consumer goods revealed Spain as a success amidst Western dictatorships: by 1976, 236 per 1,000 Spaniards owned a telephone, 248 per 1,000 a radio, and 193 per 1,000 a television, as opposed to 167 per 1,000, 163 per 1,000 and 118 per 1,000 inhabitants of Portugal, respectively.[39]

The natural death in November 1975, of western Europe's last dictator, bequeathed Spain a benign paradox. Whereas previous swings of revolution and counter-revolution in the nineteenth and early twentieth centuries had foundered in their attempts to either modernize or traditionalize a Spanish social fabric still riven in patchy social and economic development, by the 1970s the situation had clearly advanced to the other extreme. An ossified and barely softened military dictatorship governed a society which by most socio-economic measurements had become a Western consumer society.[40] Even the dwindling contingent of Spaniards who can recall the most brutal and immiserating phase of Francoism, in the immediate aftermath of the civil war, typically accord disproportionate weight to the period 1960–75 in their recollections of the past.[41] The good times of Franco's regime were those which most stood at odds with its ideological premise.

Several works produced both by historians writing under Franco's regime and by exiles abroad remained opinionated and lacking in academic objectivity. Politically motivated texts abounded, riven with historical inaccuracies and hyperbolic journalese.[42] The spectre of Spain degenerating into political turmoil, possibly even renewed civil war, which hung over the transition, in itself bestowed a certain retrospective legitimacy on the Franco regime by seemingly ratifying its boast – encapsulated in the self-congratulatory celebrations held in 1964 – that its unique achievement had been in bringing peace and stability to a country of an anarchic disposition.[43] The silence that was thus enshrined at the heart of the democratic project extended a further form of legitimacy to the Franco regime, even as it was being dismantled, by seemingly upholding the stereotype of inherent national propensity to 'pitiless blood-list and savage discord'[44] that had been manipulated by the dictatorship for decades to undergird its authoritarianism. Consequently, the Spanish state predicated the whole process of the transition on the notion that, unless the state smothered the past, Spaniards, like children who did not know any better, would re-enact the fratricidal carnage of the civil war. They would descend into a bout of the collective madness and aggression to which they were supposedly predisposed. 'Apolitical' technocracy, like a modernized form of the positivism of the Alfonso Restoration, would heal sectarianism.

A sort of apolitical civil society grew amidst the prosperity, and was even given the blessing of the dictatorship thanks to the Law of Association of 1964. Heads of family associations, neighbourhood groups and parents' and housewives' fora became a grassroots underpinning of the political corporatism of the Spanish state. In reality, as Pamela Radcliff has shown, this new civil society offered opportunities for participation which in turn undermined the old-fashioned doctrines of the regime. A kind of egalitarian citizenship, as well as a plural political culture, emerged despite the dictatorship. Ideologically Francoist families, and the much larger number of unconnected traditional Catholics, learned democratic habits via the new civil society despite their innate antipathy towards democracy.[45] When Franco died in November 1975, the foundations for a largely peaceful transition to democracy had long been laid. As British Hispanist Giles Tremlett has pointed out, conservative Spaniards saw no automatic incongruence between Francoism and democracy. Rather they believed that one was the direct result of the other. Franco, they reason, 'cured the divide between the two Spains so that, after his death, they could come together again in peace.'[46]

The significance of European, let alone British, influences in Spain's modernizing civil society should not be overstated. Many Catholic middle-class Spaniards continued to think that Franco was necessary, even though they held this conviction with decreasing degrees of enthusiasm. Not only did fears persist that drastic political change would reopen the risk of civil war, but a superficial look at the rest of Europe until the mid-1970s did not necessarily inspire confidence. 'Democracy' in Europe, whether in its unstable variety in Italy and France, or in its 'people's' variety in eastern Europe, barely seemed ideal to the Spanish middle classes desiring a quiet life. Neither the new democracy of Italy nor the old democracy of Britain inspired confidence with their militant trade unions and repeated strikes (a problem which officially could not exist in Franco's national-syndicalist state). In any case, Spain was not the only authoritarian state in non-communist Europe, as both Greece and Portugal were under dictatorships until 1974.[47] Thus, the *europeización* of Spain was not a blind acceptance of whatever current drifted across the Pyrenees. The extent to which it impacted civil society lay more in the individual entanglements of Spaniards returning from work and study abroad, to interactions with foreign tourists and to the growing popularity of foreign media despite ongoing Francoist attempts at censorship.

Over a million Spaniards emigrated to western European countries during the period of the 'Stabilization Plan' of 1959 and the Oil Crisis of 1973. The economic flight of so many young Spaniards, themselves often internally displaced by Spain's rapid urbanization and rural depopulation, was more than twice the size of the republican exile of 1939.[48] In many ways, the impact on Spain of this voluntary exile was greater than the involuntary exodus at the end of the civil war. Just as French, Swiss, West German and British economies and societies benefited from the influx of young Spanish workers and students, Spaniards also gained an appreciation of a freer and generally more prosperous way of life. The long-running Spanish TV drama *Cuéntame Como Pasó* ('Tell me How It Happened'), a partly nostalgic look at middle-class Madrid life from late-Francoism until the twenty-first century, captured the dynamic of a 'better Europe' perfectly. A conversation on a Spanish beach at the end of the 1960s between the head of a middle-class Madrid family ('Antonio', played by the actor, Imanol Arias) and a Swedish tourist couple was a revelation for the Spaniard. The Swedish man had the same career as Antonio, and yet afforded regular foreign holidays, worked fewer hours (and without the extra job – the *pluriempleo* common in Spain – with which Antonio was burdened) and both husband and wife had personal cars. The better way of life was also expressed through the doted daughter Inés (played by the actor, Irene Visedo), who studies in London and brings home a free-spirited British boyfriend, leading to all such humorous taboos as the stuffy Antonio protesting Mike's overnight presence in his house.[49]

The European themes in *Cuéntame* reflected a reality of European, and (of interest to this study) British entanglements as Spain journeyed from dictatorship towards democracy. Britain's role in helping to normalize the idea of democracy did not end with the influx of tourists. From the early 1970s, the BBC's Spanish-language service gained loyal listeners in Franco's Spain. Some 300,000 Spaniards routinely tuned in, which made Spain the largest of all the BBC's 'World Service' markets.[50] The divergence between a Spain under dictatorship and democratic western Europe – which in the early 1970s extended to their populations social as well as political rights – became 'unbridgeable' in Tom Buchanan's view.[51] The *Economist* magazine barely commented on Spain at all in the 1960s. Yet, its coverage increased during late-Francoism and the transition to democracy until, by the 1990s, Spain was firmly rooted in the regular 'Europe' section of the weekly journal.[52]

In many ways, the transition to democracy after Franco's death made less of an impression than such sudden revolutions as the army overthrow of the Portuguese dictatorship in 1974 or the demise of the Greek junta. Buttressed by the unwavering allegiance of the army, cushioned by a relatively favourable international context and, crucially, yoked to the life force of the *Caudillo*, Francoism was able to stagger on until the dictator's natural death. Even after November 1975, Francoist political institutions and culture continued to overshadow the transition in what Helen Graham has described as the 'framework of meaning'.[53] The ideological edifice of propaganda and myths endured into the 1980s and occasionally became a source of Anglo-Spanish tension. Post-Francoist Spain and Britain continued to experience tension over the status of Gibraltar. The Falklands War of 1982 placed these in sharp relief. Spain's new democracy abstained from voicing diplomatic support for Britain, in contrast to other European allies, whilst the streets of Madrid were the scene of pan-Hispanic nationalist demonstrations in favour of Argentina. Some five thousand nostalgic Francoists protested in the centre of Madrid, shouting 'Long Live the Argentine Army!', 'The Malvinas Belong to Argentina!' and by direct analogy, 'Gibraltar Is Spanish!'[54]

10

Conclusion

Anglo-Spanish cultural and social relations between the era of the Catholic monarchs and the cold war were either framed by mutual attitudes dating from earlier wars or mediated through renewed war and military encounters, either as allies or enemies. The British Army, with its notoriously aristocratic elites forged in exclusive public schools, normally offered little prospect for advancement for enlisted men. But the written word offered a tiny but growing number of common soldiers a later career or afterlife. A kind of veteran class identity therefore emerged via lengthy campaigns in Spain, as well as opportunities to forge new patterns of society and soldiering during 1936–9. In some ways, these are harder to trace given the paucity of literacy in earlier campaigns, the self-censorship or external vetting of letters and the reliability of memoirs published years after the event. But Britain's four major interventions in Iberia between the 1700s and 1930s bestowed lessons of strategy, tactics and entangled cultures. Spain's bloody wars were a reminder of the horrors of guerrilla-style warfare, the agency and victimhood of civilians and the vanishing distinctions between civilian and soldier.

Of course, the demands of war offered a counter-narrative to the Black Legend and Romanticism. The political continuities between the wars of Spain's nation-building, revolutionary and counter-revolutionary wars are plain to see even as other context changed, as are some of the continuities of foreign participation, even though most histories were opposed to the demarcated accounts existing at the moment. This book has united the vast body of research concerning Anglo-Spanish experiences in the 'ideological' Spanish civil war (1936–9), with the substantial amount in Spain's 'national' War of Independence (1808–14), and with the sparse accounts concerning Spain's 'Romantic' Carlist War (1833–40) and the 'dynastic' War of Spanish Succession (1700–14). Renewed war in Iberia and renewed British involvement underlines the reality of a *longue durée* of transnational soldiering, even at a time when most foreign observers mostly continued to view Spain as sui generis. The fact that British soldiers deployed in Spain complained of draughty windows in 1812, again in 1836 and once more in 1937 may seem a trivial anecdote. But the dialectic of one Spain imagined by British writers, strategists and propagandists, and another Spain experienced by soldiers, travellers and tourists offers a richer entangled history than an adoption of only one angle would permit. The presence in Spain of large numbers of British troops (in the wars of 1701–13, 1808–14, 1833–40 and 1936–9) produced a plebeian dimension to Anglo-Hispanic entanglements.

This book has tried to explore the main sources of conflict and collaboration between both countries using an Anglo-Hispanic viewpoint of views from outstanding political and cultural opinion makers, travellers, soldiers and ordinary people. Thus the dynastic and diplomatic tussles of the era do not by themselves explain animosity any more than the propagandistic Black Legend, except in the ways that they influenced prejudices before interactions took place. Of course, this plebeian interest does not detract from the striking similarities that pertained in both countries' royal and imperial positions. Both countries spawned empires out of dynastic politics and the aggregation of kingdoms with distinct constitutions and legal traditions. Both Spain and Britain were major non-European powers undergoing the unification of their composite monarchies, with heady blends of religious patriotism besides.

Yet, these similarities were overlooked by elites bent on emphasizing differences rather than similarities. Anglo views of Spain as a land of bigotry and despotism, of corrupt institutions and perennial instability were certainly overborne by nineteenth-century Romantics. But Romantics were impressed by what they liked to see, not what really lay before their eyes. British writers and travellers tended to avoid controversial political topics and focus instead on quaint folkloric aspects of Spanish life. The anti-modern charms represented in literature and tourism swept aside previous centuries of Anglo-Hispanic enmity and imperial rivalry, not least because Spain's global position was diminished without hope of repair by the events of 1808. But for all the accounts speaking to cultural perceptions and stereotypes, there were other records of mutual understanding, from the similar evangelizing aims in the New World, to aristocratic solidarity in the Campo de Gibraltar and to the leftist unity of Anglo-Hispanic Civil War veterans in the defence of Britain in 1940 and in later operations in the Mediterranean. The intertwined and ongoing nature of British and Spanish historical actors is in many ways more interesting than mutual alienation. The highly delicate transition to democracy in Spain after 1975, which saddled all individuals and parties with a responsibility not to endanger the process by reviving the conflictive enmities of the past made the country a model to emulate in sectarian conflicts ranging from Northern Ireland to South Africa.

Britain was therefore eyewitness, when not an outright protagonist, in the wars which caused or bequeathed so much sociopolitical unrest to Spain. Such turmoil was held up as the difference between Spain and the rest of western Europe, especially on the thorny topic of national identity. In effect, as Spain began losing its colonies, what it meant to be a nation underwent the sort of post-imperial overhaul which would not await Britain until the wake of the Second World War. Until further studies on Anglo-Hispanic entanglements come forward, along with comparisons of Anglo-Spanish and selective remembrance of different pasts, this study should conclude with some general observations about the contemporary resonance of Anglo-Hispania.

Both Britain and Spain, in the best-kept secrets of their national cultures, have a morbid tendency to talk their own countries down. 'Declinism' affected Britain's self-image in the world during the second half of the twentieth century as assuredly as Spaniards during the same time yearned for *convergencia* with western Europe. For centuries, introspective Spaniards were aided in the task of self-criticism by other Europeans who depreciated Hispanic culture via the 'Black Legend'. The Anglophobic 'Perfidious Albion' trope never acquired the same persistence or prevalence. The wake of the Brexit decision of 2016 has redressed the balance at least temporarily. The half of the British population who thought that the decision to leave the European Union was evidence of something being wrong with Britain (instead of something being wrong with the European Union) have been aided by a universally Europhile and soft Anglophobic response in the Spanish media (along with that of the other remaining EU member states). But even as the Anglophobia of EU institutions was faithfully echoed in the Spanish press, other glimpses of ongoing and positive Anglo-Hispanic entanglements were visible beyond the opinion pieces and editorials of major newspapers. Spain adopted a pragmatic position towards Gibraltar during the Brexit negotiations, despite ongoing EU insistence on terming the Overseas Territory as a 'colony', and tended towards flexibility rather than EU norms when dealing with border controls, residency rights and public health checks for UK nationals. Equally, Britain's soft Hispanophilia has remained unaffected by the EU question. Spanish is the only European language holding its own in British education amidst a decline in the learning of French,

German and Italian. Spain remains the most popular destination for British travellers, and bilateral trade and investment remain strong. Anglo-Hispanic entanglements have strengthened amidst Russian aggression in Ukraine and a reinvigorated role for the NATO alliance (which, unlike the EU, has enjoyed overwhelming support in British public opinion).

Notes

1 Introduction

1 For a conceptual analysis of travel theory and its cultural transfer, see James Clifford, *Routes: Travel and Translation in the Late Twentieth Century* (Cambridge, MA: Harvard University Press, 1997).
2 Hayden White, *Metahistory: The Historical Imagination in Nineteenth-Century Europe* (London: Johns Hopkins University Press, 1973), p. 65.
3 Maurizio Isabella, *Risorgimento in Exile: Italian Émigrés and the Liberal International in the Post-Napoleonic Era* (Oxford: Oxford University Press, 2016).
4 Andrew Ginger and Geraldine Lawless (eds), *Spain in the Nineteenth Century: New Essays on Experience of Culture and Society* (Manchester: Manchester University Press, 2018).
5 Sean Griffin, *The Liturgical Past in Byzantium and Early Rus* (Cambridge: Cambridge University Press, 2019).
6 Fernando Sánchez Dragó and Santiago Abascal, *España vertebrada* (Madrid: Planeta, 2019), p. 124.
7 https://williamchislett.com/2015/06/03/the-gap-between-spains-image-and-the-countrys-reality/ (accessed 10 June 2020).
8 Charles Petrie, *The Spanish Royal House* (London: Geoffrey Bles, 1958), p. 248.
9 George Orwell, *The Lion and the Unicorn: Socialism and the English Genius* (London: Secker and Warburg, 1941), p. 11.
10 As a recent edited collection, focusing mostly on British interactions with modern Spanish America, shows: Graciela Iglesias-Rogers (ed.), *The Hispanic Anglosphere from the Eighteenth to the Twentieth Century: An Introduction* (London: Routledge, 2021).
11 For an excellent collection of earlier Anglo-Iberian encounters, see Maria Bullón-Fernández (ed.), *England and Iberia in the Middle Ages, 12th–15th Century: Cultural, Literary, and Political Exchanges* (New York: Palgrave, 2007).
12 For example, John H. Elliot, *Scots and Catalans: Union and Disunion* (Yale: Yale University Press, 2018).
13 For an American perspective on a similar theme, see Richard L. Kagan, *The Spanish Craze: America's Fascination with the Hispanic World, 1779–1939* (Lincoln: University of Nebraska Press, 2019), pp. 18–19.

14 Ilya Berkovich, *Motivation in War: The Experience of Common Soldiers in Old-Regime Europe* (Cambridge: Cambridge University Press, 2017), p. 54.
15 Charles J. Esdaile, 'Recent Works of Note on the Peninsular War (1808–1815)', *Journal of Military History*, 74: 4 (October 2010), 143–1252, 1274.
16 For more discussion, see Nigel Townson (ed.), *Is Spain Different?: A Comparative Look at the 19th and 20th Centuries* (Brighton: Sussex Academic Press, 2015).
17 Luis G. Martínez del Campo, 'De hispanófilo a hispanista: la construcción de una comunidad profesional en Gran Bretaña', *Ayer*, 93: 19 (2014), pp. 139–61.
18 Paul Preston, *We Saw Spain Die* (London: Constable, 2008), p. 14.
19 Eduardo Haro Tegglen, *El Refugio. Situaciones: momentos de una vida* (Madrid: Aguilar, 1999), p. 240.
20 Richard Evans, *Cosmopolitan Islanders: British Historians and the European Continent* (Cambridge: Cambridge University Press, 2009), pp. 41–4.
21 Manuel Ortuño Martínez (ed.), *Servando Teresa de Mier: Memorias. Un fraile mexicano desterrado en Europa* (Madrid: Trama, 2006), pp. 62–3.
22 The phrase is usually attributed to Alexander Dumas, but there is some controversy over its origins; https://elorganillero.com/blog/2010/05/02/the-true-origins-of-africa-begins-at-the-pyrenees/ (accessed 17 September 2019).
23 José Álvarez-Junco, *Spanish Identity in the Age of Nations* (Manchester: Manchester University Press, 2011), pp. 16–48.
24 Carlos de Ayala, *Las cruzadas* (Madrid: Sílex, 2014); Henry Kamen, *La invención de España: Leyendas e ilusiones que han construido la realidad española* (Madrid: Espasa, 2020).
25 Modesto Lafuente, *Historia general de España desde los tiempos primitivos hasta la muerte de Fernando VII* (Barcelona: Montaner y Simon, 1883), Vol. I, discurso preliminar.
26 Henry Kamen, *Golden Age Spain* (London: Palgrave, 2005), pp. 7–19.
27 Xosé M. Núñez Seixas, *Suspiros de España: el nacionalismo español, 1808–2018* (Barcelona: Crítica, 2018), p. 50.
28 Jorge Cañizares-Esguerra, 'Introduction', in Jorge Cañizares-Esguerra (ed.), *Entangled Empires: The Anglo-Iberian Atlantic, 1500–1830* (Philadelphia: University of Pennsylvania Press, 2018), p. 4.
29 For example, Claudio Sánchez-Albornoz, *España, un enigma histórico* (Buenos Aires: Edhasa, 1960); or Nigel Townson (ed.), *Is Spain Different? A Comparative Look at the 19th and 20th Centuries* (Brighton: Sussex Academic Press, 2015).
30 Richard L. Kagan, 'Prescott's Paradigm: American Historical Scholarship and the Decline of Spain', *American Historical Review*, 101: 2 (April 1996), pp. 430–1.
31 George Ticknor, *Life, Letters and Journals of George Ticknor* (Boston: J. R. Osgood, 1876), p. 198.

32 Andrew Hilen (ed.), *The Letters of Henry Wadsworth Longfellow*, v. 1 (Cambridge, MA: Harvard University Press, 1966), p. 222.
33 Edward Callwell, *Small Wars: Their Principles and Practice* (London: His Majesty's Stationery Office, 1899), p. 41.
34 Lord Mahon, *The War of the Spanish Succession* (London: John Murray, 1836), p. 326.
35 W. H. Auden, *Spain* (London: Faber and Faber, 1937).
36 Thames TV (1977) interview between Mavis Nicholson and V. S. Pritchett, https://www.youtube.com/watch?v=zqQxhXiqOmc (accessed 11 May 2023).
37 Eduardo de Mesa Gallego (2021), 'English Military Interventions in the Wars of the Spanish Monarchy, 1500–1600', in B. Tauler Cid (ed.), *Presencia Británica en la Milicia Española* (Madrid: Comisión Internacional de Historia Militar), p. 70.

2 Anglo-Spanish relations and the Black Legend between the Habsburg alliances, 1489–1714

1 Reginald Merton, *Cardinal Ximenes and the Making of Spain* (London: Kegan Paul, 1934), p. 31.
2 António Henriques, 'Comparative European Institutions and the Little Divergence, 1385–1800', Centre for Global Economic History, Working paper no. 84, August 2019; https://nofuturepast.wordpress.com/2019/08/28/comparative-european-institutions-and-the-little-divergence-1385-1800/ (accessed 26 September 2019).
3 Barbara Fuchs, *The Poetics of Piracy: Emulating Spain in English Literature* (Philadelphia: University of Pennsylvania Press, 2013).
4 Wayne M. M. Kilne, 'The English Crown's Foreign Debt, 1544–1557 (1992)'. Dissertations and Theses. Portland State University. Paper 4366, pp. 36–58.
5 James A. O. C. Brown, 'Morocco and Atlantic History', in D'Maris Coffman, Adrian Leonard and William O'Reilly (eds), *The Atlantic World* (London: Routledge, 2015), pp. 191–3.
6 Mark Sheaves, 'The Anglo-Iberian Atlantic as a Hemisphere System: English Merchants Navigating the Iberian Atlantic', in Jorge Cañizares-Esguerra (ed.), *Entangled Empires: The Anglo-Iberian Atlantic, 1500–1830* (Philadelphia: University of Pennsylvania Press, 2018), pp. 20–6, 34.
7 Christopher Heaney, 'Marrying Utopia', in Jorge Cañizares-Esguerra (ed.), *Entangled Empires: The Anglo-Iberian Atlantic, 1500–1830* (Philadelphia: University of Pennsylvania Press, 2018), pp. 84–8; Heather Dalton, *Merchants and Explorers: Roger Barlow, Sebastian Cabot, and Networks of Atlantic Exchange, 1500–1560* (Oxford: Oxford University Press, 2016).
8 Alexander Samson, *Mary and Philip: The Marriage of Tudor England and Habsburg Spain* (Manchester: Manchester University Press, 2020), chapter 6.

9 For example, Nicolás González Ruiz, *Dos reinas. La católica y la protestante: Isabel de España. Isabel de Inglaterra* (Madrid: Editorial Cervantes, 1947).
10 William S. Maltby, *The Black Legend in England: The Development of Anti-Spanish Sentiment, 1558–1660* (Durham, NC: Duke University Press, 1971), pp. 3–12; Julián Juderías, *La leyenda negra* (Madrid: Editora Nacional, 1967).
11 The work of such historians as Fernández Sebastián and Capellán de Miguel has buried the 'Black Legend' myth (Javier Fernández Sebastián and Gonzalo Capellán de Miguel, 'The Notion of Modernity in Nineteenth-Century Spain. An Example of Conceptual History', *Contributions to the History of Concepts*, 1: 2 (October 2005), pp. 159–84).
12 María Elvira Roca Barea, *Imperiofobia y Leyenda Negra: Roma, Rusia, Estados Unidos y el Imperio español* (Madrid: Siruela, 2016), p. 459.
13 María Elvira Roca Barea, *Imperiofobia y Leyenda Negra: Roma, Rusia, Estados Unidos y el Imperio español* (Madrid: Siruela, 2016), p. 227.
14 Mark G. Sánchez, 'Anti-Spanish Sentiment in English Political and Literary Writing, 1553–1603' (unpublished PhD thesis, University of Leeds, 2004), p. 225.
15 B. de Las Casas, *A Short Account of the Destruction of the Indies* (London: Harmondsworth, 1992), p. 48.
16 Robert Goodwin, *Spain: The Centre of the World, 1519–1682* (London: Bloomsbury, 2015), p. 216.
17 Walter Raleigh, *The Discovery of Guiana, and the Journey of the Second Voyage Thereto* (London: Cassell & Company, 1887).
18 John Foxe, *Actes and Monuments of These Latter and Perillous Days, Touching Matters of the Church* (London: John Day, 1563), chapter 5.
19 Charles Kingsley, *Westward Ho!* (London: Macmillan, 1878).
20 David J. Weber, *Spanish Bourbons and Wild Indians* (Waco: Baylor University Press, 2004), p. 15.
21 Paul Preston, *A People Betrayed: A History of Corruption, Political Incompetence and Social Division in Modern Spain* (London: HarperCollins, 2020), p. 2.
22 Peter Pierson, *Commander of the Armada: The Seventh Duke of Medina Sidonia* (New Haven, CT: Yale University Press, 1989), pp. 56–7.
23 William S. Maltby, *The Black Legend in England: The Development of Anti-Spanish Sentiment, 1558–1660* (Durham, NC: Duke University Press, 1971), pp. 3, 12.
24 Giles Tremlett, *A Brief History of Spain* (London: Apollo, 2022), p. 121.
25 Luis Gorrochategui Santos, *The English Armada: The Greatest Naval Disaster in English History* (London: Bloomsbury, 2018), pp. 53–252.
26 Antony Wingfield (disputed), *A True Coppie of a Discourse Written by a Gentleman Employed in the Late Voyage of Spaine and Portingale: Sent to His Particular Friend, and by Him Published, for the Better Satisfaction of All Such, as Hauing Been Seduced*

by Particular Report, Haue Entred into Conceipts Tending to the Discredit of the Enterprise, and Actors of the Same (London: Thomas Orwin, 1589), p. 12.

27 Gorrochategui Santos, *The English Armada*, p. 297.
28 Brown, 'Morocco and Atlantic History', pp. 187–8.
29 Ben Wilson, *Empire of the Deep: The Rise and Fall of the British Navy* (London: Orion, 2013), pp. 146–9.
30 William S. Goldman, 'Spain and the Founding of Jamestown', *William and Mary Quarterly*, 3rd series, 68: 3 (July 2011), 427–50, 427–8, 436.
31 Óscar Alfredo Ruiz Fernández, *England and Spain in the Early Modern Era: Royal Love, Diplomacy, Trade and Naval Relations, 1604–25* (London: Bloomsbury, 2020), p. 25.
32 Adam Morton, 'Fighting Popery with Popery: Subverting Stereotypes and Contesting Anti-Catholicism in Late Seventeenth-Century England', in Koji Yamamoto (ed.), *Stereotypes and Stereotyping in Early Modern England: Puritans, Papists and Projectors* (Manchester: Manchester University Press, 2022), p. 204.
33 Ruiz Fernández, *England and Spain in the Early Modern Era*, pp. 7–8, 12–13, 59–78.
34 Calvin F. Senning, *Spain, Rumor, and Anti-Catholicism in Mid-Jacobean England: The Palatine Match, Cleves, and the Armada Scares of 1612–1613 and 1614* (London: Routledge, 2021), chapter 2.
35 Robert Cross, 'Pretense and Perception in the Spanish Match, or History in a Fake Beard', *Journal of Interdisciplinary History*, 37: 4 (Spring 2007), 563–83.
36 Ruiz Fernández, *England and Spain in the Early Modern Era*, p. 47.
37 Geoffrey Parker, *The Military Revolution: Military Innovation and the Rise of the West, 1500–1800* (Cambridge: Cambridge University Press, 1996), p. 205.
38 Ángel Alloza Aparicio, 'Guerra económica y comercio europeo en España, 1624–1674. Las grandes represalias y la lucha contra el contrabando', *Hispania: Revista Española de Historia*, 65: 219 (2005), 227–79, 248.
39 Ángel Alloza Aparicio, *Diplomacia caníbal: España y Gran Bretaña en la pugna por el dominio del mundo, 1638–1660* (Madrid: Biblioteca Nueva, 2015).
40 Jorge Cañizares-Esguerra, *Puritan Conquistadores: Iberianizing the Atlantic, 1550–1700* (Stanford: Stanford University Press, 2006), pp. 9–13.
41 William Dampier, *A New Voyage Round the World Describing Particularly the Isthmus of America* (London: James Knapton, 1703), p. 170.
42 José Antonio Maravall, *Culture of the Baroque: Analysis of a Historical Structure* (Minneapolis: University of Minnesota Press, 1986), p. 232.
43 Harald Braun, 'El pensamiento político español del siglo XVII: ¿declive y decadencia, o sabio reconocimiento de la complejidad política?', *La Clé des Langues* [en ligne], Lyon, ENS de LYON/DGESCO (ISSN 2107-7029), avril 2018. Consulté le 21/11/2022, p. 10.

44 David L. Smith, 'Diplomacy and the Religious Question: Mazarin, Cromwell and the Treaties of 1655 and 1657', *E-rea* [En ligne], 11.2 | 2014, mis en ligne le 15 juillet 2014, consulté le 10 août 2022. http://journals.openedition.org/erea/3745; DOI: https://doi.org/10.4000/erea.3745.

45 Linda Colley, *Britons: Forging the Nation, 1707–1837* (New Haven, CT: Yale University Press, 1992).

46 Hamish Scott, 'The War of the Spanish Succession: New Perspectives and Old', in Matthias Pohlig and Michael Schaich (eds), *The War of the Spanish Succession: New Perspectives* (Oxford: Oxford University Press, 2018), pp. 29–30.

47 David González Cruz, *Propaganda e información en tiempos de guerra: España y América (1700–1714)* (Madrid: Sílex, 2009), p. 28.

48 Hew Strachan, 'Scotland's Military Identity', *Scottish Historical Review*, 85: 220, Part 2 (October, 2006), pp. 315–32, 320.

49 Cited in Adrian Finucane, *The Temptations of Trade: Britain, Spain and the Struggle for Empire* (Philadelphia: University of Pennsylvania Press, 2016), p. 8.

50 Charles Esdaile, *Napoleon's Wars* (London: Allen Lane, 2008), pp. 9–10.

51 González Cruz, *Propaganda e información en tiempos de guerra*, pp. 222–3.

52 Angel Smith, *The Origins of Catalan Nationalism* (Basingstoke: Palgrave, 2014), p. 30; Joaquín Albareda Salvadó, *La Guerra de Sucesión en España (1700–1714)* (Madrid: Crítica, 2010).

53 Lord Mahon, *The War of the Succession in Spain* (London: John Murray, 1836), pp. 201–2.

54 Nicholas Dorrell, *Marlborough's Other Army* (London: Helion, 2019).

55 George Alfred Henty, *The Bravest of the Brave: Or with Peterborough in Spain* (London: Blackie, 1887).

56 W. N. Hargreaves-Mawdsley, *Eighteenth-Century Spain, 1700–1788: A Political, Diplomatic and Institutional History* (London: Macmillan, 1979), p. 2; Mahon, *War of the Succession*, pp. 51–60.

57 Andrew C. Thompson, 'War, Religion, and Public Debate in Britain during the War of the Spanish Succession', in Matthias Pohlig and Michael Schaich (eds), *The War of the Spanish Succession: New Perspectives* (Oxford, 2018), pp. 190–1, 195.

58 González Cruz, *Propaganda e información en tiempos de guerra*, pp. 142–5.

59 González Cruz, *Propaganda e información en tiempos de guerra*, p. 182.

60 John Friend, *An Account of the Earl of Peterborough's Conduct in Spain* (London: W. Wise, 1707), pp. 4–7; Julio Luis Arroyo Vozmediano, 'Francisco de Velasco y los catalanes. Sitio y capitulación de Barcelona, 1705', in *Hispania*, 74: 246 (enero-abril, 2014), pp. 69–94, 76–80.

61 Charles Petrie, *The Spanish Royal House* (London: Geoffrey Bles, 1958), p. 78.

62 Mahon, *War of the Succession*, pp. 63–4, 99–101.

63 Mahon, *War of the Succession*, p. 202.

64 Carmen Pérez Aparicio (2009), 'Don Juan Bautista Basset y Ramos. Luces y sombras del líder austracista valenciano', *Estudis: Revista de Historia Moderna*, 35, pp. 133–64.
65 Daniel Defoe, *Memoirs of Captain Carleton* (London: E. P. Dutton, 1929), pp. 149–51.
66 William Hazlitt (ed.), *The Works of Daniel Defoe: With a Memoir of His Life and Writings* (London: John Clements, 1841), Volume 2, p. 21.
67 Mahon, *War of the Succession*, pp. 231–4.
68 The union between Scotland and England commenced on 1 May 1707.
69 Arthur N. Gilbert, 'Army Impressment during the War of the Spanish Succession', in *The Historian: A Journal of History*, 38: 4 (1976), 689–708, p. 704.
70 Brian Cowan, 'The Spin Doctor: Sacheverell's Trial Speech and Political Performance in the Divided Society', *Parliamentary History*, 31: 1 (February 2012), pp. 28–46.
71 Manuel Castellano García, 'Construyendo la paz de Utrecht: las negociaciones secretas entre Francia y Gran Bretaña y la firma de los preliminares de Londres', in *Cuadernos de Historia Moderna*, 45: 1 (2020), 199–232, pp. 202–6.
72 Mark Lawrence, 'Gran Bretaña y la guerra de Sucesión española', in B. Tauler Cid (ed.), *Presencia Británica en la Milicia Española* (Madrid: Ministerio de Defensa, Comisión Internacional de Historia Militar, 2021), pp. 115–38.
73 Earl Philip Henry Stanhope, *History of the War of Succession in Spain* (London: John Murray, 1836), pp. 177–8.
74 Mahon, *War of the Succession*, pp. 351–2.
75 Stanhope, *History of the War of Succession*, pp. 393–4.
76 Cited in D. Symth,'We Are with You: Solidarity and Self-Interest in Soviet Policy towards Republican Spain, 1936–1939', in Paul Preston and Ann L. Mackenzie (eds), *The Republic Besieged: Civil War in Spain 1936–1939* (Edinburgh: Edinburgh University Press, 1996), p. 88.
77 José Cepeda Gómez, 'La historia bélica de la Guerra de Sucesión Española', in *En nombre de la paz: La Guerra de Sucesión Española y los Tratados de Madrid, Utrecht, Rastatt y Baden 1713–1715* (Madrid: Fundación Carlos Amberes, 20 December 2013–23 February 2014), pp. 119, 132.
78 Mahon, *War of the Succession*, pp. 302–4.
79 Lawrence, 'Gran Bretaña y la guerra de Sucesión española', p. 132.
80 Ilya Berkovich, *Motivation in War: the Experience of Common Soldiers in Old-Regime Europe* (Cambridge: Cambridge University Press, 2017), p. 199.
81 González Cruz, *Propaganda e información en tiempos de guerra*, p. 41.
82 Cristina Borreguero Beltrán, 'Imagen y propaganda de guerra en el conflicto sucesorio (1700–1713)', in *Manuscrits*, 21 (2003), 95–132, pp. 123–4.

83 Richard Cannon, *Historical Record of the First or the Royal Regiment of Dragoons: From Its Formation in the Reign of King Charles the Second and of Its Subsequent Services to 1839* (London: William Clowes, 1836), p. 51.
84 *New York Times*, 29 March 1937.
85 James Falkner, *Marlborough's Wars: Eyewitness Accounts 1702–1713* (Barnsley: Pen and Sword, 2005), p. 227.
86 Mahon, *War of the Succession in Spain*, pp. 347–53.
87 Berkovich, *Motivation in War*, p. 203.
88 Cited in Petrie, *Spanish Royal House*, p. 78.
89 González Cruz, *Propaganda e información en tiempos de guerra*, p. 18.
90 Michael Strubell, *The Deplorable History of the Catalans, from Their First Engaging in the War, to the Time of Their Reduction. With the Motives, Declarations, and Engagements, on Which They First Took Arms. The Letters, Treaties, &c. Relating Thereto* (London: J. Baker, 1714), preface.
91 As John Elliot explained, the differences between *aeque principaliter* and personal union are apparent. Under personal union, the constituent regions are considered to be entirely independent of one another. Under *aeque principaliter*, the regions could act and be treated with autonomy on an internal domestic level, but externally were recognized as a single entity under the unified dominion of their sovereign. One of Elliot's examples illustrating this is the marital union of Castile and Aragon. On an international level, Castile and Aragon were recast as a single entity (Spain), while domestically the internal policies of Castile and Aragon differed substantially (J. H. Elliott, 'A Europe of Composite Monarchies', *Past and Present*, 137 (November 1992), pp. 52–7).
92 John Elliott, 'The Road to Utrecht: War and Peace', in Trevor J. Dadson and J. H. Elliott (eds), *Britain, Spain and the Treaty of Utrecht, 1713–2013*, chapter 1 (New York: Legenda, 2014).
93 Esdaile, 'Conscription in Spain', pp. 102–21.
94 Saul David, *All the King's Men: The British Soldier from the Restoration to Waterloo* (London: Viking, 2013), pp. 8–9.
95 W. N. Hargreaves-Mawdsley, *Eighteenth-Century Spain, 1700–1788: A Political, Diplomatic and Institutional History* (London: Macmillan, 1979), p. 35.

3 Eighteenth-century Anglo-Hispania

1 W. N. Hargreaves-Mawdsley, *Eighteenth-Century Spain, 1700–1788: A Political, Diplomatic and Institutional History* (London: Macmillan, 1979), pp. 49–50.
2 Paul Langford (ed.), *Short History of the British Isles: The Eighteenth Century, 1688–1815* (Oxford: Oxford University Press, 2002), p. 9.

3 Bernard Mandeville, *The Fable of the Bees: Or, Private Vices, Publick Benefits* (London: Edward Parker, 1714), pp. 202–3.
4 Allan J. Kuethe and Kenneth J. Andrien, *The Spanish Atlantic World in the Eighteenth Century: War and the Bourbon Reforms, 1713–1796* (Cambridge: Cambridge University Press, 2014), pp. 1–3.
5 Adrian Finucane, *The Temptations of Trade: Britain, Spain and the Struggle for Empire* (Philadelphia: University of Pennsylvania Press, 2016), pp. 1–3.
6 Fayrer Hall, *The Importance of the British Plantations in America to This Kingdom, with the State of Their Trade, and Methods for Improving It; as also a Description of the Several Colonies There* (London: J. Peele, 1731), pp. 6, 24–5.
7 Gabriel Paquette (2004), 'The Image of Imperial Spain in British Political Thought, 1750–1800', *Bulletin of Spanish Studies*, 81: 2, 187–214, pp. 190–1.
8 Patricia T. Young and Jack S. Levy, 'Domestic Politics and the Escalation of Commercial Rivalry: Explaining the War of Jenkins' Ear, 1739–48', *European Journal of International Relations*, 17: 2 (June, 2011), pp. 209–32.
9 Allan J. Kuethe and Kenneth J. Andrien, *The Spanish Atlantic World in the Eighteenth Century: War and the Bourbon Reforms, 1713–1796* (Cambridge: Cambridge University Press, 2014), p. 147.
10 Cited in Brendan Simms, *Three Victories and a Defeat: The Rise and Fall of the First British Empire* (London: Penguin, 2008), pp. 257–8.
11 Evaristo C. Martínez-Radío Garrido, 'Españoles prisioneros y cautivos en la Inglaterra del siglo XVIII: una aproximación a su ubicación y condiciones', *Revista Universitaria de Historia Militar*, 9: 18 (Año 2020), pp. 43–65.
12 Edward Clarke, *Letters Concerning the Spanish Nation: Written at Madrid during the Years 1760 and 1761* (London: T. Becket and P. A. De Hondt, 1763), p. 251.
13 Clarke, *Letters*, pp. 251–2.
14 Anthony McFarlane, *War and Independence in Spanish America* (London: Routledge, 2013), pp. 16–21; Allan J. Kuethe and Kenneth J. Andrien, *The Spanish Atlantic World in the Eighteenth Century: War and the Bourbon Reforms, 1713–1796* (Cambridge: Cambridge University Press, 2014), pp. 236–7.
15 Leticia Villamediana González, *Anglomanía: la imagen de Inglaterra en la prensa española del siglo XVIII* (Madrid: Támesis, 2019), pp. 58–69.
16 William Coxe, *Memoirs of the Kings of Spain of the House of Bourbon*, 5 vols, Vol. 4 (London: Longman, 1815), p. 327.
17 Kristie Patricia Flannery, 'The Globalization of Anglo-Iberian Entanglement', in Jorge Cañizares-Esguerra (ed.), *Entangled Empires: The Anglo-Iberian Atlantic, 1500–1830* (Philadelphia: University of Pennsylvania Press, 2018), pp. 244–51.
18 Matthias Pohlig and Michael Schaich, 'Revisiting the War of the Spanish Succession', in Matthias Pohlig and Michael Schaich (eds), *The War of the Spanish Succession: New Perspectives* (Oxford: Oxford University Press, 2018), p. 25.

19 Adrian Shubert, '"Charity Properly Understood": Changing Ideas about Poor Relief in Liberal Spain', in *Comparative Studies in Society and History*, 33: 1 (January, 1991), pp. 36–55, 36.
20 Ruth McKay, *Lazy, Improvident People: Myth and Reality in the Writing of Spanish History* (Ithaca, NY: Cornell University Press, 2006).
21 Alexander von Humboldt, *Personal Narrative of Travels to the Equinoctial Regions of America during the Years 1799–1804* (London: William Clowes and Sons, 1851), 3 volumes, Volume 1, p. 206.
22 Joseph Clark, '"The Rage of Fanatics": Religious Fanaticism and the Making of Revolutionary Violence', *French History*, 33: 2 (June, 2019), pp. 236–58.
23 David Sorkin, *The Religious Enlightenment: Protestants, Jews and Catholics from London to Vienna* (Princeton, NJ: Princeton University Press, 2008), p. 311.
24 Clarke, '"Rage of Fanatics"', p. 247.
25 Mark Towsey, *Reading History in Britain and America, c. 1750–c. 1840* (New York: Cambridge University Press, 2019), pp. 1–24.
26 Cited in Joseph Harrison, *An Economic History of Modern Spain* (Manchester, 1978), pp. 14–15.
27 Antonio Feros, *Speaking of Spain: The Evolution of Race and Nation in the Hispanic World* (Cambridge, MA: Harvard University Press, 2017), p. 172.
28 Frederick G. Whelan, 'Eighteenth-Century Scottish Political Economy and the Decline of Imperial Spain', *Journal of Scottish Historical Studies*, 38: 1 (2018), pp. 55–72, 59–65.
29 David A. Brading, *Orbe Indiano. De la monarquía católica a la república criolla, 1492–1867* (México: Fondo de Cultura Económica, 1991).
30 For a recent positive reappraisal of the Spanish fiscal-military state, see Rafael Torres Sánchez, *Constructing a Fiscal Military State in Eighteenth-Century Spain* (Basingstoke: Palgrave, 2019).
31 Daron Acemoglu and James A. Robinson, *Why Nations Fail: The Origins of Power, Prosperity and Poverty* (London: Profile Books, 2013), pp. 218–22.
32 For example, Gabriel Tortella Casares and Clara Eugenia Nuñez, *El desarrollo de la España contemporánea: historia económica de los siglos XIX y XX* (Madrid: Alianza, 2011); David Ringrose, *Spain, Europe and the 'Spanish Miracle', 1700–1900* (Cambridge: Cambridge University Press, 1996).
33 Cited in Roy Adkins and Lesley Adkins, *Gibraltar: The Greatest Siege in British History* (London: Penguin, 2017), pp. 67–9.
34 David Allan, 'Anti-Hispanicism and the Construction of Late Eighteenth-Century British Patriotism: Robert Watson's *History of the Reign of Philip the Second*', *Bulletin of Hispanic Studies*, 77 (2000), pp. 423–49, 435.
35 Ricardo García Cárcel, 'Los fantásticos relatos acerca de nuestra patria: la leyenda negra', *Historia Social*, 3 (Winter, 1989), pp. 3–15.

36 James Baldwin Brown (ed.), *Memoirs of the Public and Private Life of John Howard the Philanthropist* (London: Thomas and George Underwood, 1823), p. 370.
37 William Coxe, *Memoirs of the Kings of Spain of the House of Bourbon, from the Accession of Philip V to the Death of Charles III. 1700 to 1788* (London: Longman, Hurst, Rees, Orme, and Brown, 1815), Volume 1, pp. xii–xiii.
38 Joaquín Varela Suanzes-Carpegna, 'The Image of the British System of Government in Spain (1759–1814)', in Jesús Astigarraga (ed.), *The Spanish Enlightenment Revisited* (Oxford: Voltaire Foundation, 2015), pp. 197–8.
39 Jean-Philippe Luis, 'The Mutations of the Spanish Monarchy (1750–1868): From the Universal Jurisdictional Monarchy to the Liberal Oligarchical Monarchy, 1780–1843', in David San Narciso and Margarita Barral Martínez (eds), *Monarchy and Liberalism in Spain: The Building of the Nation-State, 1780–1931* (London: Routledge, 2020).
40 Gabriel Paquette, 'The Image of Imperial Spain in British Political Thought, 1750–1800', *Bulletin of Spanish Studies*, 81: 2 (2004), p. 196.
41 Diego Saglia, *Poetic Castles in Spain: British Romanticism and Figurations of Iberia* (Amsterdam: Editions Rodopi, 2000), p. 32.
42 William S. Maltby, *The Black Legend in England: The Development of Anglo-Spanish Sentiment 1558–1660* (Durham, NC: Duke University Press, 1971), p. 138.
43 Henry Swinburne, *Travels through Spain, 1775 and 1776* (London: P. Elmsly, 1779), p. 238.
44 Leticia Villamediana González, *Anglomanía: la imagen de Inglaterra en la prensa española del siglo XVIII* (Madrid: Támesis, 2019), p. 21.
45 Paquette, 'Image of Imperial Spain in British Political Thought', p. 200.
46 Richard Croker, *Travels through Several Provinces of Spain and Portugal, etc.* (London: J. Robson, 1799), p. 76.
47 Maria Reyes Baztán, 'Potatoes and Nation-Building: The Case of the Spanish Omelette', *Journal of Iberian and Latin American Studies*, 27: 2 (2021), pp. 151–70, 157.
48 Federico Pablo-Marti, 'Complex Networks to Understand the Past: The Case of Roads in Bourbon Spain', *Cliometrica*, 15: 3 (September 2021), pp. 477–534.
49 Bentham Edwards (ed.), *Arthur Young's Travels in France during the Years 1787, 1788, 1789, with an Introduction, Biographical Sketch, and Notes* (London: George Bell, 1892), p. 43.
50 John Geddes, 'An Account of the Province of Biscay, in Spain to Mr Cummyg, Secretary to the Society of Scottish Antiquaries', *Archaeologia scotica or Transactions of the Society of Antiquaries of Scotland*, Edinburgh: Printed for the Society (1792), 205–15.
51 Leandro Fernández de Moratín, *Apuntaciones sueltas de Inglaterra* (Madrid: Cátedra, 2005), pp. 130, 177.

52 Charles Esdaile. 'The British Amy in the Napoleonic Wars: Approaches Old and New', *English Historical Review*, 130: 542 (February 2015), pp. 123–37.

53 Pedro Estala, *Quatro cartas de un español a un anglomano en que se manifiesta La perfidia del gobierno de la Inglaterra, como pernicioso al genero humano, potencias Europeas, y particularmente à la España* (Buenos Aires: Imprenta de Niños Expósitos, 1807).

54 Jean-Philippe Luis, 'The Mutations of the Spanish Monarchy, 1750–1868', in David San Narciso, Margarita Barral Martínez and Carolina Armenteros (eds), *Monarchy and Liberalism in Spain: The Building of the Nation-State, 1780–1931* (London: Routledge, 2020), pp. 6–7.

55 Richard Ford, *A Handbook for Travellers in Spain* (London: John Murray, 1869), Volume II, p. 131.

56 Various, 'The Act of Paris', in Sarah C. Chambers and John C. Chasteen (eds), *Latin American Independence: An Anthology of Sources* (Indianapolis: Hackett, 2010), p. 54.

57 Richard Graham, *Independence in Latin America* (London: Random House, 1971), p. 6.

58 R. A. Humphreys, 'Isolation from Spain', in R. A. Humphreys and John Lynch (eds), *The Origins of the Latin American Revolutions, 1808–1826* (New York: Alfred A. Knopf, 1965), p. 141.

59 Charles Ronald Middleton, *The Administration of British Foreign Policy, 1782–1846* (Durham, NC: Duke University Press, 1977), p. 39.

60 John Lynch, *Latin America between Colony and Nation: Selected Essays* (Basingstoke: Palgrave, 2001), p. 98.

61 Álvaro Flórez Estrada, *Examen imparcial de las disensiones de América con España, de los medios de su reconciliación, y de la prosperidad de todas las naciones* (London: Imprenta de D. Manuel Ximenez Carreño, 1811), pp. 24–33.

4 The Peninsular War and its aftermath

1 Esdaile, 'British Army in the Napoleonic Wars', p. 133; Gavin Daly, *The British Soldier in the Peninsular War: Encounters with Spain and Portugal, 1808–1814* (Basingstoke: Palgrave Macmillan, 2013), p. 5.

2 José Álvarez Junco, *Mater Dolorosa: la idea de España del siglo XIX* (Madrid: Taurus, 2002), pp. 120–5.

3 T. Kirby, *The Duke of Wellington and the Supply System during the Peninsular War* (Paris: Wagram Press, 2014), p. 22.

4 Basil Henry Liddel Hart, *The British Way in Warfare* (London: Faber and Faber, 1932), p. 7.

5 José Alberich, *Bibliografía anglo-hispánica, 1801–1850* (Oxford: Oxford University Press, 1978).
6 Charles J. Esdaile, *Women in the Peninsular War* (Norman: Oklahoma University Press, 2014).
7 Ian Robertson, *A Commanding Presence: Wellington in the Peninsula, 1808–1814* (Stroud: Spellmount, 2008).
8 Matilda Greig, *Dead Men Telling Tales: Napoleonic War Memoirs and the Military Memoir Industry, 1808–1914* (Oxford: Oxford University Press, 2021), pp. 73, 109.
9 Mahon, *The War of the Succession in Spain*, p. 85.
10 Graciela Iglesias Rogers, *British Liberators in the Age of Napoleon: Volunteering under the Spanish Flag in the Peninsular War* (London: Bloomsbury, 2012).
11 Charles Leslie, *Military Journal of Colonel Leslie, K. H., of Balquhain, whilst Serving with the Twenty-Ninth Regiment in the Peninsula and the Sixtieth Rifles in Canada, etc., 1807–1832* (Aberdeen: Aberdeen University Press, 1887), pp. 25–6, 30.
12 William Jacob, *Travels in the South of Spain in Letters written A.D. 1809 and 1810* (London: John Nichols, 1811), pp. 8–12.
13 Henry Kamen, *The Disinherited: Exile and the Making of Spanish Culture, 1492–1975* (New York: New York University Press, 2007), p. 197.
14 Jacob, *Travels in the South of Spain*, p. 202.
15 Alexander Dallas, *Felix Alvarez, or Manners in Spain* (London: Baldwin, Craddock and Joy, 1818).
16 Byron, *Childe Harold* (1812) Canto I, verse 44 (public domain access: Childe Harold's Pilgrimage by Lord Byron | The British Library (bl.uk)); https://www.bl.uk/works/childe-harolds-pilgrimage (accessed 12 May 2023).
17 Elizabeth Vassall Fox Holland, *The Journal of Elizabeth Lady Holland (1791–1811)* (London: Longmans, 1909).
18 Diego Saglia, '"O My Mother Spain!": The Peninsular War, Family Matters, and the Practice of Romantic Nation-Writing', *ELH*, 65: 2 (1998), pp. 363–93.
19 See Robert Southey, *History of the Peninsular War* (London: John Murray, 1823–32), Volume I.
20 Charles J. Esdaile, *Fighting Napoleon: Guerrillas Bandits and Adventurers in Spain 1808–1814* (London: Yale University Press, 2004), p. 4.
21 Fernando Cervantes, *Conquistadores: A New History* (London: Allen Lane, 2020), p. 353.
22 Greig, *Dead Men Telling Tales*, p. 90.
23 Robert Batty, *A Sketch of the Late Campaign in the Netherlands* (London: W. M. Clarke, 1815), pp. viii–ix.
24 Charles Esdaile, 'Prohombres, aventureros y oportunistasla influencia del trayecto personal en los orígenes del liberalismo en España', in Alda Blanco and Guy

Thomson (eds), *Visiones del liberalismo: política, identidad y cultura en la España del siglo XIX* (Valencia: PUZ, 2008), pp. 65–86.
25. *El Universal*, 14 January 1814.
26. Kevin Linch, *Britain and Wellington's Army: Recruitment, Society and Tradition, 1807–15* (Basingstoke: Palgrave, 2011), pp. 118, 132.
27. Donald D. Howard, 'British Seapower and Its Influence Upon the Peninsular War (1808–1814)', *Naval War College Review*, 31: 2 (US Naval War College Press, 1978), p. 54.
28. Verner Willoughby, *A British Rifleman: Journals and Correspondence [of George Simmons] during the Peninsular War and the Campaign of Waterloo* (London: A&C Black, 1899), p. 23.
29. Bruce Collins, *Wellington and the Siege of San Sebastián, 1813* (Barnsley: Pen and Sword, 2017), p. 7.
30. August Ludolf Friedrich Schaumann, *On the Road with Wellington: The Diary of a War Commissary in the Peninsular Campaigns* (London: William Heinemann, 1924), p. 355.
31. Carlos Santacara, *La Guerra de la Independencia vista por los británicos, 1808–1814* (Madrid: Machado, 2005), pp. 90, 110; James Wilmot Ormsby, *An Account of the Operations of the British Army and of the State and Sentiments of the People of Portugal and Spain during the Campaign of 1808–1809* (London: James Carpenter, 1809), pp. 45–69.
32. Gavin Daly, '"Barbarity More Suited to Savages": British Soldiers' Views of Spanish and Portuguese Violence during the Peninsular War, 1808–1814', *War and Society*, 35: 4 (2016), pp. 242–58, 248.
33. Gavin Daly, 'Liberators and Tourists: British Soldiers in Madrid during the Peninsular War', in Catriona Kennedy and Matthew McCormack, *Soldiering in Britain and Ireland, 1750–1850* (Basingstoke: Palgrave, 2013), pp. 118–19.
34. Basil Liddell Hart, *The Letters of Private Wheeler 1809–1828* (London: Windrush Press, 1999), p. 49.
35. Alan Forrest, 'Insurgents and Counter-Insurgents', in Erica Charters, Eve Rosenhaft and Hannah Smith (eds), *Civilians and War in Europe 1618–1815* (Liverpool: Liverpool University Press, 2012), pp. 193–4.
36. Raymond Carr, *The Spanish Tragedy: The Civil War in Perspective* (London: Phoenix Press, 1977), p. 95.
37. Charles J. Esdaile, *Napoleon's Wars: An International History, 1803–1815* (London: Allen Lane, 2008), p. 11.
38. Alicia Laspra, 'La intervención británica: ayuda material y diplomática', *Revista de historia militar*, 2 (2005), pp. 59–78.
39. Esdaile, *Fighting Napoleon*.

40 Esdaile, 'Patriots, Partisans and Land Pirates in Retrospect', in Esdaile (ed.), *Popular Resistance* (Basingstoke: Palgrave Macmillan, 2008), pp. 1–22.
41 Charles J. Esdaile, *The Duke of Wellington and the Command of the Spanish Army, 1812-1814* (London: Palgrave Macmillan, 1990), p. 81.
42 Charles J. Esdaile, *The Spanish Army in the Peninsular War* (Manchester: Manchester University Press, 1988), pp. 64–8.
43 Santacara, *La Guerra de la Independencia* , p. 736.
44 For example, Juan Romero Alpuente, *Wellington en España y Ballesteros en Ceuta* (Cádiz: Imprenta de A. Fernández Figueroa, 1813).
45 Manuel Moreno Alonso, *Blanco White: la obsesión de España* (Sevilla: Alfar, 1998), pp. 253, 295.
46 *El Observador*, 7 September 1810.
47 Gregorio Alonso, 'Corporations, Subjects, and Citizens: The Peculiar Modernity of Early Hispanic Liberalism', *Journal of Iberian and Latin American Studies*, 22: 1 (2016), 7–22, p. 13.
48 Emilio La Parra, *Fernando VII: un rey deseado y detestado* (Madrid: Tusquets, 2018).
49 Ferdinand Whittingham (ed.), *A Memoir of the Services of Lieutenant-General Sir Samuel Ford Whittingham* (London: Longmans, 1868), pp. 233–9.
50 Charles Oman, *A History of the Peninsular War: August 1813–April 14, 1814. The Capture of St. Sebastian, Wellington's Invasion of France, Battles of the Nivelle, the Nive, Orthez, and Toulouse* (London: Forgotten Books, 2018), Volume VII, p. 521.
51 Santacara, *La Guerra de la Independencia* , p. 218.
52 Mark Lawrence, 'Peninsularity and Patriotism: Spanish and British Approaches to the Peninsular War, 1808–14', *Historical Research*, 85: 229 (August 2012), pp. 453–68.
53 For example, Santacara, *La Guerra de la Independencia* , p. 152; Jacob, *Travels in the South of Spain*, pp. 31–2.
54 Daly, *British Soldier in the Peninsular War*.
55 William Napier, *History of the War in the Peninsula and in the South of France from the year 1807 to the year 1814* (London: Frederick Warne, 1828), Volume 4, p. 3.
56 Edward Tangye Lean, *The Napoleonists: A Study in Political Disaffection 1760–1960* (Oxford: Oxford University Press, 1970).
57 Cited in Santacara, *La Guerra de la Independencia* , p. 756.
58 'To the People of Spain', *Monthly Magazine*, 40 (1 October 1815), p. 237.
59 Manuel Ortuño Martínez, *Xavier Mina: fronteras de libertad* (Mexico City: Librería de Porrua Hermanos, 2003).
60 Mark Lawrence, 'Conclusion', in Mark Lawrence (ed.), *Insurgency and Counterinsurgency in the Nineteenth Century: A Global History* (London: Routledge, 2020), p. 352.

61 David A. G. Waddell, 'British Neutrality and Spanish-American Independence: The Problem of Foreign Enlistment', *Journal of Latin American Studies*, 19 (1987), pp. 1–18.

62 Juan Balansó, *Julia Bonaparte: una burguesa en el trono de España* (Barcelona: Debolsillo, 2001). This author does not support this scheme with primary evidence, but its spirit is in keeping with the adventurism of liberal exiles.

63 Karen Racine and Graham Lloyd (eds), *The Journal of James A. Brush: The Expedition and Military Operations of General Don Francisco Xavier Mina in Mexico, 1816–1817* (Albuquerque: University of New Mexico Press, 2020).

64 Klemens von Metternich, *Memoirs of Prince Metternich*, Volume 2, 1773–1815 (New York: Charles Scribner's, 1880), p. 580.

65 Charles K. Webster, *The Congress of Vienna 1814–1815* (Oxford: Oxford University Press, 1918), p. 8.

66 Dan Royle (2022), 'Winning the War and Losing the Peace: Spain and the Congress of Vienna', *The International History Review*, 44: 2, pp. 357–72.

67 Mark Lawrence, 'Peninsularity and Patriotism', p. 458.

68 Jordi Vernet Roca, 'La Restauración de Fernando VII: la transformación represiva y autoritaria de la monarquía. Barcelona, de Manuel Casamada a Luis Lacy', *Rubrica Contemporanea*, 4: 8 (2015), pp. 1–28.

69 Christopher A. Bayly, *Imperial Meridian: The British Empire and the World, 1780–1830* (London: Longman, 1989); Matthew Brown, *Adventuring through Spanish Colonies: Simón Bolívar, Foreign Mercenaries and the Birth of New Nations* (Liverpool: University of Liverpool Press, 2006).

70 Rodrigo Escribano Roca and Pablo Guerrero Oñate, 'Navalismo y panhispanismo como horizontes de regeneración imperial en España (1814–1862)', *Anuario de Estudios Americanos*, 79: 1 (Sevilla, 2022), 205–38, pp. 214–15.

71 Pío Baroja, *Siluetas románticas* (Madrid: Espasa Calpe, 1934), p. 127.

72 Pedro Rújula and Manuel Chust, *El Trienio Liberal. Revolución e independencia (1820–1823)* (Madrid: Catarata, 2020); Pedro Rújula and Ivana Frasquet (eds), *El Trienio Liberal (1820–1823): una mirada política* (Granada: Editorial Comares, 2020).

73 Mark Lawrence, 'Spanish Political Development 1808 to 1868', in Andrew Dowling (ed.), *Routledge Handbook of Spanish History* (London: Routledge, 2023).

74 Manuel Moreno Alonso, *Blanco White: la obsesión de España* (Sevilla: Alfar, 1998).

75 Gabriel Paquette, 'Introduction: Liberalism in the Early Nineteenth-Century Iberian World', *History of European Ideas* (2014), DOI: 10.1080/01916599.2014.914312, p. 11.

76 Juan Luis Simal, 'Letters from Spain: The 1820 Revolution and the Liberal International', in Maurizio Isabella and Konstantina Zanou (eds), *Mediterranean*

Diasporas: Politics and Ideas in the Long 19th Century (London: Bloomsbury, 2016), p. 33.

77 Cited in Gonzalo Butrón Prida, 'From Hope to Defensiveness: The Foreign Policy of a Beleaguered Liberal Spain, 1820–1823', *English Historical Review*, 133: 562 (2018), 567–696, p. 567.
78 Wendy Hinde, *George Canning* (London: Wiley Blackwell, 1989), p. 345.
79 Andrea Rodríguez Tapia, 'España sin América. Política y diplomacia frente a la secesión de los territorios americanos, 1823–1833' (Doctoral thesis, Colegio de México, UNAM, 2018), pp. 78–9.
80 For further analysis of global and micro history, see Jan de Vries, 'Playing with Scales: The Global and the Micro, the Macro and the Nano', *Past & Present*, 242: 14 (November 2019), pp. 23–36.
81 C. A. Bayly, *Indian Thought in the Age of Conflict and Empire* (Cambridge: Cambridge University Press, 2012), p. 47.
82 Mark Lawrence, 'Juan Álvarez Mendizábal', in José Álvarez Junco and Adrian Shubert (eds), *The History of Modern Spain: Chronologies, Themes, Individuals* (London: Bloomsbury, 2018).
83 Angel Smith, 'The Rise and Fall of "Respectable" Spanish Liberalism, 1808–1923: An Explanatory Framework', *Journal of Iberian and Latin American Studies* (2016), pp. 55–73.
84 Gonzalo Serrats Urrecha, *El general Álava y Wellington: de Trafalgar a Waterloo* (Madrid: Foro para el Estudio de la Historia Militar de España, 2014).
85 Irene Castells, *La utopía insurreccional del liberalismo: Torrijos y las conspiraciones de la década ominosa* (Barcelona: Crítica, 1989).
86 Castells, *Utopía insurreccional*, pp. 26–7.
87 Vicente Llorens, *Liberales y románticos: una emigración española en Inglaterra* (Madrid: Castalia, 1979), p. 80.
88 Cited in Rebeca Viguera Ruiz, 'Ramón Alesón y el liberalismo en los orígenes de la España contemporánea (1781–1846)' (PhD thesis, Universidad de la Rioja, 2009), chapter 3.
89 David Howard, *The Invention of Spain: Anglo-Spanish Cultural Relations, 1770–1870* (Manchester: Manchester University Press, 2007), pp. 123–5.
90 Leucadio Doblado, *Letters from Spain* (London: Colburn, 1822), pp. 8–9.
91 Juan Bautista Vilar, *La España del exilio. Las emigraciones políticas españolas en los siglos XIX y XX* (Madrid: Editorial Síntesis, 2007), p. 166.
92 AHN, Estado, leg. 217-2, No. 17: 9 March 1826 advice from *camarilla* to king on how to proceed with the manifesto of Antonio Fernández Bazán.
93 Castells, *Utopía insurreccional*, p. 153.
94 Miguel Artola-Gallego, *La España de Fernando VII* (Madrid: Espasa, 1999), pp. 724–7.

95 Álvaro París, 'King, War and Bread: Popular Royalism in Southern Europe (1789–1830)', in Andoni Artola Renedo (ed.), *Royalism, War and Popular Politics in the Age of Revolutions (1780s–1870s). In the Name of the King* (London: Palgrave, 2023), p. 84.
96 Henry David Inglis, *Spain in 1830* (London: Whittaker, Treacher and Company, 1831), Volume 2, p. 334.
97 Donald Sultana, *Benjamin Disraeli in Spain, Malta and Albania, 1830–32* (London: Tamesis Books, 1976), pp. 20, 28.
98 Conxa Rodríguez Vives, *Los exilios de Ramón Cabrera* (Zaragoza: Prensa de la Universidad de Zaragoza, 2019), p. 112.
99 Eric W. Nye (ed.), *John Kemble's Gibraltar Journal: The Spanish Expedition of the Cambridge Apostles, 1830–31* (New York: Palgrave, 2015).
100 Henry David Inglis, *Spain in 1830* (London: Whittaker, Treacher and Company, 1837), Volume 1, p. 291.
101 AHN, Estado, leg. 217-2, No. 17: intercepted correspondence between Bazán and Fransico Milans and Antonio Salinas detailing the names of sympathetic and hostile residents in Guardamar (Alicante); Castells, *Utopía insurreccional*, pp. 148, 205.
102 Castells, *Utopía insurreccional*, pp. 181–8.
103 Even so, Adam Zamowski has suggested that Torrijos's heroic failures inspired the 'Glorious' revolution in France and the independence of Belgium in 1830 (Adam Zamowski, *Holy Madness: Romantics, Patriots and Revolutionaries, 1776–1871* (London: Viking, 2000), p. 268).

5 Anglo-Hispania and the first Carlist War (1833–40)

1 Antonio Caridad Salvador, 'La historiografía reciente sobre el primer carlismo (2006–2018), *Studia Historica. Historia Contemporánea*, 38 (2020), p. 207.
2 Josep-Ramón Segarra Estarelles, 'El reverso de la nación. "Provincialismo" e "independencia" durante la revolución liberal', Javier Moreno Luzón (ed.), *Construir España: Nacionalismo español y procesos de nacionalización* (Madrid: Centro de Estudios Constitucionales, 2007), pp. 40–5.
3 Nigel Glendinning, 'Nineteenth-Century British Envoys in Spain and the Taste for Spanish Art in England', *The Burlington Magazine*, 131: 1031 (February 1989), 117–26, p. 117.
4 Richard Ford, *A Handbook for Travellers in Spain* (London: John Murray, 1855), p. 55.

5 Douglas Hilt, 'The Reception of the Spanish Theatre in European Romanticism', in Gerald Ernest and Paul Gillespie (eds), *Romantic Drama* (Philadelphia: John Benjamins, 1994), p. 25.
6 Jasper Ridley, *Lord Palmerston* (London: Book Club Associates, 1970), pp. 42–8.
7 For example, Román Oyarzun, *Historia del carlismo* (Valladolid: Maxtor, 2008); Alfonso Bullón de Mendoza, *La primera guerra carlista* (Madrid: Actas, 1992).
8 For an excellent recent analysis, see Alfonso Goizueta Alfaro, 'Forging Liberal States: Palmerston's Foreign Policy and the Rise of a Constitutional Monarchy in Spain, 1833–7', *Historical Research*, 94: 266 (November 2021), pp. 827–48.
9 *The Times*, 14 October 1834.
10 *Edinburgh Review*, 64 (1837), p. 178.
11 TNA, FO 72/443, George Villiers, doc. 55: 12 March 1836 letter from ambassador to British Foreign Office detailing the affair of Burke Honan.
12 Antonio Pirala, *Historia de la guerra civil y de los partidos liberal y carlista* (Madrid: Turner, 1984), Volume I, pp. 537–41.
13 Mariano de la Cámara, *La politica exterior del carlismo (1833–1839)* (Sevilla: Librería e imprenta Modernas, 1933), pp. 22–4.
14 William Makepeace Thackeray, *Tremendous Adventures of Major Gahagan* (London: Bradbury & Evans, 1855).
15 Antonio Caridad Salvador, 'Las mujeres durante la primera guerra carlista (1833–1840)', *Memoria y Civilización*, 14 (2011), 175–99, p. 188.
16 George Borrow, *The Bible in Spain* (London: John Murray, 1843).
17 Letter: 20th April, 1836 To the Rev. A. Brandram (Endorsed: recd. May 5, 1836) Madrid, no. 3, Calle de la Zarza, 20 April 1836 (George Borrow, *Letters of George Borrow to the Foreign and British Bible Society* (London: Hodder and Stoughton, 1911)).
18 Undated letter (summer 1837) from George Borrow to the Rev. Andrew Brandram regarding his journey from Astorga to Lugo (Borrow, *Letters*, p. 88).
19 Rory Muir, *Tactics and the Experience of Battle in the Age of Napoleon* (London: Yale University Press, 2000), p. 6.
20 Lovell Benjamin Badcock, *Rough Leaves from a Journal Kept in Spain and Portugal, during the Years 1832, 1833, and 1834* (London: Richard Bentley, 1835), pp. 82–3.
21 Letter: 26th December, 1836 To the Rev. A. Brandram (Endorsed: Recd. January 6, 1837) Madrid, December 26th, 1836 (Borrow, *Letters*).
22 Poco Mas, *Scenes and Adventures from Spain, 1835–1840* (London: Richard Bentley, 1845), Volume 1, pp. 114–15.
23 Ian Robertson, *Los curiosos impertinentes: viajeros ingleses por España, 1760–1855* (Madrid: Editora Nacional, 1975).
24 Baroja, *Siluetas*.

25 Alberto del Campo Tejedor, *La infame fama del andaluz* (Córdoba: Editorial Almuzara, 2020).
26 Antonio Luis Cortes Peña, 'Nacionalismo/regionalismo andaluz: una invención de laboratorio', *Historia Social*, 4 (2001), pp. 137–52. In some ways, the southern question in Spain compares with the Mezzogiorno in southern Italy.
27 George Dennis, *A Summer in Andalucia* (London: Richard Bentley, 1839), Volume 1, pp. 229–30.
28 Edwin M. Brett, *The British Auxiliary Legion in the First Carlist War in Spain, 1835-1838: A Forgotten Army* (Dublin: Four Courts Press, 2005).
29 Pirala, *Guerra Civil*, II, pp. 234–8.
30 Brett, *British Auxiliary Legion*, p. 26.
31 I am grateful to Dr Helen Rogers for making me aware of William Turner's testimony written in prison in 1840. For contextual information, see Helen Rogers, 'Kindness and Reciprocity: Liberated Prisoners and Christian Charity in Early Nineteenth-Century England', *Journal of Social History*, 47: 3 (Spring 2014), pp. 721–45.
32 For contextual information, see Rogers, 'Kindness and Reciprocity', pp. 721–45.
33 Pirala, *Guerra Civil*, II, pp. 238–40.
34 Pirala, *Guerra Civil*, II, pp. 495–502.
35 George de Lacy Evans, *Memoranda of the Contest in Spain* (London: James Ridgway, 1840), pp. 10–11.
36 *Hansard Parliamentary Debates* (3d ser.), LII, 552–3, in Philip E. Mosely, 'Intervention and Nonintervention in Spain, 1838–39', *Journal of Modern History*, 13: 2 (June 1941), 195–217, p. 200.
37 Edward M. Spiers, *Radical General: Sir George de Lacy Evans, 1787–1870* (Manchester: Manchester University Press, 1983), pp. 60–100, 140–71.
38 Spiers, *Radical General*, p. 168; William Bollaert, *The Wars of Succession of Portugal and Spain, from 1826 to 1840: With Résumé of the Political History of Portugal and Spain to the Present Time* (London: E. Stanford, 1870), II, p. 222, 226; Javier de Burgos, *Anales del reinado de Doña Isabel II* (Madrid: Mellado, 1850), III, p. 120.
39 Spiers, *Radical General*, pp. 77–9.
40 Spiers, *Radical General*, pp. 81–5.
41 Pirala, *Guerra Civil*, II, pp. 114–20.
42 For example, de la Cámara, *La política exterior*, pp. 69–75.
43 F. Melgar, *Pequeña historia del carlismo* (Pamplona: Editorial Gómez, 1958), pp. 44–5; Pirala, *Guerra Civil*, IV, pp. 461–6.
44 Charles K. Webster, *The Foreign Policy of Palmerston, 1830–41* (London: G. Bell, 1951), Volume I, p. 429.
45 Letter from George Villiers to Lord Palmerston (15 November 1834), in Roger Bullen and Felicity Strong (eds), *Palmerston, I: Private Correspondence with Sir*

George Villiers (Afterwards Fourth Earl of Clarendon) as Minister to Spain 1833–1837 (London: Her Majesty's Stationery Office, 1985), p. 230.
46 François Guizot, *Mémoires pour servir à l'histoire de mon temps*, IV (Paris: Michel Levy, 1861), p. 76.
47 *Eco del Comercio*, 2 September 1841.
48 Pirala, *Guerra Civil*, II, pp. 362–3.
49 Pirala, *Guerra Civil*, II, pp. 150–1.
50 Pirala, *Guerra Civil*, II, p. 170.
51 Pirala, *Guerra Civil*, II, pp. 398–401.
52 Alfonso García Tejero, *Historia politico-administrativa de Mendizábal* (Madrid: Establecimiento Tipografico de J.A. Ortigosa, 1858), 2 volumes, I, p. 182.
53 Jordi Roca Vernet, 'La milicia nacional o la ciudadanía armada. El contrapoder revolucionario frente al liberalismo institucional', 54/2020, Les espaces du politique dans l'Espagne du Trienio liberal (1820–1823); https://journals.openedition.org/bhce/2598#tocto1n4.
54 Pirala, *Guerra Civil*, II, pp. 415–22.
55 *Eco del Comercio*, 9 February 1836.
56 Pirala, *Guerra Civil*, II, pp. 465–73.
57 Letter: 22nd May, 1836 To the Rev. A. Brandram (Endorsed: Recd. June 2, 1836) 10 at night, Madrid, May 22, 1836 in Borrow, *Letters*.
58 In July 1835, for example, the British authorities foiled a plot involving exiled Portuguese miguelistas to seize the port of Algeciras (*Eco del Comercio*, 22 July 1835).
59 TNA, FO/72/459 George Villiers, Doc. 146: 12 June 1836 letter from Villiers to Palmerston.
60 Pirala, *Guerra Civil*, II, pp. 17, 21–7.
61 John Francis Bacon, *Six Years in Biscay: Comprising a Personal Narrative of the Sieges of Bilbao, in June 1835, and Oct. to Dec., 1836. And of the Principal Events which Occurred in That City and the Basque Provinces, during the Years 1830 to 1837* (London: Smith, Elder, 1838), p. 126.
62 For contextual information, see Rogers, 'Kindness and Reciprocity', pp. 721–45.
63 Richard McMahon, 'The Races of Europe: Anthropological Race Classification of Europeans, 1839–1939' (PhD thesis, European University Institute, 2006), pp. 341–2.
64 Henry John George Stobart, *Portugal and Galicia, with a review of the social and political state of the Basque provinces; and a few remarks on recent events in Spain to which is now subjoined a reply to the "Policy of England towards Spain"'* (London: John Murray, 1837), vol. II, pp. 213–217.
65 Ridley, *Lord Palmerston*, pp. 269–84.
66 Pirala, *Guerra Civil*, II, pp. 483–6.

67 *Hansard Parliamentary Debates*, 2 December 1836: Lord Londonderry speech in House of Lords.
68 Henry John George Stobart, *Portugal and Gallicia, with a Review of the Social and Political State of the Basque Provinces; and a Few Remarks on Recent Events in Spain to which Is Now Subjoined a Reply to the 'Policy of England towards Spain'* (London: John Murray, 1837), 131–138, p. 272.
69 *Hansard's Parliamentary Debates*, 19-4-1837, 64.
70 Henry John Temple Palmerston, *The Speech of the Viscount Palmerston, in the House of Commons, on Wednesday 19 April 1837 on the Civil War in Spain* (London: James Ridgway and Sons, 1837).
71 Ridley, *Lord Palmerston*, p. 70.
72 Estrella Trincado and José-Luis Ramos, 'John Stuart Mill and Nineteenth-Century Spain', *Journal of the History of Economic Thought*, 33: 4 (December 2011), pp. 507–26.
73 For contextual information, see Rogers, 'Kindness and Reciprocity', pp. 721–45.
74 Maurice Charles O'Connell was the Australian-born son of the Irish-born lieutenant governor of New South Wales, and not a direct relative of the famous radical Daniel O'Connell. But the fame of the name gave the Carlists reason to complain about the enlistment of many Irish Catholics in the ranks of the British Auxiliary Legion – which showed how Catholic Ireland was betraying its natural links to Catholic monarchies in Europe (*Gaceta Oficial*, 26 February 1836).
75 Alexander Gallardo, 'Anglo-Spanish Relations during the First Carlist War (1833–1839)' (unpublished PhD dissertation, St John's University, New York, 1977), pp. iii–vi.
76 *Papers Relating to the Convention of Bergara Presented to both Houses of Parliament by Command of Her Majesty* (London: T. R. Harrison, 1841), p. 36.
77 Mark Lawrence, *Spain's First Carlist War, 1833–40* (Basingstoke: Palgrave, 2014).
78 Charles Esdaile, book review of Edward M. Brett, *The British Auxiliary Legion in the First Carlist War, 1835–38: A Forgotten Army* (Dublin: Four Courts Press, 2005), *The English Historical Review*, 121: 492 (June 2006), pp. 951–2.
79 Alexander Ball, *A Personal Narrative of Seven Years in Spain* (London: J. Chappell, 1846), p. 371.
80 Alberto Cañas de Pablos, *Los generales políticos en Europa y América (1810–1870): Centauros carismáticos bajo la luz de Napoleón* (Madrid: Alianza, 2022).
81 Adrian Shubert, *The Sword of Luchana: Baldomero Espartero and the Making of Modern Spain, 1793–1879* (London: University of Toronto Press, 2021), p. 117.
82 John Brown, *The Life and Adventures of a Soldier; or, Struggles through Real Life: Comprising a Faithful History of the Late War in Spain. By John Brown, of the –th Light Dragoons, and Late of the 67th Foot* (London: E. Cornish, 1855), pp. 45–9, 119–25, 212–14.

83 Henry Mayhew, *London Labour and the London Poor* (London: George Woodfall and Son, 1851), Volume I, pp. 24, 415.
84 Mayhew, *London Labour*, Vol. I, p. 244.
85 Mark Lawrence, *The Spanish Civil Wars: A Comparative History of the First Carlist War and the Conflict of the 1930s* (London: Bloomsbury, 2017), pp. 184–5.
86 Melchor Ferrer, *Historia del tradicionalismo español* (Sevilla: Editorial Católica Española, 1941-1960), Volume 20, pp. 60, 67–8.
87 Rodríguez Vives, *Los exilios*, pp. 142–3.
88 Spiers, *Radical General*, pp. 100–23; Lacy-Evans, *Memoranda of the Contest in Spain* (London: James Ridgway, 1840).

6 Anglo-Hispania and the world

1 Ford, *Handbook for Travellers*, p. 79.
2 Adrian Shubert, 'Being – and Staying – Famous in 19th-Century Spain: Baldamero Espartero and the Birth of Political Celebrity', *Historia y Política*, 34, Madrid, julio-diciembre (2015), 211–37, p. 215.
3 *La Gaceta de Madrid*, 11 September 1841.
4 David Hannay, *Don Emilio Castelar* (London: Bliss, Sands and Foster, 1896), p. 19.
5 Juan Marichal, *El secreto de España: ensayos de historia intelectual y política* (Madrid: Taurus, 1995), p. 98.
6 For a more positive recent appraisal of Espartero as a constitutional regent, see Daniel Aquillué, *España con honra. Una historia del siglo XIX español, 1793–1923* (Madrid: La Esfera de los Libros, 2023).
7 Shubert, *Sword of Luchana*, p. 169.
8 AGP, Caja 28/32, No. 1, Reinados, FVII, 27: undated (1842) police transcription of the manifesto of the Sociedad de Regeneradores Españoles.
9 Isabel Burdiel, *Isabel II: una biografía* (Madrid: Taurus, 2011), pp. 245–7.
10 Richard Ford, *A Hand-book for Travellers in Spain, and Readers at Home* (London: J. Murray, 1845), Volume 2, p. 922.
11 Gonzalo Capellán, 'Introducción: Miradas a la Historia de España desde la caricatura política', in Gonzalo Capellán (ed.), *Dibujar discursos, construir imaginarios: Prensa y caricatura política en España (1836–1874)* (Santander: Editorial Universidad de Cantabria, 2022), Volume I, pp. 12–44.
12 Scott Eastman, 'Spain in World History', in Adrian Shubert and José Álvarez Junco (eds), *The History of Modern Spain: Chronologies, Themes, Individuals* (London: Bloomsbury, 2018), p. 360.
13 Alejandro Oliván, 'Ultramar. Nada tiene la España que envidiar a otras naciones respecto a posesiones ultramarinas', *La Gaceta de Madrid*, 21 May 1839.

14 Jorge A. Marbán, *Confederate Patriot, Journalist, and Poet: The Multifaceted Life of José Agustín Quintero* (Victoria, BC: Friesen Press, 2014), pp. 6–7.
15 Christopher Schmidt-Novara, 'Continental Origins of Insular Proslavery: George Dawson Flinter in Curaçao, Venezuela, Britain, and Puerto Rico, 1810s–1830s', *Almanack. Guarulhos*, 8: 2 (semestre de 2014), pp. 55–67.
16 AHN, Estado, 5448: 16 November 1838 letter from Spanish Foreign Office to consul in Bristol with observations and instructions on how to deal with Lord Brougham's slight.
17 Jesús Sanjurjo, *In the Blood of Our Brothers. Abolitionism and the End of Slave Trade in Spain's Atlantic Empire, 1800–1870* (Tuscaloosa: Alabama University Press, 2021), p. 59.
18 Letter: 13th February, 1836 To the Rev. A. Brandram (Endorsed. Recd. February 29th, 1836), Madrid, Calle de la Zarza, February 13th, 1836 in Borrow, *Letters of George Borrow*.
19 Sanjurjo, *In the Blood of Our Brothers*, p. 70.
20 Rodríguez Vives, *Los exilios*, pp. 57–8.
21 Matthew Ian Brand, 'Right-Wing Refugees and British Politics, 1830–1871' (PhD thesis, University of East Anglia, 2016), pp. 20–1.
22 Leopoldo Augusto de Centurión, *El Conde de Montemolín: historia de la vida pública y privada de D. Carlos Luis de Borbón* (Madrid: Imprenta de D. Manuel Álvarez, 1848), p. 307.
23 Roger Bullen, *Palmerston, Guizot, and the Collapse of the Entente Cordiale* (London: Athlone Press, 1974).
24 Burdiel, *Isabel II*, pp. 268–70.
25 Burdiel, *Isabel II*, p. 278.
26 Isabel Burdiel, *Isabella II: no se puede reinar inocentemente* (Madrid: Espasa, 2004).
27 TNA, FO 72/443, George Villiers, doc. 107: 10 July 1835 letter from Villiers to Lord Palmerston.
28 Miles Taylor (ed.), *The European Diaries of Richard Cobden, 1846–1849* (London: Routledge, 1994), p. 61.
29 Anthony Howe, *Free Trade and Liberal England, 1846–1946* (Oxford: Oxford University Press, 1998), pp. 70–85.
30 Mark Lawrence, *Nineteenth-Century Spain: A New History* (London: Routledge, 2019), pp. 118–20.
31 Guy Thomson, 'Mazzini and Spain, 1820–72', in C. A. Bayly and E. F. Biagini (eds), *Giuseppe Mazzini and the Globalization of Democratic Nationalism, 1830–1920* (Oxford: Oxford University Press, 2008), pp. 260–2.

32 Rodrigo Escribano Roca and Pablo Guerrero Oñate, 'Navalismo y panhispanismo como horizontes de regeneración imperial en España (1814–1862)', *Anuario de Estudios Americanos*, 79: 1 (Sevilla, 2022), 205–38, p. 220.
33 Jorge Lasso de la Vega, 'Construcción de buques de vapor en Inglaterra', *Crónica Naval de España*, Tomo VIII (1859), pp. 733–5.
34 Scott Eastman, *A Missionary Nation. Race, Religion, and Spain's Age of Liberal Imperialism, 1841–1881* (Lincoln: University of Nebraska Press, 2021).
35 Joan Serrallonga Urquidi, 'La Guerra de África (1859-1860): Una Revisión', *Ayer*, 29 (1998), 139–59, pp. 140–1.
36 V. G. Kiernan, 'The Old Alliance: England and Portugal' (discussion paper written for the conference held at Manchester in June 1973 by the Committee for Freedom in Mozambique, Angola and Guinea), pp. 270–2.
37 Cervantes, *Conquistadores*, p. 232.
38 Christopher Baker, 'The Discovery of Spain: Introduction', in *The Discovery of Spain: British Artists and Collectors, from Goya to Picasso* (Edinburgh: National Galleries of Scotland, 2009), p. 10.
39 Catherine Davies and Sarah Sánchez, 'Rafael María de Labra and Ramón Labra: Two Generations of Revolution and Liberal Reform in Spain and Cuba', *Hispanic Research Journal*, 11: 1 (February 2010), 11–24, pp. 17–18.
40 Josep Fontana, 'El Partido Popular y la Constitución de Cádiz', *El País*, 15 February 2006, p. 13.
41 C. A. M. Hennessey, *The Federal Republic in Spain: Pi y Margall and the Federal Republican Movement, 1868–1874* (Oxford: Oxford University Press, 1962).
42 Jeanne Moisand, 'Revolutions, Republics and IWMA in the Spanish Empire (around 1873)', *Studies in Global Social History*, 29 (2018), pp. 238–52.
43 Walter Laqueur, *Guerrilla Warfare: A Historical and Critical Study* (London: Transaction Publishers, 1997), p. 419.
44 Vincent Kennett-Barrington, *Letters from the Carlist War (1874–76)* (Exeter: Exeter University Press, 1967), p. xi.
45 Alexandre Dupont, *La internacional blanca: contrarrevolución más allá de las fronteras (España y Francia, 1868–1876)* (Zaragoza: Prensas de la Universidad de Zaragoza, 2020), pp. 252–7.

7   Anglo-Hispania between disaster and civil war

1 Scott Eastman, 'Spain in World History', in Adrian Shubert and José Álvarez Junco (eds), *The History of Modern Spain: Chronologies, Themes, Individuals* (London: Bloomsbury, 2018), p. 360.

2 Xosé M. Núñez Seixas, *Suspiros de España: el nacionalismo español, 1808–2018* (Barcelona: Crítica, 2018), pp. 27–8.
3 Nick Sharman, *Britain's Informal Empire in Spain, 1830–1950: Free Trade, Protectionism and Military Power* (Basingstoke: Palgrave Macmillan, 2021), pp. 5–8.
4 Kirsty Hooper, 'A Tale of Two Empires? The Earl's Court Spanish Exhibition (1889)', *Modern Languages Open*, 1 (2014); 421a64bff580f55636ffa5e20c8374e7b6d8.pdf (semanticscholar.org) (accessed 15 May 2023).
5 Geoffrey Wawro, *Warfare and Society in Europe, 1792–1914* (London: Routledge, 1999), p. 169.
6 Javier Moreno Luzón, *Modernizing the Nation: Spain during the Reign of Alfonso XIII, 1902–1931* (Brighton: Sussex Academic Press, 2016), p. 10.
7 Rosario de la Torre, 'La prensa madrileña y el discurso de Lord Salisbury sobre las naciones moribundas', *Cuadernos de Historia Moderna y Contemporánea*, 6 (1985), pp. 163–80.
8 F. J. Schrijver, *Regionalism after Regionalisation: Spain, France and the United Kingdom* (Amsterdam: University of Amsterdam Press, 2006).
9 María Reyes Baztán, 'Anti-colonial Imagination and Internationalism in Basque Radical Nationalism (1892–1939)' (PhD thesis, University of Warwick, 2021). As Dr Reyes explains, the Irish Nationalist revolt ('Easter Rising') of 1916 turned a radical element of Basque nationalism against British colonialism.
10 Joaquín Costa, *Oligarquía y caciquismo como la forma actual de gobierno en España* (Madrid: Imprenta de los Hijos de M. G Hernández. 1909), p. 19.
11 Cited in Julio Crespo MacLennan, *Spain and the Process of European Integration, 1957–85* (London: Palgrave, 2000), foreword.
12 Geoffrey Jensen, 'Moral Strength through Material Defeat? The Consequences of 1898 for Spanish Military Culture', *War & Society*, 17: 2 (1999), pp. 25–39; Geoffrey Jensen, *Irrational Triumph: Cultural Despair, Military Nationalism and the Ideological Origins of Franco's Spain* (Reno: University of Nevada Press, 2002), p. 7.
13 Carlos García-Martí, 'Arrival of the International Team of English Boxing in Spain in 1911: Boxing Bans and Clashes over Bullfighting, Regeneration and Europe', *Sport in History*, 41: 1 (2021), pp. 25–49.
14 Josefina Gómez Mendoza, 'Regeneracionismo y Regadíos', in Antonio Gil Olcina and Alfredo Morales Gil (eds), *Hitos históricos de los regadíos españoles* (Madrid: Ministerio de Agricultura, 1992), pp. 249–50.
15 José Álvarez Junco, *Mater Dolorosa: la idea de España del siglo XIX* (Madrid: Taurus, 2001).
16 Charles Petrie, *The Spanish Royal House* (London: Geoffrey Bles, 1958), p. 207.
17 Arturo Zoffmann Rodríguez, '"The Anarchist Feedback Loop": Spanish Solidarity Campaigns in London and the Birth of Revolutionary Syndicalism, 1896–1913', in

Graciela Iglesias-Rogers (ed.), *The Hispanic Anglosphere from the Eighteenth to the Twentieth Century: An Introduction* (London: Routledge, 2021), pp. 188–202.

18 Daniel Laqua, 'Freethinkers, Anarchists and Francisco Ferrer: The Making of a Transnational Solidarity Campaign', *European Review of History: Revue européenne d'histoire*, 21: 4, pp. 467–84.

19 Jean-Louis Guereña, 'Las Casas del Pueblo y la educación obrera a principios del siglo XX', *Hispania*, 51: 178 (1991), pp. 645–92.

20 Ángel Herrerín, 'Anarchist Sociability in Spain. In Times of Violence and Clandestinity', *Bulletin for Spanish and Portuguese Historical Studies*, 38: 1 (2013), p. 165.

21 J. Lomas (ed.), *O Shea's Guide to Spain and Portugal* (London: Adam and Charles Black, 1899), p. 43.

22 Margarita Parral, 'Royal Travels: The Modern Staging and Legitimation of the Spanish Monarchy, 1858–1931', in David San Narciso, Margarita Barral Martínez and Carolina Armenteros (eds), *Monarchy and Liberalism in Spain: The Building of the Nation-State, 1780–1931* (London: Routledge, 2022), pp. 202–20.

23 Raymond Carr, *Spain, 1808–1975* (Oxford: Clarendon Press, 1982), p. 369.

24 José Antonio Rodríguez Martín, 'Una aproximación al bandolerismo en España', *Iberoamericana*, 8: 31 (2008), 85–105, p. 86–7.

25 Kirsty Hooper, *The Edwardians and the Making of a Spanish Obsession* (Liverpool: Liverpool University Press, 2020), pp. x–xii.

26 Sandie Holguín, *Flamenco Nation: The Construction of Spanish National Identity* (Madison: University of Wisconsin Press, 2019), pp. 112, 150.

27 María Sierra, 'Hombres arcaicos en tiempos modernos. La construcción romántica de la masculinidad gitana', *Historia Social*, 93 (2019), 51–66, p. 62.

28 José María Jover, *España en la política internacional, siglos XVIII–XX* (Madrid: Marcial Pons, 1999), p. 136.

29 Sebastian Balfour, *Deadly Embrace: Morocco and the Road to the Spanish Civil War* (Oxford: Oxford University Press, 2002), p. 5.

30 TNA, FO 371/171, No. 208: 27 December 1905 letter from Sir A. Nicolson to Sir Edward Grey.

31 William George Clark, *Gazpacho: or, Summer Months in Spain* (London: George Parker, 1850), p. 173.

32 Sasha D. Pack, 'The Making of the Gibraltar–Spain Border: Cholera, Contraband, and Spatial Reordering, 1850–1873', *Mediterranean Historical Review*, 29: 1 (2014), 71–88, p. 75.

33 Pack, 'Making of the Gibraltar–Spain Border', pp. 71–88.

34 Gareth Stockey and Nicholas Rankin, *Defending the Rock* (London: Faber and Faber, 2017), pp. 28–101.

35 Francisco J. Romero Salvadó, *Spain 1914–1918: Between War and Revolution* (London: Routledge, 1999), p. 13.
36 Javier Moreno-Luzón, 'The Two Monarchies of Alfonso XIII (1902–1931)', in David San Narciso, Margarita Barral Martínez and Carolina Armenteros (eds), *Monarchy and Liberalism in Spain: The Building of the Nation-State, 1780–1931* (London: Routledge, 2022), pp. 93–110.
37 Francisco J. Romero Salvadó, 'The Organic Crisis of the Liberal State in Spain: Between the Catalan Quagmire and the Red Spectre (November 1918–April 1919)', *Historical Journal*, 60: 3 (2017), pp. 795–815.
38 Arturo Barea, *The Forging of a Rebel: The Clash* (London: Faber and Faber, 1946), p. 439.
39 Charles Edmund Richard Pennell, 'A Critical Investigation of the Opposition of the Rifi Confederation led by Muhammad Bin Abd-El Karim Al-Khattabi to Spanish Colonial Expansion in northern Morocco, 1920–1925, and Its Political and Social Background', Volume I (PhD thesis, University of Leeds, November 1979), pp. 58, 426.
40 Rhea Marsh Smith, *The Day of the Liberals in Spain* (Philadelphia: University of Pennsylvania Press, 1938), pp. 77–83, 100.
41 Alejandro Quiroga, *Making Spaniards: Primo de Rivera and the Nationalization of the Masses, 1923–30* (New York: Palgrave, 2007), pp. 83–92.
42 Alejandro Quiroga, *Miguel Primo de Rivera. Dictadura, Populismo y Nación* (Barcelona: Crítica, 2022).
43 Muirhead Bone and Lady Gertrude Helena Bone, *Old Spain* (London: Macmillan, 1936), p. 1.
44 Sharman, *Britain's Informal Empire*, p. 199.
45 Adrian Pole (2019), 'Leicestershire People and the Spanish Civil War', *Leicestershire Historian*, 55, 50–56, p. 50.
46 V. S. Pritchett, *The Spanish Temper* (New York: Alfred Knopf, 1954), p. 68.
47 Laurie Lee, *As I Walked Out on Midsummer Morning* (London: Andre Deutsch, 1969).
48 Peter Chalmers Mitchell, *My House in Málaga* (London: Faber and Faber, 1938).
49 Archivo Histórico Provincial de Las Palmas (AHPLP), 554, 134/0, Secretaría General, 11 May 1936 instruction from civil governor of Las Palmas to chief of Las Palmas Guardias de Asalto.
50 AHPLP, 554, 134/0, Secretaría General, doc. 1791: May 1936 'muy urgente' instruction from Director General of Aeronautics to Director of Aerodrome of Gando, Las Palmas.

8 Anglo-Hispania during civil war and world war

1. Chalmers Mitchell, *My House in Málaga*, p. 53.
2. David Deacon, *British News Media and the Spanish Civil War* (Edinburgh: Edinburgh University Press, 2008), pp. 48–9.
3. W. C. Frank, Jr., 'Multinational Naval Cooperation in the Spanish Civil War', *Naval College Review*, 47: 2 (Spring 1994), pp. 74–7.
4. Chris Ealham, 'Myth of the Maddened Crowd', in Chris Ealham and Michael Richards (eds), *The Splintering of Spain* (Cambridge: Cambridge University Press, 2005), pp. 112–13.
5. Hugh Thomas, *The Spanish Civil War* (London: Penguin, 1977), pp. 366–7.
6. Nancy Johnstone, *Hotel in Flight* (London: Longmans, Green, 1940), p. 13.
7. Tom Buchanan, *Britain and the Spanish Civil War* (Cambridge: Cambridge University Press, 2008), p. 1.
8. Cited in Richard Baxell, *Unlikely Warriors: The Extraordinary Story of the Britons Who Fought in the Spanish Civil War* (London: Autumn Press, 2014), p. 44.
9. Buchanan, *Britain and the Spanish Civil War*, p. 12.
10. Peter Day, *Franco's Friends: How British Intelligence Helped Bring Franco to Power in Spain* (London: Biteback Publishing, 2012).
11. E. N. Dzelepy, *Britain in Spain: A Study of the National Government's Spanish Policy by an Unknown Diplomat* (London: Hamish Hamilton, 1939), pp. 13–14.
12. Daniel Kowalsky, 'Stalin and the Spanish Civil War: The New Historiography' (LSE Canada Blanch Centre, 13 February 2020); Tim Bouverie's much-acclaimed work on appeasement, for example, hardly mentions the Spanish civil war, even though Prime Minister Baldwin's attitude to the conflict was central (Tim Bouverie, *Appeasing Hitler: Chamberlain, Churchill and the Road to War* (London: Bodley Head, 2019)).
13. Francisco J. Romero Salvadó, *The Spanish Civil War: Origins, Course and Outcomes* (London: Macmillan, 2005), pp. 66–98.
14. Emily Mason, *Democracy, Deeds and Dilemmas: Support for the Spanish Republic within British Civil Society, 1936–1939* (Brighton: Sussex Academic Press, 2017), pp. 12–13.
15. Mason, *Democracy, Deeds and Dilemmas*, p. 145.
16. Mason, *Democracy, Deeds and Dilemmas*, pp. 34–5.
17. Chalmers Mitchell, *My House in Málaga*, p. 39.
18. Henry Gannes and Theodore Repard, *Spain in Revolt: A History of the Civil War in Spain in 1936 and a Study of Its Political and Economic Causes* (London: Victory Gollancz, 1936), p. 15.
19. Arquivo Torre dos Tombos, Arquico Oliveira Salazar, August 1936 Report on the Reception at the Royal British Club, Lisbon.

20 Richard L. Kagan, *The Spanish Craze: America's Fascination with the Hispanic World, 1779-1939* (Lincoln: University of Nebraska Press, 2019), pp. 21–2.
21 George Orwell, 'Homage to Catalonia', in Peter Davison (ed.), *Orwell in Spain* (London: Penguin, 2001), pp. 32–3.
22 John Langdon Davies, *Behind the Spanish Barricades* (London: Reportage Press, 2007), p. 136.
23 Maria Mercedes Aguirre Alastuey, 'The Spanish Civil War in the Works of Nancy Cunard, Martha Gellhorn, and Sylvia Townsend Warner' (PhD dissertation, University College London, Department of English, 2015), p. 125.
24 Mary Nash, '"Milicianas" and Homefront Heroines: Images of Women in Revolutionary Spain 1936–1939', *History of European Ideas*, 11 (1989), pp. 235–44.
25 Richard Kisch, *They Shall Not Pass: The Spanish People at War, 1936–39* (London: Wayland, 1974), p. 129.
26 Jason Gurney, *Crusade in Spain* (London: Faber and Faber, 1974), p. 39.
27 Judith Cook, *Apprentices of Freedom* (London: Quartet Books, 1979), pp. vii–ix.
28 Dan Richardson, for example, published cold-war history with his focus largely on the role played by the Comintern in the organization of the International Brigades (Dan Richardson, *Comintern Army: The International Brigades and the Spanish Civil War* (Lexington: University Press of Kentucky, 1982)).
29 Nicola Barker, *Five Miles from Outer Hope* (London: Faber and Faber, 2000), p. 112.
30 See, for example, Fraser Raeburn, '"Fae nae Hair te Grey Hair They Answered the Call": International Brigade Volunteers from the West Central Belt of Scotland in the Spanish Civil War, 1936–9', *Journal of Scottish Historical Studies*, 35: 1 (2015), 92–114; Hywel Francis, 'Welsh Miners and the Spanish Civil War', *Journal of Contemporary History*, 5:3 (1970), 177–91; as well as Gerben Zaagsma, *Jewish Volunteers of the International Brigades and the Spanish Civil War* (London: Bloomsbury 2017).
31 Helen Graham, *The War and Its Shadow: Spain's Civil War in Europe's Long Twentieth Century* (Brighton: Sussex Academic Press, 2012), pp. 75–6, 82.
32 Esmond Romilly, *Boadilla* (London: Hamish Hamilton, 1937), p. 130.
33 Hugh Thomas, *The Spanish Civil War* (London: Eyre & Spottiswoode, 1961), pp. 454–6.
34 Richard Baxell, *British Volunteers in the Spanish Civil War: The British Battalion in the International Brigades 1936–1939* (London: Warren and Pell, 2007), pp. 9–14.
35 James K. Hopkins, *Into the Heart of the Fire: The British in the Spanish Civil War* (Stanford: Stanford University Press, 1998), p. xi.
36 Buchanan, *Britain and the Spanish Civil War*, p. 126.
37 Anthony Beevor, *The Battle for Spain: The Spanish Civil War 1936–1939* (London: Weidenfeld & Nicolson, 2006), p. 178.

38 W. Aycock and J. Perez (eds), *The Spanish Civil War in Literature* (Texas: Texas Tech University Press, 1990), p. 1.
39 Aycock and Perez (eds), *The Spanish Civil War in Literature*, p. 1.; *El Mundo*, 18 May 2019.
40 Gisèle Freund, *Photography and Society* (London: D. R. Godine, 1980), p. 115.
41 Irme Schaber, *Gerda Taro: With Robert Capa as Photojournalist in the Spanish Civil War* (Stuttgart: Edition Axel Menges, 2019), pp. 73–4.
42 Paul Preston, *We Saw Spain Die: Foreign Correspondents in the Spanish Civil War* (London: Skyhorse Publishing, 2009).
43 Susan Sontag, *Essays on Photography* (New York: Picador, 2001), p. 14.
44 Phillip Knightley, *The First Casualty: The War Correspondent as Hero and Myth-Maker from the Crimea to Kosovo* (London: Prion Books, 2000), p. 193.
45 Buchanan, *Britain and the Spanish Civil War*, p. 35.
46 'Clergy Tainted by the Red Virus', *Saturday Review of Politics, Literature, Science and Art*, 21 November 1936, p. 648.
47 Christian Leitz, *Economic Relations between Nazi Germany and Franco's Spain, 1936–1945* (Oxford: Oxford University Press, 1996), p. 102.
48 Deacon, *British News Media*, p. 2.
49 Deacon, *British News Media*, p. 161.
50 Caroline Brothers, *War and Photography: A Cultural History* (London: Routledge, 1996), p. 41.
51 'Civil War in Spain: The Suppression of the Rebel Rising', *Illustrated London News*, 3 August 1936, p. 183.
52 Robert Stradling, *Your Children Will Be Next: Bombing and Propaganda in the Spanish Civil War 1936–1939* (Cardiff: University of Wales Press, 2008), p. 13.
53 Tom Buchanan, *The British Labour Movement and the Spanish Civil War* (Cambridge: Cambridge University Press, 1991), p. 127.
54 Vincent Brome, *The International Brigades: Spain 1936–1939* (London: Heinemann, 1965), p. 47.
55 Baxell, *British Volunteers in the Spanish Civil War*, p. 12.
56 Bob Clarke, *No Boots on My Feet: Experiences of a Britisher in Spain, 1937–38* (Newcastle: The People's Publications, 1984), pp. 24–5.
57 Clarke, *No Boots on My Feet*, p. 117.
58 Ben Hughes, *They Shall Not Pass the British Battalion at Jarama* (Oxford: Osprey, 2011), pp. 180, 193.
59 Walter Gregory, *The Shallow Grave: A Memoir of the Spanish Civil War* (London: Victor Gollancz, 1986), p. 130.
60 Javier Pérez-López, 'Creating an International Harmony: Music in the International Brigades', *Past and Memory*, 11 (2012), 239–254, p. 244.

61 Josie McLellan, '"I Wanted to Be a Little Lenin": Ideology and the German International Brigade Volunteers', *Journal of Contemporary History*, 41: 2 (April, 2006), 287–304, p. 301.
62 Contrary to modern versions, the original Jarama Valley song speaks less about land 'where our brave comrades fell' and in more comically bitter terms about a battalion whose leave has been cancelled and who have grown old in the line from waiting. For the original lyrics, see Richard Baxell, *Unlikely Warriors* (London: Aurum Press, 2012), pp. 172–3.
63 William Rust, *Britons in Spain: The History of the British Battalion of the XV International Brigade* (London: Laurence and Wishart 1939), p. 33.
64 Fred Thomas, *To Tilt at Windmills: A Memoir of the Spanish Civil War* (East Lansing: Michigan State University Press, 1996), p. 21.
65 Hughes, *They Shall Not Pass*, p. 57; Baxell, *Unlikely Warriors*, p. 137.
66 Clarke, *No Boots on My Feet*, pp. 33, 179.
67 Gurney, *Crusade in Spain*, p. 115.
68 Orwell, *Homage to Catalonia*, p. 17; Thomas, *To Tilt at Windmills*, p. 47.
69 Rust, *Britons in Spain*, pp. 33–4; Thomas, *To Tilt at Windmills*, p. 21.
70 Thomas, *To Tilt at Windmills*, pp. 21, 26.
71 Gregory, *The Shallow Grave*, pp. 128–31.
72 James Mathews, *Reluctant Warriors: Republican Popular Army and Nationalist Army Conscripts in the Spanish Civil War, 1936–1939* (Oxford: Oxford University Press, 2012), pp. 112–13.
73 Jesús Baigorri-Jalón, *Languages in the Crossfire: Interpreters in the Spanish Civil War, 1936–1939* (London: Routledge, 2021).
74 Robert Stradling (ed.), Frank Thomas, Frank Thomas, *Brother against Brother: Experiences of a British Volunteer in the Spanish Civil War* (Stroud: Sutton Publishing, 1998), pp. 163–71.
75 Peter Kemp, *Thorns of Memory* (London: Sinclair Stevenson, 1990).
76 Baxell, *Unlikely Warriors*, pp. 247–50.
77 Baxell, *Unlikely Warriors*, pp. 165–73.
78 Gregory, *The Shallow Grave*, p. 125.
79 Mathews, *Reluctant Warriors*, pp. 106–7; Michael Alpert, *The Republican Army in the Spanish Civil War, 1936–1939* (Cambridge: Cambridge University Press 2013), pp. 162–4.
80 Clarke, *No Boots on My Feet*, p. 57.
81 Stradling (ed.), Thomas, *Brother against Brother*, p. 119; Thomas, *To Tilt against Windmills*.
82 For an analysis of Spanish hospitals, see Sebastian Browne, *Medicine and Conflict: The Spanish Civil War and Its Traumatic Legacy* (London: Routledge, 2019).

83 Michael Seidman, *Republic of Egos: A Social History of the Spanish Civil War* (Madison: University of Wisconsin Press, 2002), p. 113.
84 Baxell, *Unlikely Warriors*, pp. 207–8.
85 Baxell, *Unlikely Warriors*, pp. 208–10.
86 Rust, *Britons in Spain*, p. 30.
87 Brome, *International Brigades*, pp. 65–7.
88 Baxell, *Unlikely Warriors*, p. 260. Ryan was executed for this incident, although he did not kill anyone and was still remembered fondly by many surviving brigadiers for his joking attitude.
89 Jorge Marco, *Paraísos en el infierno. Drogas y Guerra Civil española* (Granada: Comares, 2021); Stradling (ed.), Thomas, *Brother against Brother*, p. 167.
90 Clarke, *No Boots on My Feet*, p. 72; Baxell, *Unlikely Warriors*, p. 215.
91 Rust, *Britons in Spain*, p. 19.
92 Richardson, *Comintern Army*, pp. 90–177; Robert Stradling, 'English-Speaking Units of the International Brigades', *Journal of Contemporary History*, 45: 4 (October, 2010), 744–67, p. 753.
93 James Matthews, 'The Vanguard of Sacrifice'? Political Commissars in the Republican Popular Army during the Spanish Civil War, 1936–1939', *War in History*, 21: 1 (2014), 82–101, p. 99.
94 Cited in Baxell, *Unlikely Warriors*, p. 244; Dan Richardson observed that good commissars could be compared to priests in other armies (Richardson, *Comintern Army*, p. 128).
95 Richardson, *Comintern Army*, p. 132.
96 Richardson, *Comintern Army*, p. 128.
97 Rust, *Britons in Spain*, pp. 31–3.
98 Hugh Purcell, *The Last English Revolutionary: Tom Wintringham 1898–1949* (Gloucestershire: Sutton Publishing, 2004), p. 110.
99 Helen Graham, '"Against the State": A Genealogy of the Barcelona May Days', *European History Quarterly*, 29: 4 (1999).
100 John Campbell, 'Is the ILP for Winning the War or Aiding Franco', and R. Palme Dutt, 'Spain Organises for Victory', *The Daily Worker*, 22 May 1937, pp. 1–3.
101 Santos Juliá, *La Guerra Civil Española de la Segunda República a la dictadura de Franco* (Barcelona: Emse Edapp, 2019).
102 GeorgeOrwell, *Homage to Catalonia* (London: Secker & Warburg 1986).
103 Tom Buchanan, "A Far Away Country of Which We Know Nothing'? Perceptions of Spain and Its Civil War in Britain, 1931–1939', *Twentieth Century British History*, 4: 1 (1993), pp. 1–24.
104 José Martín Blázquez, *I Helped to Build an Army* (London: Secker and Warburg, 1939), p. 324.

105 A. Durgan, 'Freedom Fighters or Comintern Army?,' *International Socialism*, 84 (1999), p. 127.
106 Rust, *Britons in Spain*, pp. 4–7.
107 Tom Buchanan, 'Holding the Line: The Political Strategy of the International Brigade Association, 1939–1977,' *Labour History Review*, 66 (2001), pp. 294–6.
108 Gordon F. Sander, *The Hundred Day Winter War* (Lawrence: University of Kansas Press, 2013), pp. 112–13.
109 Peter Anderson, 'The Struggle over the Evacuation to the United Kingdom and Repatriation of Basque Refugee Children in the Spanish Civil War: Symbols and Souls', *Journal of Contemporary History*, 52: 2 (April, 2017), pp. 297–318.
110 Ander González Fernández and Guillermo Tabernilla, *Combatientes vascos en la Segunda Guerra Mundial* (Madrid: Desperta Ferro, 2018), p. 75.
111 *ARP and AFS Review (Civil Defence Journal)*, 1 June 1940, p. 11.
112 *ARP and AFS Review (Civil Defence Journal)*, 1 June 1940, p. 11.
113 Tom Wintringham, *New Ways of War* (London: Penguin, 1940).
114 *Daily Mirror*, 28 May 1940.
115 Penny Summerfield and Corinna Peniston-Bird, *Contesting Home Defence: Men, Women and the Home Guard in the Second World War* (Manchester: Manchester University Press, 2013), pp. 40–3.
116 Jonathan Whitehead, *Spanish Republicans and the Second World War: Republic across the Mountains* (Barnsley: Pen and Sword, 2021), pp. 197–8.
117 John Langdon Davies, *The Home Guard Training Manual* (London: John Murray, 1942), pp. 159, 182.
118 Scott Soo, *The Routes to Exile: France and the Spanish Civil War Refugees, 1939–2009* (Manchester: Manchester University Press, 2013).
119 *Hansard Parliamentary Debates*, 10 July 1940 (https://hansard.parliament.uk/commons/1940-07-10/debates/513c14f4-f07b-48c8-bf14-f863b62ffa58/Refugees).
120 Whitehead, *Spanish Republicans and the Second World War*, pp. 160–1.
121 Michael Davie (ed.), *The Diaries of Evelyn Waugh* (London: Weidenfeld and Nicholson, 1976), p. 494.
122 Tim Moreman, *British Commandos, 1940–46* (London: Bloomsbury, 2006); Daniel Arasa, *Los españoles de Churchill* (Mexico City: Editorial Armonía, 1991).
123 Charles Messenger, *The Middle East Commandos* (London: William Kimber, 1988), p. 92; Antony Beevor, *Crete: The Battle and the Resistance* (London: John Murray, 2011), p. 228.
124 Norman J. W. Goda, *Tomorrow the World: Hitler, Northwest Africa and the Path Toward America* (College Station: Texas A&M University Press, 1998).
125 Davie (ed.), *Diaries of Evelyn Waugh*, p. 484.
126 *Civil and Military Gazette*, 7 May 1941.
127 *The Civil and Military Gazette*, 10 April 1942.

128 Stanley G. Payne and Jesús Palacios, *Franco: A Personal and Political Biography* (Madison: University of Wisconsin Press, 2014), pp. 277–9.
129 *Rock Magazine*, 3: 6 (August 1943).
130 Jo Fox (keynote conference address, Propaganda and Neutrality: Alternative Battlegrounds and Active Deflection, University of Kent, 24–25 June 2021). See also the Leverhulme Trust project currently led by Dr James Smith of the University of Durham ('The Political Warfare Executive, Covert Propaganda, and British Culture', 2018).
131 Edward Corse, *A Battle for Neutral Europe: British Cultural Propaganda during the Second World War* (London: Bloomsbury, 2012).
132 Christopher Bannister, 'Diverging Neutrality in Iberia: The British Ministry of Information in Portugal and Spain during the Second World War', in Simon Eliot and Marc Wiggam (eds), *Allied Communication to the Public during the Second World War: National and Transnational Networks* (London: Bloomsbury, 2020), pp. 167–84.
133 João Arthur Ciciliato Franzolin, 'Signal, Em Guarda, Victory and the Transnational Struggle of the Axis and the Allies to Influence Readers in Neutral and Occupied Countries during World War II' (conference paper, Propaganda and Neutrality: Alternative Battlegrounds and Active Deflection, University of Kent, 24–25 June 2021).
134 Miguel Ángel del Arco Blanco and Peter Anderson, 'Introduction: Famine, not Hunger?', in Miguel Ángel del Arco Blanco and Peter Anderson (eds), *Franco's Famine: Malnutrition, Disease and Starvation in Post-Civil War Spain* (London: Bloomsbury, 2021), pp. 7–8.
135 Miguel Ángel del Arco Blanco, 'Famine in Spain during Franco's Dictatorship, 1939–52', *Journal of Contemporary History*, 56: 1 (January 2021), pp. 3–27.
136 *ABC*, 15 February 1941.
137 María Antonia Paz, 'La propaganda francesa en España', *Mélanges de la Casa de Velázquez*, Année 1995, 31–3, 219–279, pp. 231–4.
138 Claudia Baldoli and Andrew Knapp, *Forgotten Blitzes: France and Italy under Allied Air Attack, 1940–1945* (London: Continuum, 2012), p. 195.
139 *Guinea Gold: Australian Edition*, 1: 203, 8 June 1943, p. 4.
140 Marta García Cabrera, 'Operation Warden: British Sabotage Planning in the Canary Islands during the Second World War', *Intelligence and National Security*, 5: 2 (2020), pp. 252–68.
141 Manuel Leguineche, *Gibraltar: La roca en el zapato de España* (Barcelona: Planeta, 2002), pp. 113–17.
142 Paul Preston, *A People Betrayed: A History of Corruption, Political Incompetence and Social Division in Modern Spain* (London: HarperCollins, 2020), pp. 352–3.

143 For example, Rolf-Dieter Müller, *The Unknown Eastern Front* (London: I. B. Tauris, 2015), pp. 110–11.

144 S. O'Connor and M. Gutmann, 'Under a Foreign Flag: Integrating Foreign Units and Personnel in the British and German Armed Forces, 1940–1945', *Journal of Modern European History*, 14: 3(2016), 321–41, p. 331.

145 Stanley Payne, *The Franco Regime, 1936–1975* (Madison: University of Wisconsin Press, 1987), pp. 231–342.

146 *The Civil and Military Gazette*, 6 May 1944, vol. LXV, no. 6193, p. 2.

147 José Ferri Verdú, Àngel Beneito Lloris and Richard Cleminson (eds), *Republicanos españoles prisioneros de guerra en Inglaterra: las memorias de José Ferri* (Alcoi: Ajuntament d'Alcoi, 2019), pp. 147–8.

148 Ferri Verdú, Beneito Lloris and Cleminson (eds), *Republicanos españoles prisioneros*, pp. 147–8.

149 Ferri Verdú, Beneito Lloris and Cleminson (eds), *Republicanos españoles prisioneros*, pp. 46, 130, 148–9.

150 Richard Cleminson, 'Spanish Anti-fascist "Prisoners of War" in Lancashire, 1944–46', *International Journal of Iberian Studies*, 22: 3 (2009), pp. 163–83.

9 Anglo-Hispania and Franco's Spain

1 Manuel Azaña, *Causas de la guerra de España* (Paris: Biblioteca de Bolsillo, 1941), pp. 158–60, 175–6 and 177–9.

2 *The Civil and Military Gazette*, 28 December 1945, vol. LXVI, no. 304, p. 2.

3 P. A. M. van der Esch, *Prelude to War, the International Repercussions of the Spanish Civil War (1936–1939)* (The Hague: Martinus Nijhoff, 1951), p. 32.

4 TNA, Vol. 5, Reference: [Z 9536/537/41]. (Aug 14, 1945): Sr V. Mallet (San Sebastián (telegramme to Aneurin Bevan).

5 *Union Jack* (Greece edition), 23 August 1945, no. 193, p. 4.

6 *Times*, 5 March 1946.

7 J. A. Pitt-Rivers, *The People of the Sierra* (New York: Criterion Books, 1954), pp. 26, 58.

8 Gerald Brenan, 'Spain and Its Future', published in *Tripoli Times*, 30 December 1945, 908, p. 2.

9 Bastian Matteo Scianna, 'Stuck in the Past? British Views on the Spanish Army's Effectiveness and Military Culture, 1946–1983', *War and Society*, 38: 1 (February 2019), 41–56, pp. 43–4.

10 David Brydan, *Franco's Internationalists: Social Experts and Spain's Search for Legitimacy* (Oxford: Oxford University Press, 2019).

11 David J. Dunthon, *Britain and the Spanish Anti-Franco Opposition, 1940–1950* (Basingstoke: Palgrave, 2000), pp. 66, 130–7.
12 Tom Buchanan, 'Receding Triumph: British Opposition to the Franco Regime, 1945–59', *Twentieth-Century British History*, 12: 2 (2001), 163–84, pp. 170–2.
13 Petrie, *Spanish Royal House*, p. 211.
14 Graham, *The War and Its Shadow*.
15 TNA, KV2/896: 10 August 1949 'Secret' intelligence report (PF48909 MOSELY) report on the movements of Oswald and Diana Mosley.
16 Pablo del Hierro, 'The Neofascist Network and Madrid, 1945–1953: From City of Refuge to Transnational Hub and Centre of Operations', *Contemporary European History*, 31 (2022), 171–94, pp. 171–2.
17 Luis G. Martínez del Campo, *Cultural Diplomacy: A Hundred Years of British-Spanish Society* (Liverpool: Liverpool University Press, 2015), pp. 53–61.
18 Crespo MacLennan, *Spain and the Process of European Integration*, pp. 41, 44.
19 For example, Roberto Bolaño, *Amulet* (London: Picador, 2009).
20 Olga Glondys, 'Cold War Controversies in the Pro-Amnesty Campaigns of the Spanish Political Prisoners (1961) and the Erosion of Spanish Exiles' Leadership in the Anti-Francoist Policies', *Journal of Iberian and Latin American Studies*, 27: 1 (2021), pp. 63–77.
21 Petrie, *Spanish Royal House*, pp. 107–8.
22 William Buckley in *Firing Line* debate with Staughton Lynd, recorded 23 May 1966, accessed courtesy of the Hoover Institution Archives via: https://www.youtube.com/watch?v=f-iYnB2wqNU (accessed 9 October 2019).
23 Luis Arias González, *Gonzalo de Aguilera Munro: XI Conde de Alba de Yeltes (1886–1965)* (Universidad de Salamanca, 2013), p. 172.
24 Arnold Lunn in interview with William F. Buckley, *Firing Line*, recorded 28 November 1966 (https://www.youtube.com/watch?v=bH3nWA465nQ, accessed 22 October 2019).
25 María Elvira Roca Barea, *Imperiofobia y Leyenda Negra: Roma, Rusia, Estados Unidos y el Imperio español* (Madrid: Siruela, 2016).
26 Holguín, *Flamenco Nation*, p. 217.
27 Nigel Townson, 'Spain Is Different? The Franco Dictatorship', in Nigel Townson (ed.), *Is Spain Different? A Comparative Look at the 19th and 20th Centuries* (Brighton: Sussex Academic Press, 2015), p. 136.
28 Carolin Viktorin, '"All Publicity Is Good Publicity?" Advertising, Public Relations and Branding of Spain in the United Kingdom, 1945–1969', in Carolin Viktorin (ed.), *Nation Branding in Modern History* (New York: Bergahn Books, 2018), p. 139.
29 Dominic Sandbrook, *White Heat: A History of Britain in the Swinging Sixties, 1964–1970* (London: Abacus, 2009), pp. 193–4.

30 Sasha D. Pack, *Tourism and Dictatorship: Europe's Peaceful Invasion of Franco's Spain* (Basingstoke: Palgrave, 2006), p. 71.
31 Jacqueline Waldren, *Insiders and Outsiders: Paradise and Reality in Mallorca* (New York: Berghahn, 1996), pp. 190–1, 206–7.
32 Peter Beneson, *Persecution, 1961* (London: Penguin, 1961).
33 *Economist*, 25 August 1973.
34 *Hansard Parliamentary Debates*, 18 July 1973, vol. 860, c128W.
35 Gordon Carr, *The Angry Brigade* (London: PM Press, 2010), pp. 45–9; J. D. Taylor, 'The Party's Over? The Angry Brigade, The Counterculture, and the British New Left, 1967–72', *Historical Journal*, 58: 3 (2015), 877–900, p. 889.
36 Gerard de Groot, *The Seventies Unplugged* (New York: Pan Books, 2010), pp. 146–7.
37 Michael Richards, *After the Civil War: Making Memory and Re-Making Spain since 1936* (New York: Cambridge University Press, 2013) pp. 316–17
38 Pablo Martín Aceña and Elena Martínez Ruiz, 'The Golden Age of Spanish Capitalism: Economic Growth without Political Freedom', in Nigel Townson (ed.), *Spain Transformed: The Late-Franco Dictatorship, 1959–1975* (Basingstoke: Palgrave, 2007), p. 34.
39 David H. Close, *Greece since 1945: Politics, Economy and Society* (London: Routledge, 2014), p. 77.
40 Kenneth Maxwell and Steven Spiegel, *The New Spain: From Isolation to Influence* (New York: Council on Foreign Relations Press, 1994), pp. 1–9.
41 Ofelia Ferrán, *Working through Memory: Writing and Remembrance in Contemporary Spanish Narrative* (Cranbury: Associated University Presses, 2007), p. 34.
42 For example, Pío Moa, *Los mitos de la Guerra Civil* (Madrid: Esfera de los Libros, 2004).
43 Julián Casanova and Carlos Gil Andrés, *Twentieth-Century Spain: A History* (Cambridge: Cambridge University Press, 2014), p. 267.
44 Paul Preston, *The Politics of Revenge: Fascism and the Military in 20th Century Spain* (London: Routledge, 1995), p. 30.
45 Pamela Radcliff, *Making Democratic Citizens in Spain. Civil Society and the Popular Origins of the Transition, 1960–78* (New York: Palgrave, 2011).
46 Giles Tremlett, *Ghosts of Spain: Travels through a Country's Hidden Past* (London: Faber and Faber, 2012), pp. 54–5.
47 Nigel Townson, '"Spain Is Different?" The Franco Dictatorship', in Nigel Townson (ed.), *Is Spain Different?: A Comparative Look at the 19th and 20th centuries* (Brighton: Sussex Academic Press, 2015) .
48 José Babiano y Sebastian, 'La emigración española a Europa durante los años sesenta: Francia y Suiza como países de acogida', *Historia Social*, 42 (2002), pp. 81–98.

49 *Cuéntame cómo pasó* – Web Oficial – RTVE.es (accessed 18 December 2022).
50 Martín García, Óscar, 'Emisarios de la moderación. La diplomacia pública británica ante el fin de las dictaduras ibéricas', *Hispania: Revista Española de Historia*, 72: 242 (2012), pp. 798–9.
51 Tom Buchanan, 'The Late-Franco Regime in International Context', in Nigel Townson (ed.), *Spain Transformed: The Late-Franco Dictatorship, 1959–1975* (Basingstoke: Palgrave, 2007), pp. 88–9.
52 Gema Cano Jiménez, 'Del Spain Is Different al Party's Over: La imagen de España a través de *The Economist* (2008–2009)', *Textual & Visual Media*, 3 (2010), pp. 63–80.
53 Graham, *War and Its Shadow*, p. 126.
54 Leguineche, *Gibraltar*, pp. 210–11.

Bibliography

Sources available in the public domain

Byron, George Gordon Noel, *Childe Harold* (1812) Canto I, verse LIV; public domain access: Manuscript of Childe Harold's Pilgrimage by Byron, Cantos I and II | The British Library (bl.uk) (accessed 15 May 2023).

Cuéntame cómo pasó – Web Oficial – RTVE.es https://elorganillero.com/blog/2010/05/02/the-true-origins-of-africa-begins-at-the-pyrenees/, accessed 17 September 2019.

Henriques, António, 'Comparative European Institutions and the Little Divergence, 1385–1800', Centre for Global Economic History, Working paper no. 84, August 2019; showcased online at: https://nofuturepast.wordpress.com/2019/08/28/comparative-european-institutions-and-the-little-divergence-1385-1800/, accessed 26 September 2019.

Hoover Institution Archives, https://www.youtube.com/watch?v=f-iYnB2wqNU Parliamentary Papers - Parliament Archives, accessed 12 October 2022.

Thames TV interview with writer, https://www.youtube.com/watch?v=zqQxhXiqOmc; https://williamchislett.com/2015/06/03/the-gap-between-spains-image-and-the-countrys-reality/, accessed 10 June 2020.

Papers Relating to the Convention of Bergara Presented to both Houses of Parliament by Command of Her Majesty (London: T. R. Harrison, 1841), p. 36.

Archive sources

Archivo General del Palacio (Madrid) (AGP).
Archivo Histórico Nacional (Madrid) (AHN), Estado, leg. 217-2, No. 17.
Archivo Histórico Provincial de Las Palmas (AHPLP).
Arquivo Torre dos Tombos.
Real Academia de la Historia (Madrid) (RAH).
The National Archives (Kew) (TNA).

Conference papers

Ciciliato, Franzolin, and João, Arthur, 'Signal, Em Guarda, Victory and the Transnational Struggle of the Axis and the Allies to Influence Readers in Neutral and Occupied Countries during World War II' (conference paper, Propaganda and Neutrality: Alternative Battlegrounds and Active Deflection, University of Kent, 24–25 June 2021).

Fox, Jo (keynote conference address, Propaganda and Neutrality: Alternative Battlegrounds and Active Deflection, University of Kent, 24–25 June 2021).

Kowalsky, Daniel, 'Stalin and the Spanish Civil War: The New Historiography' (LSE Canada Blanch Centre, 13 February 2020).

Novels/novellas/plays

Barker, Nicola, *Five Miles from Outer Hope* (London: Faber and Faber, 2000).
Bolaño, Roberto, *Amulet* (London: Picador, 2009).
Doblado, Leucadio, *Letters from Spain* (London: Colburn, 1822).
Henty, George Alfred, *The Bravest of the Brave: Or with Peterborough in Spain* (London: Blackie and Son, 1887).
Kingsley, Charles, *Westward Ho!* (London: Macmillan, 1878).
Pritchett, V. S., *The Spanish Temper* (New York: Alfred Knopf, 1954).
Thackeray, William Makepeace, *Tremendous Adventures of Major Gahagan* (London: Bradbury & Evans, 1855).

Newspapers/magazines/pamphlets

ABC.
ARP and AFS Review (Civil Defence Journal).
Daily Mirror.
Eco del Comercio.
El Observador.
El País.
El Universal.
Gaceta Oficial.
Guinea Gold: Australian Edition.
Hansard Parliamentary Debates.
La Gaceta de Madrid.
New York Times.
Picture Post.

Saturday Review.
Civil and Military Gazette.
Daily Worker.
Economist.
Edinburgh Review.
Guardian.
Illustrated London News.
Rock Magazine.
Times.
'To the People of Spain', *Monthly Magazine*, 40 (1 October 1815).
Tripoli Times.
Union Jack (Greece Edition).

Published primary sources

Álvarez del Vayo, Julio, *Freedom's Battle* (London: William Heinemann, 1940).
Auden, W. H., *Spain* (London: Faber and Faber, 1937).
Azaña, Manuel, *Causas de la guerra de España* (Paris: Biblioteca de Bolsillo, 1941).
Bacon, John Francis, *Six Years in Biscay: Comprising a Personal Narrative of the Sieges of Bilbao, in June 1835, and Oct. to Dec., 1836. And of the Principal Events which Occurred in That City and the Basque Provinces, during the Years 1830 to 1837* (London: Smith, Elder, 1838).
Badcock, Lovell Benjamin, *Rough Leaves from a Journal Kept in Spain and Portugal, during the Years 1832, 1833, and 1834* (London: Richard Bentley, 1835).
Baldwin Brown, James (ed.), *Memoirs of the Public and Private Life of John Howard the Philanthropist* (London: Thomas and George Underwood, 1823).
Ball, Alexander, *A Personal Narrative of Seven Years in Spain* (London: J. Chappell, 1846).
Barea, Arturo, *The Forging of A Rebel: The Clash* (London: Faber and Faber, 1946).
Batty, Robert, *A Sketch of the Late Campaign in the Netherlands* (London: W. M. Clarke, 1815).
Beneson, Peter, *Persecution, 1961* (London: Penguin, 1961).
Blázquez, José Martín, *I Helped to Build an Army* (London: Secker and Warburg, 1939).
Bollaert, William, *The Wars of Succession of Portugal and Spain, from 1826 to 1840: With Résumé of the Political History of Portugal and Spain to the Present Time* (London: E. Stanford, 1870), Volume 2.
Bone, Muirhead, and Bone, Lady Gertrude Helena, *Old Spain* (London: Macmillan, 1936).
Borrow, George, *Letters of George Borrow to the Foreign and British Bible Society* (London: Hodder and Stoughton, 1911).

Borrow, George, *The Bible in Spain* (London: John Murray, 1843).

Brand, Matthew Ian, 'Right-Wing Refugees and British Politics, 1830–1871' (PhD thesis, University of East Anglia, 2016).

Brown, James A. O. C., 'Morocco and Atlantic History', in D'Maris Coffman, Adrian Leonard and William O'Reilly (eds), *The Atlantic World* (London: Routledge, 2015), pp. 191–3.

Brown, John, *The Life and Adventures of a Soldier; or, Struggles through Real Life: Comprising a Faithful History of the Late War in Spain. By John Brown, of the –th Light Dragoons, and Late of the 67th Foot* (London: E. Cornish, 1855).

Bullen, Roger, and Strong, Felicity (eds), *Palmerston, I: Private Correspondence with Sir George Villiers (afterwards Fourth Earl of Clarendon) as Minister to Spain 1833–1837* (London: Her Majesty's Stationery Office, 1985).

Burgos, Javier de, *Anales del reinado de Doña Isabel II* (Madrid: Mellado, 1850), Volume 3.

Centurión, Leopoldo Augusto de, *El Conde de Montemolín: historia de la vida pública y privada de D. Carlos Luis de Borbón* (Madrid: Imprenta de D. Manuel Álvarez, 1848).

Chalmers Mitchell, Peter, *My House in Málaga* (London: Faber and Faber, 1938).

Clark, William George, *Gazpacho: or, Summer Months in Spain* (London: George Parker, 1850).

Clarke, Bob, *No Boots on My Feet: Experiences of a Britisher in Spain, 1937–38* (Newcastle: The People's Publications, 1984).

Clarke, Edward, *Letters Concerning the Spanish Nation: Written at Madrid during the Years 1760 and 1761* (London: T. Becket and P. A. De Hondt, 1763).

Costa, Joaquín, *Oligarquía y caciquismo como la forma actual de gobierno en España* (Madrid: Imprenta de los Hijos de M. G Hernández, 1909).

Croker, Richard, *Travels through Several Provinces of Spain and Portugal, etc.* (London: J. Robson, 1799).

Dallas, Alexander, *Felix Alvarez, or Manners in Spain* (London: Baldwin, Craddock and Joy, 1818).

Dampier, William, *A New Voyage Round the World Describing Particularly the Isthmus of America* (London: James Knapton, 1703).

Davie, Michael (ed.), *The Diaries of Evelyn Waugh* (London: Weidenfeld and Nicholson, 1976).

Defoe, Daniel, *Memoirs of Captain Carleton* (London: E. P. Dutton, 1929).

de Las Casas, B., *A Short Account of the Destruction of the Indies* (London: Harmondsworth, 1992).

Dennis, George, *A Summer in Andalucía* (London: Richard Bentley, 1839), Volume 1.

Dzelepy, E. N., *Britain in Spain: A Study of the National Government's Spanish Policy by an Unknown Diplomat* (London: Hamish Hamilton, 1939).

Edwards, Bentham (ed.), *Arthur Young's Travels in France during the Years 1787, 1788, 1789, with an Introduction, Biographical Sketch, and Notes* (London: George Bell, 1892).

Estala, Pedro (1807), *Quatro cartas de un español a un anglomano en que se manifiesta La perfidia del gobierno de la Inglaterra, como pernicioso al genero humano, potencias Europeas, y particularmente à la España* (Buenos Aires: Imprenta de Niños Expósitos,).

Fernández de Moratín, Leandro, *Apuntaciones sueltas de Inglaterra* (Madrid: Cátedra, 2005).

Ferri Verdú, José, Beneito Lloris, Àngel and Cleminson, Richard (eds), *Republicanos españoles prisioneros de guerra en Inglaterra: las memorias de José Ferri* (Alcoi: Ajuntament d'Alcoi, 2019).

Flórez Estrada, Álvaro, *Examen imparcial de las disensiones de América con España, de los medios de su reconciliación, y de la prosperidad de todas las naciones* (London: Imprenta de D. Manuel Ximenez Carreño, 1811).

Ford, Richard, *A Handbook for Travellers in Spain* (London: John Murray, 1869), Volume II.

Foxe, John, *Actes and Monuments of These Latter and Perilous Days, Touching Matters of the Church* (London: John Day, 1563).

Gannes, Henry, and Repard, Theodore, *Spain in Revolt: A History of the Civil War in Spain in 1936 and a Study of Its Political and Economic Causes* (London: Victory Gollancz, 1936).

Geddes, John, 'An Account of the Province of Biscay, in Spain to Mr Cummyg, Secretary to the Society of Scottish Antiquaries', *Archaeologia Scotica or Transactions of the Society of Antiquaries of Scotland* (Edinburgh: Printed for the Society, 1792), 205–15.

Gregory, Walter, *The Shallow Grave: A Memoir of the Spanish Civil War* (London: Victor Gollancz, 1986).

Guizot, François, *Mémoires pour servir à l'histoire de mon temps* (Paris: Michel Levy, 1861), Volume IV.

Gurney, Jason, *Crusade in Spain* (London: Faber and Faber, 1974).

Hall, Fayrer, *The Importance of the British Plantations in America to This Kingdom, with the State of Their Trade, and Methods for Improving It; as also a Description of the Several Colonies There* (London: J. Peele, 1731).

Hannay, David, *Don Emilio Castelar* (London: Bliss, Sands and Foster, 1896).

Haro Tegglen, Eduardo, *El Refugio. Situaciones: momentos de una vida* (Madrid: Aguilar, 1999).

Hazlitt, William (ed.), *The Works of Daniel Defoe: With a Memoir of His Life and Writings* (London: John Clements, 1841), Volume II.

Heaney, Christopher, 'Marrying Utopia', in Jorge Cañizares-Esguerra (ed.), *Entangled Empires: The Anglo-Iberian Atlantic, 1500–1830* (Philadelphia: University of Pennsylvania Press, 2018), pp. 84–8.

Hilen, Andrew (ed.), *The Letters of Henry Wadsworth Longfellow* (Cambridge, MA: Harvard University Press, 1966), Volume 1.

Humboldt, Alexander von, *Personal Narrative of Travels to the Equinoctial Regions of America during the Years 1799–1804* (London: William Clowes, 1851), 3 volumes.

Inglis, Henry David, *Spain in 1830* (London: Whittaker, Treacher, 1831), Volume 2.
Jacob, William, *Travels in the South of Spain in Letters Written AD 1809 and 1810* (London: John Nichols, 1811).
Johnstone, Nancy, *Hotel in Flight* (London: Longmans, Green, 1940).
Kemp, Peter, *Thorns of Memory* (London: Sinclair Stevenson, 1990).
Kosetler, Arthur, *Spanish Testament* (London: Victor Gollancz, 1937).
Lacy Evans, George de, *Memoranda of the Contest in Spain* (London: James Ridgway, 1840).
Langdon Davies, John, *Behind the Spanish Barricades* (London: Reportage Press, 2007).
Langdon Davies, John, *The Home Guard Training Manual* (London: John Murray, 1942).
Lasso de la Vega, Jorge, 'Construcción de buques de vapor en Inglaterra', *Crónica Naval de España* (Madrid: Imprenta de la viuda de Calero, 1859), Tomo VIII.
Lee, Laurie, *As I Walked Out One Midsummer Morning* (London: Andre Deutsch, 1969).
Leslie, Charles, *Military Journal of Colonel Leslie, K. H., of Balquhain, whilst Serving with the Twenty-Ninth Regiment in the Peninsula and the Sixtieth Rifles in Canada, etc., 1807–1832* (Aberdeen: Aberdeen University Press, 1887).
Liddell Hart, Basil (ed.), *The Letters of Private Wheeler 1809–1828* (London: Windrush Press, 1999).
Lomas, J. (ed.), *O Shea's Guide to Spain and Portugal* (London: Adam and Charles Black, 1899).
Luis Simal, Juan, 'Letters from Spain: The 1820 Revolution and the Liberal International', in Maurizio Isabella and Konstantina Zanou (eds), *Mediterranean Diasporas: Politics and Ideas in the Long 19th Century* (London: Bloomsbury, 2016), p. 33.
Mandeville, Bernard, *The Fable of the Bees: or, Private Vices, Publick Benefits* (London: Edward Parker, 1714).
Mas, Poco, *Scenes and Adventures from Spain, 1835–1840* (London: Richard Bentley, 1845), Volume 1.
Mayhew, Henry, *London Labour and the London Poor* (London: George Woodfall, 1851), Volume I.
Metternich, Klemens von, *Memoirs of Prince Metternich II, 1773–1815* (New York: Charles Scribner's, 1880).
Morton, Adam, 'Fighting Popery with Popery: Subverting Stereotypes and Contesting Anti-Catholicism in Late Seventeenth-Century England', in Koji Yamamoto (ed.), *Stereotypes and Stereotyping in Early Modern England: Puritans, Papists and Projectors* (Manchester: Manchester University Press, 2022), p. 204.
Napier, W. F. P., *History of the War in the Peninsula and in the South of France: From the Year 1807–1814* (London: Frederick Warne, 1892), Volume 6.
Nye, Eric W. (ed.), *John Kemble's Gibraltar Journal: The Spanish Expedition of the Cambridge Apostles, 1830–31* (New York: Palgrave, 2015).

Ortuño Martínez, Manuel (ed.), *Servando Teresa de Mier: Memorias. Un fraile mexicano desterrado en Europa* (Madrid: Trama, 2006).
Orwell, George, *Homage to Catalonia* (London: Secker & Warburg, 1986).
Orwell, George, *The Lion and the Unicorn: Socialism and the English Genius* (London: Secker and Warburg, 1941).
Palmerston, Henry John Temple, *The Speech of the Viscount Palmerston, in the House of Commons, on Wednesday 19 April 1837 on the Civil War in Spain* (London: James Ridgway, 1837).
Pirala, Antonio, *Historia de la guerra civil y de los partidos liberal y carlista* (Madrid: Turner, 1984), 6 volumes.
Racine, Karen, and Lloyd, Graham (eds), *The Journal of James A. Brush: The Expedition and Military Operations of General Don Francisco Xavier Mina in Mexico, 1816–1817* (Albuquerque: University of New Mexico Press, 2020).
Raleigh, Walter, *The Discovery of Guiana, and the Journey of the Second Voyage Thereto* (London: Cassell, 1887).
Romero Alpuente, Juan, *Wellington en España y Ballesteros en Ceuta* (Cádiz: Imprenta de A. Fernández Figueroa, 1813).
Romilly, Esmond, *Boadilla* (London: Hamish Hamilton, 1937).
Rust, William, *Britons in Spain: The History of the British Battalion of the XV International Brigade* (London: Laurence and Wishart, 1939).
Schaumann, August Ludolf Friedrich, *On the Road with Wellington: The Diary of a War Commissary in the Peninsular Campaigns* (London: William Heinemann, 1924).
Serrats Urrecha, Gonzalo, *El general Álava y Wellington: de Trafalgar a Waterloo* (Madrid: Foro para el Estudio de la Historia Militar de España, 2014).
Sheaves, Mark, 'The Anglo-Iberian Atlantic as a Hemisphere System: English Merchants Navigating the Iberian Atlantic', in Jorge Cañizares-Esguerra (ed.), *Entangled Empires: The Anglo-Iberian Atlantic, 1500–1830* (Philadelphia: University of Pennsylvania Press, 2018), pp. 20–6, 34.
Smith, Rhea Marsh, *The Day of the Liberals in Spain* (Philadelphia: University of Pennsylvania Press, 1938).
Stobart, Henry John George, *Portugal and Galicia, with a Review of the Social and Political State of the Basque Provinces; and a Few Remarks on Recent Events in Spain to Which Is Now Subjoined a Reply to the 'Policy of England towards Spain'* (London: John Murray, 1837), Volume 2.
Stradling, Robert (ed.), Frank Thomas, *Brother against Brother: Experiences of a British Volunteer in the Spanish Civil War* (Stroud: Sutton Publishing, 1998).
Strubell, Michael, *The Deplorable History of the Catalans, from Their First Engaging in the War, to the Time of Their Reduction. With the Motives, Declarations, and Engagements, on Which They First Took Arms. The Letters, Treaties, &c. Relating Thereto* (London: J. Baker, 1714).
Sultana, Donald, *Benjamin Disraeli in Spain, Malta and Albania, 1830–32* (London: Tamesis Books, 1976).

Swinburne, Henry, *Travels through Spain, 1775 and 1776* (London: P. Elmsly, 1779).
Taylor, Miles (ed.), *The European Diaries of Richard Cobden, 1846–1849* (London: Routledge, 1994).
Thomas, Fred, *To Tilt at Windmills: A Memoir of the Spanish Civil War* (East Lansing: Michigan State University Press, 1996).
Ticknor, George, *Life, Letters and Journals of George Ticknor* (Boston: J. R. Osgood, 1876).
Whittingham, Ferdinand (ed.), *A Memoir of the Services of Lieutenant-General Sir Samuel Ford Whittingham* (London: Longmans, 1868).
Willoughby, Verner, *A British Rifleman: Journals and Correspondence [of George Simmons] during the Peninsular War and the Campaign of Waterloo* (London: A&C Black, 1899).
Wilmot Ormsby, James, *An Account of the Operations of the British Army and of the State and Sentiments of the People of Portugal and Spain during the Campaign of 1808–1809* (London: James Carpenter, 1809).
Wingfield, Antony (disputed), *A True Coppie of a Discourse Written by a Gentleman Employed in the Late Voyage of Spaine and Portingale: Sent to His Particular Friend, and by Him Published, for the Better Satisfaction of All Such, as Hauing Been Seduced by Particular Report, Haue Entred into Conceipts Tending to the Discredit of the Enterprise, and Actors of the Same* (London: Thomas Orwin, 1589).
Wintringham, Tom, *New Ways of War* (London: Penguin, 1940).

Published secondary sources

Acemoglu, Daron, and Robinson, James A., *Why Nations Fail: The Origins of Power, Prosperity and Poverty* (London: Profile Books, 2013).
Adkins, Roy, and Adkins, Lesley, *Gibraltar: The Greatest Siege in British History* (London: Penguin, 2017).
Aguirre Alastuey, Maria Mercedes, 'The Spanish Civil War in the Works of Nancy Cunard, Martha Gellhorn, and Sylvia Townsend Warner' (PhD Thesis, University College London Department of English, 2015).
Albareda Salvadó, Joaquín, *La Guerra de Sucesión en España (1700–1714)* (Madrid: Crítica, 2010).
Alberich, José, *Bibliografía anglo-hispánica, 1801–1850* (Oxford: Oxford University Press, 1978).
Allan, David, 'Anti-Hispanicism and the Construction of Late Eighteenth-Century British Patriotism: Robert Watson's *History of the Reign of Philip the Second*', *Bulletin of Hispanic Studies*, 77 (2000), 423–49.
Alloza Aparicio, Ángel, *Diplomacia caníbal: España y Gran Bretaña en la pugna por el dominio del mundo, 1638–1660* (Madrid: Biblioteca Nueva, 2015).

Alloza Aparicio, Ángel, 'Guerra económica y comercio europeo en España, 1624–1674. Las grandes represalias y la lucha contra el contrabando', *Hispania: Revista Española de Historia*, 65: 219 (2005), 227–79.

Alonso, Gregorio, 'Corporations, Subjects, and Citizens: The Peculiar Modernity of Early Hispanic Liberalism', *Journal of Iberian and Latin American Studies*, 22: 1 (2016), 7–22.

Alpert, Michael, *The Republican Army in the Spanish Civil War, 1936–1939* (Cambridge: Cambridge University Press, 2013).

Álvarez Junco, José, *Mater Dolorosa: la idea de España del siglo XIX* (Madrid: Taurus, 2002).

Álvarez-Junco, José, *Spanish Identity in the Age of Nations* (Manchester: Manchester University Press, 2011).

Álvarez Junco, José, and Shubert, Adrian (eds), *Spanish History since 1808* (London: Bloomsbury, 2000).

Álvarez Junco, José, and Shubert, Adrian (eds), *The History of Modern Spain: Chronologies, Themes, Individuals* (London: Bloomsbury, 2018).

Anderson, Peter, 'The Struggle over the Evacuation to the United Kingdom and Repatriation of Basque Refugee Children in the Spanish Civil War: Symbols and Souls', *Journal of Contemporary History*, 52: 2 (April, 2017), pp. 297–318.

Aquillué, Daniel, *España con honra. Una historia del siglo XIX español, 1793–1923* (Madrid: La Esfera de los Libros, 2023).

Arasa, Daniel, *Los españoles de Churchill* (Mexico City: Editorial Armonía, 1991).

Arias González, Luis, *Gonzalo de Aguilera Munro: XI Conde de Alba de Yeltes (1886–1965)* (Salamanca: Universidad de Salamanca, 2013).

Arco Blanco, Miguel Ángel del, 'Famine in Spain during Franco's Dictatorship, 1939–52', *Journal of Contemporary History*, 56: 1 (January 2021), 3–27.

Arco Blanco, Miguel Ángel del, and Anderson, Peter (eds), *Franco's Famine: Malnutrition, Disease and Starvation in Post-Civil War Spain* (London: Bloomsbury, 2021).

Arroyo Vozmediano, Julio Luis, 'Francisco de Velasco y los catalanes. Sitio y capitulación de Barcelona, 1705', *Hispania*, 74: 246 (enero-abril 2014), 69–94.

Artola-Gallego, Miguel, *La España de Fernando VII* (Madrid: Espasa, 1999).

Artola Renedo, Andoni (ed.), *Royalism, War and Popular Politics in the Age of Revolutions (1780s–1870s). In the Name of the King* (London: Palgrave, 2023).

Ayala, Carlos de, *Las cruzadas* (Madrid: Sílex, 2014).

Babiano y Sebastian, José, 'La emigración española a Europa durante los años sesenta: Francia y Suiza como países de acogida', *Historia Social*, 42 (2002), 81–98.

Baker, Christopher, 'The Discovery of Spain: Introduction', in *The Discovery of Spain: British Artists and Collectors, from Goya to Picasso* (Edinburgh: National Galleries of Scotland, 2009).

Baigorri-Jalón, Jesús, *Languages in the Crossfire: Interpreters in the Spanish Civil War, 1936–1939* (London: Routledge, 2021).

Balansó, Juan, *Julia Bonaparte: una burguesa en el trono de España* (Barcelona: Debolsillo, 2001).

Baldoli, Claudia, and Knapp, Andrew, *Forgotten Blitzes: France and Italy under Allied Air Attack, 1940–1945* (London: Continuum, 2012).

Balfour, Sebastian, *Deadly Embrace: Morocco and the Road to the Spanish Civil War* (Oxford: Oxford University Press, 2002).

Bannister, Christopher, 'Diverging Neutrality in Iberia: The British Ministry of Information in Portugal and Spain during the Second World War', in Simon Eliot and Marc Wiggam (eds), *Allied Communication to the Public during the Second World War: National and Transnational Networks* (London: Bloomsbury, 2020), pp. 167–84.

Baroja, Pío, *Siluetas románticas* (Madrid: Espasa Calpe, 1934).

Bautista Vilar, Juan, *La España del exilio. Las emigraciones políticas españolas en los siglos XIX y XX* (Madrid: Editorial Síntesis, 2007), 166.

Bayly, Christopher A., *Imperial Meridian: The British Empire and the World, 1780–1830* (London: Longman, 1989).

Bayly, Christopher A., *Indian Thought in the Age of Conflict and Empire* (Cambridge: Cambridge University Press, 2012).

Bayly, Christoper A., and Biagini, E. F. (eds), *Giuseppe Mazzini and the Globalization of Democratic Nationalism, 1830–1920* (Oxford: Oxford University Press, 2008).

Baxell, Richard, *British Volunteers in the Spanish Civil War: The British Battalion in the International Brigades 1936–1939* (London: Warren and Pell, 2007).

Baxell, Richard, *Unlikely Warriors: The British in the Spanish Civil War and the Struggle against Fascism* (London: Aurum, 2012).

Baxell, Richard, *Unlikely Warriors: The Extraordinary Story of the Britons Who Fought in the Spanish Civil War* (London: Autumn Press, 2014).

Beevor, Antony, *Crete: The Battle and the Resistance* (London: John Murray, 2011).

Beevor, Anthony, *The Battle for Spain: The Spanish Civil War 1936–1939* (London: Weidenfeld & Nicolson, 2006).

Bensimon, Fabrice, Quentin, Deluermoz, and Moisand, Jeanne (eds), '"Arise Ye Wretched of the Earth": The First International in a Global Perspective', *Studies in Global Social History*, 29 (2018), pp. 238–52.

Berkovich, Ilya, *Motivation in War: the Experience of Common Soldiers in Old-Regime Europe* (Cambridge: Cambridge University Press, 2017).

Black, Jeremy, *European Warfare 1660–1815* (London: Routledge, 2002).

Blanco, Alda, and Thomson, Guy (eds), *Visiones del liberalismo: política, identidad y cultura en la España del siglo XIX* (Valencia: PUZ, 2008).

Borreguero Beltrán, Cristina, 'Imagen y propaganda de onfli en el onflict sucesorio (1700–1713)', *Manuscrits*, 21 (2003), pp. 95–132.

Bouverie, Tim, *Appeasing Hitler: Chamberlain, Churchill and the Road to War* (London: Bodley Head, 2019).

Brading, David A., *Orbe Indiano: De la monarquía católica a la república criolla, 1492–1867* (México: Fondo de Cultura Económica, 1991).

Braun, Harald, 'El pensamiento político español del siglo XVII: ¿declive y decadencia, o sabio reconocimiento de la complejidad política?', *La Clé des Langues* [en ligne], Lyon, ENS de LYON/DGESCO (ISSN 2107-7029), avril 2018

Brenan, Gerald, 'Spain and Its Future', published in *Tripoli Times*, 30 December 1945, 908, p. 2.

Brett, Edwin M., *The British Auxiliary Legion in the First Carlist War in Spain, 1835–1838: A Forgotten Army* (Dublin: Four Courts Press, 2005).

Brome, Vincent, *The International Brigades: Spain 1936–1939* (London: Heinemann, 1965).

Brothers, Caroline, *War and Photography: A Cultural History* (London: Routledge, 1996).

Brown, Matthew, *Adventuring through Spanish Colonies: Simón Bolívar, Foreign Mercenaries and the Birth of New Nations* (Liverpool: University of Liverpool Press, 2006).

Browne, Sebastian, *Medicine and Conflict: The Spanish Civil War and Its Traumatic Legacy* (London: Routledge, 2019).

Brydan, David, *Franco's Internationalists: Social Experts and Spain's Search for Legitimacy* (Oxford: Oxford University Press, 2019).

Buchanan, Tom, ' "A Far Away Country of Which We Know Nothing"? Perceptions of Spain and Its Civil War in Britain, 1931–1939', *Twentieth Century British History*, 4: 1 (1993), 1–24.

Buchanan, Tom, *Britain and the Spanish Civil War* (Cambridge: Cambridge University Press, 2008).

Buchanan, Tom, 'Holding the Line: The Political Strategy of the International Brigade Association, 1939–1977', *Labour History Review*, 66 (2001), pp. 294–6.

Buchanan, Tom, 'Receding Triumph: British Opposition to the Franco Regime, 1945–59', *Twentieth-Century British History*, 12: 2 (2001), pp. 163–84.

Buchanan, Tom, *The British Labour Movement and the Spanish Civil War* (Cambridge: Cambridge University Press, 1991).

Buchanan, Tom, 'The Late-Franco Regime in International Context', in Nigel Townson (ed.), *Spain Transformed: The Late-Franco Dictatorship, 1959–1975* (Basingstoke: Palgrave, 2007), pp. 88–9.

Bullen, Roger, *Palmerston, Guizot, and the Collapse of the Entente Cordiale* (London: Athlone Press, 1974).

Bullón de Mendoza, Alfonso, *La primera guerra carlista* (Madrid: Actas, 1992).

Bullón-Fernández, Maria (ed.), *England and Iberia in the Middle Ages, 12th–15th Century: Cultural, Literary, and Political Exchanges* (New York: Palgrave, 2007).

Burdiel, Isabel, *Isabella II: no se puede reinar inocentemente* (Madrid: Espasa, 2004).

Burdiel, Isabel, *Isabel II: una biografía* (Madrid: Taurus, 2011).

Butrón Prida, Gonzalo, 'From Hope to Defensiveness: the Foreign Policy of a Beleaguered Liberal Spain, 1820–1823', *English Historical Review*, 133: 562 (2018), pp. 567–696.

Cabrera, Miguel A., 'Developments in Contemporary Spanish Historiography: From Social History to the New Cultural History', *Journal of Modern History* 77 (December, 2005), pp. 988–1023.

Callwell, Edward, *Small Wars: Their Principles and Practice* (London: His Majesty's Stationery Office, 1899).

Cámara, Mariano de la, *La política exterior del carlismo (1833–1839)* (Sevilla: Librería e imprenta moderna, 1933).

Campbell, John, 'Is the ILP for Winning the War or Aiding Franco', *The Daily Worker*, 22 May 1937, pp. 1–3.

Campo Tejedor, Alberto del, *La infame fama del andaluz* (Córdoba: Editorial Almuzara, 2020).

Cañas de Pablos, Alberto, *Los generales políticos en Europa y América (1810–1870): Centauros carismáticos bajo la luz de Napoleón* (Madrid: Alianza, 2022).

Cañizares-Esguerra, Jorge (ed.), *Entangled Empires: The Anglo-Iberian Atlantic, 1500–1830* (Philadelphia: University of Pennsylvania Press, 2018).

Cañizares-Esguerra, Jorge, *Puritan Conquistadores: Iberianizing the Atlantic, 1550–1700* (Stanford: Stanford University Press, 2006).

Cannon, Richard, *Historical Record of the First or the Royal Regiment of Dragoons: From Its Formation in the Reign of King Charles the Second and of Its Subsequent Services to 1839* (London: William Clowes, 1836).

Cano Jiménez, Gema, 'Del Spain Is Different al Party's Over: La imagen de España a través de *The Economist* (2008–2009)', *Textual & Visual Media*, 3 (2010), pp. 63–80.

Capellán, Gonzalo (ed.), *Dibujar discursos, construir imaginarios: Prensa y caricatura política en España (1836–1874)* (Santander: Editorial Universidad de Cantabria, 2022), Volume 1.

Caridad Salvador, Antonio, 'La historiografía reciente sobre el primer carlismo (2006–2018), *Studia Historica. Historia Contemporánea*, 38 (2020), pp. 203–43.

Caridad Salvador, Antonio, 'Las mujeres durante la primera guerra carlista (1833–1840), *Memoria y Civilización*, 14 (2011), pp. 175–99.

Carr, Gordon, *The Angry Brigade* (London: PM Press, 2010).

Carr, Raymond, *Spain, 1808–1975* (Oxford: Oxford University Press, 1982).

Carr, Raymond, *The Spanish Tragedy: The Civil War in Perspective* (London: Phoenix Press, 1977).

Casanova, Julián, and Gil Andrés, Carlos, *Twentieth-Century Spain: A History* (Cambridge: Cambridge University Press, 2014).

Castellano García, Manuel, 'Construyendo la paz de Utrecht: las negociaciones secretas entre Francia y Gran Bretaña y la firma de los preliminares de Londres', *Cuadernos de Historia Moderna*, 45: 1 (2020), 199–232.

Castells, Irene, *La utopía insurreccional del liberalismo: Torrijos y las conspiraciones de la década ominosa* (Barcelona: Crítica, 1989).
Cepeda Gómez, José, 'La historia bélica de la Guerra de Sucesión Española', in *En nombre de la paz: La Guerra de Sucesión Española y los Tratados de Madrid, Utrecht, Rastatt y Baden 1713-1715* (Madrid: Fundación Carlos Amberes, 20 December 2013-23 February 2014).
Cervantes, Fernando, *Conquistadores: A New History* (London: Allen Lane, 2020).
Chambers, Sarah C., and Chasteen, John C. (eds), *Latin American Independence: An Anthology of Sources* (Indianapolis: Hackett, 2010).
Charters, Erica, Rosenhaft, Eve, and Smith, Hannah (eds), *Civilians and War in Europe 1618-1815* (Liverpool: Liverpool University Press, 2012).
Clark, Joseph, ' "The Rage of Fanatics": Religious Fanaticism and the Making of Revolutionary Violence', *French History*, 33: 2 (June, 2019), pp. 236-58.
Cleminson, Richard (2009), 'Spanish Anti-fascist "Prisoners of War" in Lancashire, 1944-46', *International Journal of Iberian Studies*, 22: 3, pp. 163-83.
Clifford, James, *Routes: Travel and Translation in the Late Twentieth Century* (Cambridge, MA: Harvard University Press, 1997).
Close, David H., *Greece since 1945: Politics, Economy and Society* (London: Routledge, 2014).
Coffman, D'Maris, Leonard, Adrian, and O'Reilly, William (eds), *The Atlantic World* (London: Routledge, 2015).
Colley, Linda, *Britons: Forging the Nation, 1707-1837* (New Haven, CT: Yale University Press, 1992).
Collins, Bruce, *Wellington and the Siege of San Sebastián, 1813* (Barnsley: Pen and Sword, 2017).
Cook, Judith, *Apprentices of Freedom* (London: Quartet Books, 1979).
Corse, Edward, *A Battle for Neutral Europe: British Cultural Propaganda during the Second World War* (London: Bloomsbury, 2012).
Cortes Peña, Antonio Luis, 'Nacionalismo/regionalismo andaluz: una invención de laboratorio', *Historia Social*, 4 (2001), pp. 137-52.
Cowan, Brian, 'The Spin Doctor: Sacheverell's Trial Speech and Political Performance in the Divided Society', *Parliamentary History*, 31: 1 (February, 2012), pp. 28-46.
Coxe, William, *Memoirs of the Kings of Spain of the House of Bourbon: From the Accession of Philip V to the Death of Charles III: 1700 to 1788* (London: Longman, 1815), 5 volumes.
Cross, Robert, 'Pretense and Perception in the Spanish Match, or History in a Fake Beard', *Journal of Interdisciplinary History*, 37: 4 (Spring, 2007), pp. 563-83.
Dadson, Trevor J., and Elliott, John H. (eds), *Britain, Spain and the Treaty of Utrecht, 1713-2013* (New York: Legenda, 2014).
Dalton, Heather, *Merchants and Explorers: Roger Barlow, Sebastian Cabot, and Networks of Atlantic Exchange, 1500-1560* (Oxford: Oxford University Press, 2016).

Daly, Gavin, '"Barbarity More Suited to Savages": British Soldiers' Views of Spanish and Portuguese Violence during the Peninsular War, 1808–1814', *War and Society*, 35:4 (2016), pp. 242–58.

Daly, Gavin, *The British Soldier in the Peninsular War: Encounters with Spain and Portugal, 1808–1814* (Basingstoke: Palgrave Macmillan, 2013).

David, Saul, *All the King's Men: The British Soldier from the Restoration to Waterloo* (London: Viking, 2013).

Davies, Catherine, and Sánchez, Sarah, 'Rafael María de Labra and Ramón Labra: Two Generations of Revolution and Liberal Reform in Spain and Cuba', *Hispanic Research Journal*, 11: 1 (February 2010), pp. 11–24.

Davison, Peter (ed.), *Orwell in Spain* (London: Penguin, 2001).

Day, Peter, *Franco's Friends: How British Intelligence Helped Bring Franco to Power in Spain* (London: Biteback Publishing, 2012).

Deacon, David, *British News Media and the Spanish Civil War* (Edinburgh: Edinburgh University Press, 2008).

de la Torre, Rosario, 'La prensa madrileña y el discurso de Lord Salisbury sobre las naciones moribundas', *Cuadernos de Historia Moderna y Contemporánea*, 6 (1985), pp. 163–80.

del Arco Blanco, Miguel Ángel, and Anderson, Peter, 'Introduction: Famine, not Hunger?', in Miguel Ángel del Arco Blanco and Peter Anderson (eds), *Franco's Famine: Malnutrition, Disease and Starvation in Post-Civil War Spain* (London: Bloomsbury, 2021), pp. 7–8.

de Mendoza, Alfonso Bullón, *La primera guerra carlista* (Madrid: Actas, 1992).

de Pablos, Alberto Cañas, *Los generales políticos en Europa y América (1810–1870): Centauros carismáticos bajo la luz de Napoleón* (Madrid: Alianza, 2022).

Dorrell, Nicholas, *Marlborough's Other Army* (London: Helion, 2019).

Dowling, Andrew (ed.), *Routledge Handbook of Spanish History* (London: Routledge, 2023).

Dunthon, David J., *Britain and the Spanish Anti-Franco Opposition, 1940–1950* (Basingstoke: Palgrave, 2000).

Dupont, Alexandre, *La internacional blanca: contrarrevolución más allá de las fronteras (España y Francia, 1868–1876)* (Zaragoza: Prensas de la Universidad de Zaragoza, 2020).

Durgan, Andy, 'Freedom Fighters or Comintern Army?', *International Socialism*, 84 (1999), pp. 1–16.

Ealham, Chris, and Richards, Michael (eds), *The Splintering of Spain* (Cambridge: Cambridge University Press, 2005).

Eastman, Scott, *A Missionary Nation. Race, Religion, and Spain's Age of Liberal Imperialism, 1841–1881* (Lincoln: University of Nebraska Press, 2021).

Eastman, Scott, 'Spain in World History', in Adrian Shubert and José Álvarez Junco (eds), *The History of Modern Spain: Chronologies, Themes, Individuals* (London: Bloomsbury, 2018), p. 360.

Elliot, John H., *Scots and Catalans: Union and Disunion* (Yale: Yale University Press, 2018).
Eliot, Simon, and Wiggam, Marc (eds), *Allied Communication to the Public during the Second World War: National and Transnational Networks* (London: Bloomsbury, 2020).
Elliott, John, 'The Road to Utrecht: War and Peace', in Trevor J. Dadson and J. H. Elliott (eds), *Britain, Spain and the Treaty of Utrecht, 1713-2013* (New York: Legenda, 2014).
Elliott, John H., 'A Europe of Composite Monarchies', *Past and Present*, 137, The Cultural and Political Construction of Europe (November, 1992).
Ernest, Gerald, and Gillespie, Paul (eds), *Romantic Drama* (Philadelphia: John Benjamins, 1994).
Escribano Roca, Rodrigo, and Guerrero Oñate, Pablo, 'Navalismo y panhispanismo como horizontes de regeneración imperial en España (1814-1862)', *Anuario de Estudios Americanos*, 79: 1 (Sevilla, 2022), pp. 205-38.
Esdaile, Charles J., 'Book Review of Edward M. Brett, *The British Auxiliary Legion in the First Carlist War, 1835-38: A Forgotten Army* (Dublin: Four Courts Press, 2005)', *English Historical Review*, 121: 492 (June, 2006).
Esdaile, Charles J., *Fighting Napoleon: Guerrillas Bandits and Adventurers in Spain 1808-1814* (London: Yale University Press, 2004).
Esdaile, Charles J., *Napoleon's Wars: An International History, 1803-1815* (London: Allen Lane, 2008).
Esdaile, Charles J., 'The British Army in the Napoleonic Wars: Approaches Old and New', *English Historical Review*, 130: 542 (February, 2015), pp. 123-37.
Esdaile, Charles, 'Conscription in Spain in the Napoleonic Era', in Donald Stoker, Frederick Schneid and Harold Blanton (eds), *Conscription in the Napoleonic Era* (London: Routledge, 2008).
Esdaile, Charles J., *The Duke of Wellington and the Command of the Spanish Army, 1812-1814* (London: Palgrave Macmillan, 1990).
Esdaile, Charles J., *The Spanish Army in the Peninsular War* (Manchester: Manchester University Press, 1988).
Esdaile, Charles J., *The Spanish Civil War: A Military History* (London: Routledge, 2018).
Esdaile, Charles J., *Women in the Peninsular War* (Norman: Oklahoma University Press, 2014).
Esdaile, Charles, 'Prohombres, aventureros y oportunistasla influencia del trayecto personal en los orígenes del liberalismo en España', in Alda Blanco and Guy Thomson (eds), *Visiones del liberalismo: política, identidad y cultura en la España del siglo XIX* (Valencia: PUZ, 2008), pp. 65-86.
El Universal, 14 January 1814.
Evans, Richard, *Cosmopolitan Islanders: British Historians and the European Continent* (Cambridge: Cambridge University Press, 2009).

Falkner, James, *Marlborough's Wars: Eyewitness Accounts 1702–1713* (Barnsley: Pen and Sword, 2005).

Fernández Sebastián, Javier, and Capellán de Miguel, Gonzalo, 'The Notion of Modernity in Nineteenth-Century Spain. An Example of Conceptual History', *Contributions to the History of Concepts*, 1: 2 (October 2005), pp. 159–84.

Feros, Antonio, *Speaking of Spain: The Evolution of Race and Nation in the Hispanic World* (Cambridge, MA: Harvard University Press, 2017).

Ferrán, Ofelia, *Working through Memory: Writing and Remembrance in Contemporary Spanish Narrative* (Cranbury: Associated University Presse, 2007).

Ferrer, Melchor, *Historia del tradicionalismo español* (Sevilla: Editorial Católica Española, 1941–60), Volume 20.

Finucane, Adrian, *The Temptations of Trade: Britain, Spain and the Struggle for Empire* (Philadelphia: University of Pennsylvania Press, 2016).

Fontana, Josep, 'El Partido Popular y la Constitución de Cádiz', *El País*, 15 February 2006, p. 13.

Francis, Hywel, 'Welsh Miners and the Spanish Civil War', *Journal of Contemporary History*, 5: 3 (1970), pp. 177–91.

Frank Jr., W. C., 'Multinational Naval Cooperation in the Spanish Civil War', *Naval College Review*, 47: 2 (Spring, 1994), pp. 72–101.

Freund, Gisèle, *Photography and Society* (London: D. R. Godine, 1980).

Friend, John, *An Account of the Earl of Peterborough's Conduct in Spain* (London: W. Wise, 1707).

Fuchs, Barbara, *The Poetics of Piracy: Emulating Spain in English Literature* (Philadelphia: University of Pennsylvania Press, 2013).

Gallardo, Alexander, 'Anglo-Spanish Relations during the First Carlist War (1833–1839)' (unpublished PhD dissertation, St John's University, New York, 1977).

García Cabrera, Marta, 'Operation Warden: British Sabotage Planning in the Canary Islands during the Second World War', *Intelligence and National Security*, 5: 2 (2020), pp. 252–68.

García Cárcel, Ricardo, 'Los fantásticos relatos acerca de nuestra patria: la leyenda negra', *Historia Social*, 3 (Winter, 1989), pp. 3–15.

García-Martí, Carlos, 'Arrival of the International Team of English Boxing in Spain in 1911: Boxing Bans and Clashes over Bullfighting, Regeneration and Europe', *Sport in history*, 41: 1 (2021), pp. 25–49.

García, Óscar Martín, 'Emisarios de la moderación: La diplomacia pública británica ante el fin de las dictaduras ibéricas', *Hispania: Revista Española de Historia*, 72: 242 (2012), pp. 789–816.

García Tejero, Alfonso, *Historia politico-administrativa de Mendizábal* (Madrid: Establecimiento Tipografico de J. A. Ortigosa, 1858), 2 volumes.

Gil Olcina, Antonio, and Morales Gil, Alfredo (eds), *Hitos históricos de los regadíos españoles* (Madrid: Ministerio de Agricultura, 1992).

Gilbert, Arthur N., 'Army Impressment during the War of the Spanish Succession', in *The Historian: A Journal of History*, 38: 4 (1976), pp. 689–708.

Ginger, Andrew, and Lawless, Geraldine (eds), *Spain in the Nineteenth Century: New Essays on Experience of Culture and Society* (Manchester: Manchester University Press, 2018).

Glendinning, Nigel, 'Nineteenth-Century British Envoys in Spain and the Taste for Spanish Art in England', *Burlington Magazine*, 131: 1031 (February, 1989), pp. 117–26.

Glondys, Olga, 'Cold War Controversies in the Pro-amnesty Campaigns of the Spanish Political Prisoners (1961) and the Erosion of Spanish Exiles' Leadership in the Anti-Francoist Policies', *Journal of Iberian and Latin American Studies*, 27: 1 (2021), pp. 63–77.

Goda, Norman J. W., *Tomorrow the World: Hitler, Northwest Africa and the Path Toward America* (College Station: Texas A&M University Press, 1998).

Goizueta Alfaro, Alfonso, 'Forging Liberal States: Palmerston's Foreign Policy and the Rise of a Constitutional Monarchy in Spain, 1833–7', *Historical Research*, 94: 266 (November 2021), pp. 827–48.

Goldman, William S., 'Spain and the Founding of Jamestown', *William and Mary Quarterly*, 3rd series, 68: 3 (July, 2011), pp. 427–50.

Gómez Mendoza, Josefina, 'Regeneracionismo y Regadíos', in Antonio Gil Olcina and Alfredo Morales Gil (eds), *Hitos históricos de los regadíos españoles* (Madrid: Ministerio de Agricultura, 1992), pp. 249–50.

González Cruz, David, *Propaganda e información en tiempos de guerra: España y América (1700–1714)* (Madrid: Sílex, 2009).

González Fernández, Ander, and Tabernilla, Guillermo, *Combatientes vascos en la Segunda Guerra Mundial* (Madrid: Desperta Ferro, 2018), p. 75.

González, Luis Arias, *Gonzalo de Aguilera Munro: XI Conde de Alba de Yeltes (1886–1965)* (Universidad de Salamanca, 2013), p. 172.

González Ruiz, Nicolás, *Dos reinas. La católica y la protestante: Isabel de España. Isabel de Inglaterra* (Madrid: Editorial Cervantes, 1947).

Goodwin, Robert, *Spain: The Centre of the World, 1519–1682* (London: Bloomsbury, 2015).

Gorrochategui Santos, Luis, *The English Armada: The Greatest Naval Disaster in English History* (London: Bloomsbury, 2018).

Graham, Richard, *Independence in Latin America* (London: Random House, 1971).

Graham, Helen, '"Against the State": A Genealogy of the Barcelona May Days', *European History Quarterly*, 29: 4 (1999), pp. 485–542.

Graham, Helen, *The War and Its Shadow: Spain's Civil War in Europe's Long Twentieth Century* (Brighton: Sussex Academic Press, 2012).

Greig, Matilda, *Dead Men Telling Tales: Napoleonic War Memoirs and the Military Memoir Industry, 1808–1914* (Oxford: Oxford University Press, 2021).

Griffin, Sean, *The Liturgical Past in Byzantium and Early Rus* (Cambridge: Cambridge University Press, 2019).

Groot, Gerard de, *The Seventies Unplugged* (New York, 2010).
Guereña, Jean-Louis, 'Las Casas del Pueblo y la educación obrera a principios del siglo XX', *Hispania*, 51: 178 (1991), pp. 645–92.
Hargreaves-Mawdsley, W. N., *Eighteenth-Century Spain, 1700–1788: A Political, Diplomatic and Institutional History* (London: Macmillan, 1979).
Harrison, Joseph, *An Economic History of Modern Spain* (Manchester: Manchester University Press, 1978).
Hennessey, C. A. M., *The Federal Republic in Spain: Pi y Margall and the Federal Republican Movement, 1868–1874* (Oxford: Oxford University Press, 1962).
Herrerín, Ángel, 'Anarchist Sociability in Spain. In Times of Violence and Clandestinity', *Bulletin for Spanish and Portuguese Historical Studies*, 38: 1 (2013), pp. 155–74.
Hierro, Pablo del, 'The Neofascist Network and Madrid, 1945–1953: From City of Refuge to Transnational Hub and Centre of Operations', *Contemporary European History*, 31 (2022), pp. 171–94.
Hilt, Douglas, 'The Reception of the Spanish Theatre in European Romanticism', in Gerald Ernest and Paul Gillespie (eds), *Romantic Drama* (Philadelphia: John Benjamins, 1994), p. 25.
Hinde, Wendy, *George Canning* (London: Wiley Blackwell, 1989).
Holguín, Sandie, *Flamenco Nation: The Construction of Spanish National Identity* (Madison: University of Wisconsin Press, 2019).
Hooper, Kirsty, 'A Tale of Two Empires? The Earl's Court Spanish Exhibition (1889)', *Modern Languages Open*, 1 (2014), pp. 1–27.
Hooper, Kirsty, *The Edwardians and the Making of a Spanish Obsession* (Liverpool: Liverpool University Press, 2020).
Hopkins, James K., *Into the Heart of the Fire: The British in the Spanish Civil War* (Stanford: Stanford University Press, 1998).
Howard, David, *The Invention of Spain: Anglo-Spanish Cultural Relations, 1770–1870* (Manchester: Manchester University Press, 2007).
Howard, Donald D., 'British Seapower and Its Influence Upon the Peninsular War (1808–1814)', *Naval War College Review*, 31: 2 (1978), pp. 54–71.
Howe, Anthony, *Free Trade and Liberal England, 1846–1946* (Oxford: Oxford University Press, 1998).
Hughes, Ben, *They Shall Not Pass The British Battalion at Jarama* (Oxford: Osprey, 2011).
Humphreys, R. A., and Lynch, John (eds), *The Origins of the Latin American Revolutions, 1808–1826* (New York: Alfred A. Knopf, 1965).
Iglesias-Rogers, Graciela (ed.), *The Hispanic Anglosphere from the Eighteenth to the Twentieth Century: An Introduction* (London: Routledge, 2021).
Iglesias Rogers, Graciela, *British Liberators in the Age of Napoleon: Volunteering under the Spanish Flag in the Peninsular War* (London: Bloomsbury, 2012).
Izabella, Maurizio, and Zanou, Konstantina (eds), *Mediterranean Diasporas: Politics and Ideas in the Long 19th Century* (London: Bloomsbury, 2016).

Izabella, Maurizio, *Risorgimento in Exile: Italian Émigrés and the Liberal International in the Post-Napoleonic Era* (Oxford: Oxford University Press, 2016).

James, Richard, 'Public Opinion and the British Legion in Spain 1835–1838' (unpublished PhD thesis, McGill University, March 1996).

Jensen, Geoffrey, *Irrational Triumph: Cultural Despair, Military Nationalism and the Ideological Origins of Franco's Spain* (Reno: University of Nevada Press, 2002).

Jensen, Geoffrey, 'Moral Strength through Material Defeat? The Consequences of 1898 for Spanish Military Culture', *War & Society*, 17: 2 (1999), pp. 25–39.

Jover, José María, *España en la política internacional, siglos XVIII–XX* (Madrid: Marcial Pons, 1999).

Juderías, Julián, *La leyenda negra* (Madrid: Editora Nacional, 1967).

Juliá, Santos, *La Guerra Civil Española de la Segunda República a la dictadura de Franco* (Barcelona: Emse Edapp, 2019).

Kagan, Richard L., 'Prescott's Paradigm: American Historical Scholarship and the Decline of Spain', in *The American Historical Review*, 101: 2 (April, 1996), pp. 423–46.

Kagan, Richard L., *The Spanish Craze: America's Fascination with the Hispanic World, 1779–1939* (Lincoln: University of Nebraska Press, 2019).

Kamen, Henry, *Golden Age Spain* (London: Palgrave, 2005).

Kamen, Henry, *La invención de España: Leyendas e ilusiones que han construido la realidad española* (Madrid: Espasa, 2020).

Kamen, Henry, *The Disinherited: Exile and the Making of Spanish Culture, 1492–1975* (New York: New York University Press, 2007).

Keene, Judith, *Fighting for Franco: International Volunteers in Nationalist Spain during the Spanish Civil War* (London: Hambledon Continuum 2007).

Kennedy, Catriona, and McCormack, Matthew, *Soldiering in Britain and Ireland, 1750–1850* (Basingstoke: Palgrave, 2013).

Kennett-Barrington, Vincent, *Letters from the Carlist War (1874–76)* (Exeter: Exeter University Press, 1967), p. xi.

Kiernan, V. G., 'The Old Alliance: England and Portugal' (discussion paper written for the conference held at Manchester in June 1973 by the Committee for Freedom in Mozambique, Angola and Guinea).

Kilne, Wayne M. M., 'The English Crown's Foreign Debt, 1544–1557' (1992). Dissertations and Theses. Portland State University. Paper 4366.

Kirby, T., *The Duke of Wellington and the Supply System during the Peninsular War* (Paris: Wagram Press, 2014).

Kisch, Richard, *They Shall Not Pass: The Spanish People at War, 1936–39* (London: Wayland, 1974).

Knightley, Phillip, *The First Casualty: The War Correspondent as Hero and Myth-Maker from the Crimea to Kosovo* (London: Prion Books, 2000).

Kuethe, Allan J., and Andrien, Kenneth J., *The Spanish Atlantic World in the Eighteenth Century: War and the Bourbon Reforms, 1713–1796* (Cambridge: Cambridge University Press, 2014).

La Parra, Emilio, *Fernando VII: un rey deseado y detestado* (Madrid: Tusquets, 2018).
Lafuente, Modesto, *Historia general de España desde los tiempos primitivos hasta la muerte de Fernando VII* (Barcelona: Montaner y Simon, 1883), Volume 1.
Langford, Paul (ed.), *Short History of the British Isles: The Eighteenth Century, 1688-1815* (Oxford: Oxford University Press, 2002).
Laqua, Daniel (2014), 'Freethinkers, Anarchists and Francisco Ferrer: The Making of a Transnational Solidarity Campaign', *European Review of History: Revue européenne d'histoire*, 21: 4, pp. 467–84.
Laqueur, Walter, *Guerrilla Warfare: a Historical and Critical Study* (London: Transaction Publishers, 1997).
Laspra, Alicia, 'La intervención británica: ayuda material y diplomática', *Revista de historia militar*, 2 (2005), 59–78.
Lawrence, Mark, 'Gran Bretaña y la guerra de Sucesión española', in B. Tauler Cid (ed.) *Presencia Británica en la Milicia Española* (Madrid: Comisión Internacional de Historia Militar, 2021), 115–38.
Lawrence, Mark (ed.), *Insurgency and Counterinsurgency in the Nineteenth Century: A Global History* (London: Routledge, 2020).
Lawrence, Mark, 'Juan Álvarez Mendizábal', in José Álvarez Junco and Adrian Shubert (eds), *The History of Modern Spain: Chronologies, Themes, Individuals* (London: Bloomsbury, 2018).
Lawrence, Mark, *Nineteenth-Century Spain: A New History* (London: Routledge, 2019).
Lawrence, Mark, 'Peninsularity and Patriotism: Spanish and British Approaches to the Peninsular War, 1808–14', *Historical Research*, 85: 229 (August 2012), 453–68.
Lawrence, Mark, 'Spanish Political Development 1808 to 1868', in Andrew Dowling (ed.), *Routledge Handbook of Spanish History* (London: Routledge, 2023).
Lawrence, Mark, *The Spanish Civil Wars: A Comparative History of the First Carlist War and the Conflict of the 1930s* (London: Bloomsbury, 2017).
Lean, Edward Tangye, *The Napoleonists: A Study in Political Disaffection 1760–1960* (Oxford: Oxford University Press, 1970).
Leguineche, Manuel, *Gibraltar: La roca en el zapato de España* (Barcelona: Planeta, 2002).
Leitz, Christian, *Economic Relations between Nazi Germany and Franco's Spain, 1936–1945* (Oxford: Oxford University Press, 1996).
Liddel Hart, Basil Henry, *The British Way in Warfare* (London: Faber and Faber, 1932).
Linch, Kevin, *Britain and Wellington's Army: Recruitment, Society and Tradition, 1807–15* (Basingstoke: Palgrave, 2011).
Llorens, Vicente, *Liberales y románticos: una emigración española en Inglaterra* (Madrid: Castalia, 1979).
Lynch, John, *Latin America between Colony and Nation: Selected Essays* (Basingstoke: Palgrave, 2001).
MacLennan, Julio Crespo, *Spain and the Process of European Integration, 1957–85* (London: Palgrave, 2000).

Mahon, Lord, *The War of the Spanish Succession* (London: John Murray, 1836).
Maltby, William S., *The Black Legend in England: The Development of Anti-Spanish Sentiment, 1558-1660* (Durham, NC: Duke University Press, 1971).
Maravall, José Antonio, *Culture of the Baroque: Analysis of a Historical Structure* (Minneapolis: University of Minnesota Press, 1986).
Marbán, Jorge A., *Confederate Patriot, Journalist, and Poet:: The Multifaceted Life of José Agustín Quintero* (Victoria, BC: Friesen Press, 2014).
Marco, Jorge, *Paraísos en el infierno. Drogas y Guerra Civil española* (Granada: Comares, 2021).
Marichal, Juan, *El secreto de España: ensayos de historia intelectual y política* (Madrid: Taurus, 1995).
Martínez del Campo, Luis G., *Cultural Diplomacy: A Hundred Years of British-Spanish Society* (Liverpool: Liverpool University Press, 2015).
Martínez del Campo, Luis G., 'De hispanófilo a hispanista: la construcción de una comunidad profesional en Gran Bretaña', *Ayer*, 93 (2014), 139-61.
Martínez-Radío Garrido, Evaristo C., 'Españoles prisioneros y cautivos en la Inglaterra del siglo XVIII: una aproximación a su ubicación y condiciones', *Revista Universitaria de Historia Militar*, 9: 18 (Año 2020), 43-65.
Mas, Poco, *Scenes and Adventures from Spain, 1835-1840* (London: Richard Bentley, 1845), Volume 1, pp. 114-15.
Mason, Emily, *Democracy, Deeds and Dilemmas: Support for the Spanish Republic within British Civil Society, 1936-1939* (Brighton: Sussex Academic Press, 2017).
Mathews, James, *Reluctant Warriors: Republican Popular Army and Nationalist Army Conscripts in the Spanish Civil War, 1936-1939* (Oxford: Oxford University Press, 2012).
Matthews, James, 'The Vanguard of Sacrifice'? Political Commissars in the Republican Popular Army during the Spanish Civil War, 1936-1939', *War in History*, 21: 1 (2014), 82-101.
Maxwell, Keneth, and Spiegel, Steven, *The New Spain: From Isolation to Influence* (New York: Council on Foreign Relations Press, 1994).
McFarlane, Anthony, *War and Independence in Spanish America* (London: Routledge, 2013).
McKay, Ruth, *Lazy, Improvident People: Myth and Reality in the Writing of Spanish History* (Ithaca: Cornell University Press, 2006).
McMahon, Richard, 'The Races of Europe: Anthropological Race Classification of Europeans, 1839-1939' (PhD thesis, European University Institute, 2006).
McLellan, Josie, '"I Wanted to Be a Little Lenin" Ideology and the German International Brigade Volunteers', *Journal of Contemporary History*, 41: 2 (April, 2006), 287-304.
Melgar, F., *Pequeña historia del carlismo* (Pamplona: Editorial Gómez, 1958).
Merton, Reginald, *Cardinal Ximenes and the Making of Spain* (London: Kegan Paul, 1934).

Mesa Gallego, Eduardo de, 'English Military Interventions in the Wars of the Spanish Monarchy, 1500–1600', in B. Tauler Cid (ed.), *Presencia Británica en la Milicia Española* (Madrid: Comisión Internacional de Historia Militar, 2021).

Messenger, Charles, *The Middle East Commandos* (London: William Kimber, 1988).

Middleton, Charles Ronald, *The Administration of British Foreign Policy, 1782–1846* (Durham, NC: Duke University Press, 1977).

Moa, Pío, *Los mitos de la Guerra Civil* (Madrid: Esfera de los Libros, 2004).

Moreman, Tim, *British Commandos, 1940–46* (London: Bloomsbury, 2006).

Moreno Alonso, Manuel, *Blanco White: la obsesión de España* (Sevilla: Alfar, 1998).

Moreno Luzón, Javier (ed.), *Construir España: Nacionalismo español y procesos de nacionalización* (Madrid: Centro de Estudios Constitucionales, 2007).

Moreno Luzón, Javier, *Modernizing the Nation: Spain during the Reign of Alfonso XIII, 1902–1931* (Brighton: Sussex Academic Press, 2016).

Moreno-Luzón, Javier, 'The Two Monarchies of Alfonso XIII (1902–1931)', in David San Narciso, Margarita Barral Martínez and Carolina Armenteros (eds), *Monarchy and Liberalism in Spain: The Building of the Nation-State, 1780–1931* (London: Routledge, 2022), pp. 93–110.

Mosely, Philip E., 'Intervention and Nonintervention in Spain, 1838–39', *Journal of Modern History*, 13: 2 (June, 1941), 195–217.

Muir, Rory, *Tactics and the Experience of Battle in the Age of Napoleon* (London: Yale University Press, 2000).

Müller, Rolf-Dieter, *The Unknown Eastern Front* (London: I. B. Tauris, 2015).

Nash, Mary, '"Milicianas" and Homefront Heroines: Images of Women in Revolutionary Spain 1936–1939', *History of European Ideas*, 11 (1989), 235–44.

Núñez Seixas, Manuel, *¡Fuera el invasor! Nacionalismos y movilización bélica durante la guerra civil española (1936–1939)* (Madrid: Marcial Pons, 2006).

Núñez Seixas, Xosé M., *Suspiros de España: el nacionalismo español, 1808–2018* (Barcelona: Crítica, 2018).

O'Connor, S., and Gutmann, M., 'Under a Foreign Flag: Integrating Foreign Units and Personnel in the British and German Armed Forces, 1940–1945', *Journal of Modern European History*, 14: 3(2016), 321–41.

Oman, Charles, *A History of the Peninsular War: August 1813–April 14, 1814. The Capture of St. Sebastian, Wellington's Invasion of France, Battles of the Nivelle, the Nive, Orthez, and Toulouse* (London: Forgotten Books, 2018), Volume 7.

Ortuño Martínez, Manuel, *Xavier Mina: fronteras de libertad* (Mexico City: Librería de Porrua Hermanos, 2003).

Othen, Christopher, *Franco's International Brigades – Adventurers, Fascists and Christian Crusaders in the Spanish Civil War* (London: Hurst Publishers 2013).

Oyarzun, Román, *Historia del carlismo* (Valladolid: Maxtor, 2008).

Pablo-Marti, Federico, 'Complex Networks to Understand the Past: The Case of Roads in Bourbon Spain', *Cliometrica*, 15: 3 (September, 2021), 477–534.

Pack, Sasha D., 'The Making of the Gibraltar–Spain Border: Cholera, Contraband, and Spatial Reordering, 1850–1873', *Mediterranean Historical Review*, 29: 1 (2014), 71–88.

Pack, Sasha D., *Tourism and Dictatorship: Europe's Peaceful Invasion of Franco's Spain* (Basingstoke: Palgrave, 2006).

Palme Dutt, R., 'Spain Organises for Victory', *The Daily Worker*, 22 May 1937, pp. 1–3.

Paquette, Gabriel, 'Introduction: Liberalism in the Early Nineteenth-Century Iberian World', *History of European Ideas* (2014), 1–13; doi: 10.1080/01916599.2014.914312.

Paquette, Gabriel, 'The Image of Imperial Spain in British Political Thought, 1750–1800', *Bulletin of Spanish Studies*, 81:2 (2004), 187–214.

París, Álvaro, 'King, War and Bread: Popular Royalism in Southern Europe (1789–1830)', in Andoni Artola Renedo (ed.), *Royalism, War and Popular Politics in the Age of Revolutions (1780s–1870s). In the Name of the King* (London: Palgrave, 2023), p. 84.

Parker, Geoffrey, *The Military Revolution: Military Innovation and the Rise of the West, 1500–1800* (Cambridge: Cambridge University Press, 1996).

Parral, Margarita, 'Royal Travels: The Modern Staging and Legitimation of the Spanish Monarchy, 1858–1931', in David San Narciso, Margarita Barral Martínez and Carolina Armenteros (eds), *Monarchy and Liberalism in Spain: The Building of the Nation-State, 1780–1931* (London: Routledge, 2022), pp. 202–20.

Payne, Stanley G., and Palacios, Jesús, *Franco: A Personal and Political Biography* (Madison: University of Wisconsin Press, 2014).

Payne, Stanley G., *The Franco Regime, 1936–1975* (Madison: University of Wisconsin Press, 1987).

Payne, Stanley, *The Spanish Civil War, the Soviet Union, and Communism* (New Haven, CT: Yale University Press, 2004).

Paz, María Antonia, 'La propaganda francesa en España', *Mélanges de la Casa de Velázquez*, 31: –3 (Année 1995), 219–79.

Pennell, Charles Edmund Richard, 'A Critical Investigation of the Opposition of the Rifi Confederation led by Muhammad Bin Abd-El Karim Al-Khattabi to Spanish Colonial Expansion in Northern Morocco, 1920–1925, and Its Political and Social Background' (PhD thesis, University of Leeds, November 1979), Volume I.

Pérez Aparicio, Carmen, 'Don Juan Bautista Basset y Ramos. Luces y sombras del líder austracista valenciano', *Estudis: Revista de Historia Moderna*, 35 (2009), 133–64.

Pérez-López, Javier, 'Creating an International Harmony: Music in the International Brigades', *Past and Memory*, 11 (2012), 239–54.

Petrie, Charles, *The Spanish Royal House* (London: Geoffrey Bles, 1958).

Pierson, Peter, *Commander of the Armada: The Seventh Duke of Medina Sidonia* (New Haven, CT: Yale University Press, 1989).

Pitt-Rivers, J. A., *The People of the Sierra* (New York: Criterion Books, 1954).

Pohlig, Matthias, and Schaich, Michael (eds), *The War of the Spanish Succession: New Perspectives* (Oxford: Oxford University Press, 2018).

Pole, Adrian, 'Leicestershire People and the Spanish Civil War', *Leicestershire Historian*, 55 (2019), 50–6.

Preston, Paul, *A People Betrayed: A History of Corruption, Political Incompetence and Social Division in Modern Spain* (London: Harper Collins, 2020).

Preston, Paul, *Comrades: Portraits from the Spanish Civil War* (London: Fontana, 2000).

Preston, Paul, *The Politics of Revenge: Fascism and the Military in 20th Century Spain* (London: Routledge, 1995).

Preston, Paul, and Mackenzie, Ann L. (eds), *The Republic Besieged: Civil War in Spain 1936–1939* (Edinburgh: Edinburgh University Press, 1996).

Preston, Paul, *The Spanish Holocaust: Inquisition and Extermination in Twentieth-Century Spain* (London: Harper Press, 2012).

Preston, Paul, *We Saw Spain Die: Foreign Correspondents and the Spanish Civil War* (London: Constable, 2008).

Purcell, Hugh, *The Last English Revolutionary: Tom Wintringham 1898–1949* (Gloucestershire: Sutton Publishing, 2004).

Quiroga, Alejandro, *Making Spaniards: Primo de Rivera and the Nationalization of the Masses, 1923–30* (New York: Palgrave, 2007).

Quiroga, Alejandro, *Miguel Primo de Rivera. Dictadura, Populismo y Nación* (Barcelona: Crítica, 2022).

Radcliff, Pamela, *Making Democratic Citizens in Spain. Civil Society and the Popular Origins of the Transition, 1960–78* (New York: Palgrave, 2011).

Raeburn, Fraser, '"Fae nae hair te Grey Hair They Answered the Call": International Brigade Volunteers from the West Central Belt of Scotland in the Spanish Civil War, 1936–9', *Journal of Scottish Historical Studies*, 35: 1 (2015), 92–114.

Reyes Baztán, María, 'Anti-colonial Imagination and Internationalism in Basque Radical Nationalism (1892–1939)' (PhD thesis, University of Warwick, 2021).

Reyes Baztán, María, 'Potatoes and Nation-Building: The Case of the Spanish Omelette', *Journal of Iberian and Latin American Studies*, 27:2 (2021), 151–70.

Richards, Michael, *After the Civil War* (2013).

Richardson, Dan, *Comintern Army: The International Brigades and the Spanish Civil War* (Lexington: University Press of Kentucky, 1982).

Ridley, Jasper, *Lord Palmerston* (London: Book Club Associates, 1970).

Ringrose, David, *Spain, Europe and the 'Spanish Miracle', 1700–1900* (Cambridge: Cambridge University Press, 1996).

Robertson, Ian, *A Commanding Presence: Wellington in the Peninsula, 1808–1814* (Stroud: Spellmount, 2008).

Robertson, Ian, *Los curiosos impertinentes: viajeros ingleses por España, 1760–1855* (Madrid: Editora Nacional, 1975).

Roca Barea, María Elvira, *Imperiofobia y Leyenda Negra: Roma, Rusia, Estados Unidos y el Imperio español* (Madrid: Siruela, 2016).

Roca Vernet, Jordi, 'La milicia nacional o la ciudadanía armada. El contrapoder revolucionario frente al liberalismo institucional', *Les espaces du politique dans*

l'Espagne du Trienio liberal (1820–1823), 54 (2020), https://journals.openedition.org/bhce/2598#tocto1n4 (accessed 15 May 2023).
Rodríguez Martín, José Antonio, 'Una aproximación al bandolerismo en España', *Iberoamericana*, 8: 31 (2008), 85–105.
Rodríguez Tapia, Andrea, 'España sin América. Política y diplomacia frente a la secesión de los territorios americanos, 1823–1833' (PhD thesis, Colegio de México, UNAM, 2018).
Rodríguez Vives, Conxa, *Los exilios de Ramón Cabrera* (Zaragoza: Prensa de la Universidad de Zaragoza, 2019).
Rogers, Helen, 'Kindness and Reciprocity: Liberated Prisoners and Christian Charity in Early Nineteenth-Century England', *Journal of Social History*, 47:3 (Spring, 2014), 721–45.
Romero Salvadó, Francisco J., *Spain 1914–1918: Between War and Revolution* (London: Routledge, 1999).
Romero Salvadó, Francisco J., 'The Organic Crisis of the Liberal State in Spain: Between the Catalan Quagmire and the Red Spectre (November 1918–April 1919)', *Historical Journal*, 60: 3 (2017), 795–815.
Romero Salvadó, Francisco J., *The Spanish Civil War: Origins, Course and Outcomes* (London: Macmillan, 2005).
Royle, Dan, 'Winning the War and Losing the Peace: Spain and the Congress of Vienna', *International History Review*, 44: 2 (2022), 357–72.
Ruiz Fernández, Óscar Alfredo, *England and Spain in the Early Modern Era: Royal Love, Diplomacy, Trade and Naval Relations, 1604–25* (London: Bloomsbury, 2020).
Rújula, Pedro, and Chust, Manuel, *El Trienio Liberal. Revolución e independencia (1820–1823)* (Madrid: Catarata, 2020).
Rújula, Pedro, and Frasquet, Ivana (eds), *El Trienio Liberal. (1820–1823): una mirada política* (Granada: Editorial Comares, 2020).
Saglia, Diego, ' "O My Mother Spain!": The Peninsular War, Family Matters, and the Practice of Romantic Nation-Writing', *ELH*, 65: 2 (1998), 363–93.
Saglia, Diego, *Poetic Castles in Spain: British Romanticism and Figurations of Iberia* (Amsterdam: Editions Rodopi, 2000).
Samson, Alexander, *Mary and Philip: The Marriage of Tudor England and Habsburg Spain* (Manchester: Manchester University Press, 2020).
San Narciso, David, and Barral Martínez, Margarita (eds), *Monarchy and Liberalism in Spain: The Building of the Nation-State, 1780–1931* (London: Routledge, 2020).
Sánchez-Albornoz, Claudio, *España, un enigma histórico* (Buenos Aires: Edhasa, 1960).
Sánchez Dragó, Fernando, and Abascal, Santiago, *España vertebrada* (Madrid: Planeta, 2019).
Sánchez, Mark G., 'Anti-Spanish Sentiment in English Political and Literary Writing, 1553–1603' (unpublished PhD thesis, University of Leeds, 2004).
Sandbrook, Dominic, *White Heat: A History of Britain in the Swinging Sixties, 1964–1970* (London: Abacus, 2009).

Sander, Gordon F., *The Hundred Day Winter War* (Lawrence: University of Kansas Press, 2013).

Sanjurjo, Jesús, *In the Blood of Our Brothers: Abolitionism and the End of the Slave Trade in Spain's Atlantic Empire, 1800–1870* (Tuscaloosa: University of Alabama Press, 2021).

Santacara, Carlos, *La Guerra de la Independencia vista por los británicos, 1808–1814* (Madrid: Machado, 2005).

Schaber, Irme, *Gerda Taro: With Robert Capa as Photojournalist in the Spanish Civil War* (Stuttgart: Edition Axel Menges, 2019).

Schmidt-Novara, Christopher, 'Continental Origins of Insular Proslavery: George Dawson Flinter in Curaçao, Venezuela, Britain, and Puerto Rico, 1810s–1830s', *Almanack. Guarulhos*, 8: 2 (semestre de 2014), 55–67.

Schrijver, F. J., *Regionalism after Regionalisation: Spain, France and the United Kingdom* (Amsterdam: University of Amsterdam Press, 2006).

Scott, Hamish, 'The War of the Spanish Succession: New Perspectives and Old', in Matthias Pohlig and Michael Schaich (eds), *The War of the Spanish Succession: New Perspectives* (Oxford, 2018), pp. 29–30.

Scianna, Bastian Matteo, 'Stuck in the Past? British Views on the Spanish Army's Effectiveness and Military Culture, 1946–1983', *War and Society*, 38: 1 (February 2019), 41–56.

Segarra Estarelles, Josep-Ramón, 'El reverso de la nación. "Provincialismo" e "independencia" durante la revolución liberal', Javier Moreno Luzón (ed.), *Construir España: Nacionalismo español y procesos de nacionalización* (Madrid: Centro de Estudios Constitucionales, 2007), pp. 40–5.

Seidman, Michael, *Republic of Egos: A Social History of the Spanish Civil War* (Madison: University of Wisconsin Press, 2002).

Senning, Calvin F., *Spain, Rumor, and Anti-Catholicism in Mid-Jacobean England: The Palatine Match, Cleves, and the Armada Scares of 1612–1613 and 1614* (London: Routledge, 2021).

Serrallonga Urquidi, Joan, 'La Guerra de África (1859–1860): Una Revisión', *Ayer*, 29 (1998), 139–59.

Sharman, Nick, *Britain's Informal Empire in Spain, 1830–1950: Free Trade, Protectionism and Military Power* (Basingstoke: Palgrave Macmillan, 2021).

Shubert, Adrian, 'Being – and Staying– Famous in 19th-Century Spain: Baldomero Espartero and the Birth of Political Celebrity', *Historia y Política*, 34 (julio-diciembre, 2015), 211–37.

Shubert, Adrian, 'Charity Properly Understood": Changing Ideas about Poor Relief in Liberal Spain', *Comparative Studies in Society and History*, 33: 1 (January 1991), 36–55.

Shubert, Adrian, *The Sword of Luchana: Baldomero Espartero and the Making of Modern Spain, 1793–1879* (London: University of Toronto Press, 2021).

Sierra, María, 'Hombres arcaicos en tiempos modernos: La construcción romántica de la masculinidad gitana', *Historia Social*, 93 (2019), 51–66.

Simms, Brendan, *Three Victories and a Defeat: the Rise and Fall of the First British Empire* (London: Penguin, 2008).

Smith, Angel, *The Origins of Catalan Nationalism* (Basingstoke: Palgrave, 2014).

Smith, Angel, 'The Rise and Fall of "Respectable" Spanish Liberalism, 1808–1923: An Explanatory Framework', *Journal of Iberian and Latin American Studies*, 1 (2016), 55–73.

Smith, David L., 'Diplomacy and the Religious Question: Mazarin, Cromwell and the Treaties of 1655 and 1657', *E-rea* [En ligne], 11.2 | 2014, mis en ligne le 15 juillet 2014, consulté le 10 août 2022 (accessed 10 August 2022).

Symth, D., 'We Are with You: Solidarity and Self-Interest in Soviet Policy towards Republican Spain, 1936–1939', in Paul Preston and Ann L. Mackenzie (eds), *The Republic Besieged: Civil War in Spain 1936–1939* (Edinburgh: Edinburgh University Press, 1996), p. 88.

Snyder, Timothy, *Bloodlands: Europe between Hitler and Stalin* (New York: Vintage, 2011).

Sontag, Susan, *Essays on Photography* (New York: Picador, 2001).

Soo, Scott, *The Routes to Exile: France and the Spanish Civil War Refugees, 1939–2009* (Manchester: Manchester University Press, 2013).

Sorkin, David, *The Religious Enlightenment: Protestants, Jews and Catholics from London to Vienna* (Princeton: University Press, 2008).

Southey, Robert, *History of the Peninsular War* (London: John Murray, 1823–32), Volume 1.

Spiers, Edward M., *Radical General: Sir George de Lacy Evans, 1787–1870* (Manchester: Manchester University Press, 1983).

Stanhope, Earl Philip Henry (Lord Mahon), *The War of the Spanish Succession* (London: John Murray, 1836).

Stockey, Gareth, and Rankin, Nicholas, *Defending the Rock* (London: Faber and Faber, 2017).

Stoker, Donald, Schneid, Frederick, and Blanton, Harold (eds), *Conscription in the Napoleonic Era* (London: Routledge, 2008).

Strachan, Hew, 'Scotland's Military Identity', *Scottish Historical Review*, 85: 220, Part 2 (October, 2006), 315–32.

Stradling, Robert, 'English-Speaking Units of the International Brigades War, Politics and Discipline', *Journal of Contemporary History*, 45: 4 (2010), 744–67.

Stradling, Robert, *Your Children Will Be Next: Bombing and Propaganda in the Spanish Civil War 1936–1939* (Cardiff: University of Wales Press, 2008).

Summerfield, Penny, and Peniston-Bird, Corinna, *Contesting Home Defence: Men, Women and the Home Guard in the Second World War* (Manchester: Manchester University Press, 2013).

Taylor, J. D., 'The Party's Over? The Angry Brigade, the Counterculture, and the British New Left, 1967–72', *Historical Journal*, 58: 3 (2015), 877–900.

Thomas, Hugh, *The Spanish Civil War* (London: Penguin, 1977).

Thompson, Andrew C., 'War, Religion, and Public Debate in Britain during the War of the Spanish Succession', in Matthias Pohlig and Michael Schaich (eds), *The War of the Spanish Succession: New Perspectives* (Oxford, 2018), pp. 190–1, 195.

Thomson, Guy, 'Mazzini and Spain, 1820–72', in C. A. Bayly and E. F. Biagini (eds), *Giuseppe Mazzini and the Globalization of Democratic Nationalism, 1830–1920* (Oxford: Oxford University Press, 2008), pp. 260–2.

Torre, Rosario de la, 'La prensa madrileña y el discurso de Lord Salisbury sobre las naciones moribundas', *Cuadernos de Historia Moderna y Contemporánea*, 6 (1985), 163–80.

Torres Sánchez, Rafael, *Constructing a Fiscal Military State in Eighteenth-Century Spain* (Basingstoke: Palgrave, 2019).

Tortella Casares, Gabriel, and Eugenia Nuñez, Clara, *El desarrollo de la España contemporánea: historia económica de los siglos XIX y XX* (Madrid: Alianza, 2011).

Townson, Nigel (ed.), *Is Spain Different?: A Comparative Look at the 19th and 20th Centuries* (Brighton: Sussex Academic Press, 2015).

Townson, Nigel (ed.), *Spain Transformed: The Late-Franco Dictatorship, 1959–1975* (Basingstoke: Palgrave, 2007).

Towsey, Mark, *Reading History in Britain and America, c. 1750–c. 1840* (New York: Cambridge University Press, 2019).

Tremlett, Giles, *A Brief History of Spain* (London: Apollo, 2022).

Tremlett, Giles, *Ghosts of Spain: Travels through a Country's Hidden Past* (London: Faber and Faber, 2012).

Trincado, Estrella, and Ramos, José-Luis, 'John Stuart Mill and Nineteenth-Century Spain', *Journal of the History of Economic Thought*, 33: 4 (December, 2011), 507–26.

van der Esch, P. A. M., *Prelude to War, the International Repercussions of the Spanish Civil War (1936–1939)* (The Hague: Martinus Nijhoff, 1951).

Vernet Roca, Jordi, 'La Restauración de Fernando VII: la transformación represiva y autoritaria de la monarquía. Barcelona, de Manuel Casamada a Luis Lacy', *Rubrica Contemporanea*, 4: 8 (2015), 5–28.

Viguera Ruiz, Rebeca, 'Ramón Alesón y el liberalismo en los orígenes de la España contemporánea (1781–1846)' (PhD thesis, Universidad de la Rioja, 2009).

Viktorin, Carolin, '"All Publicity Is Good Publicity?" Advertising, Public Relations and Branding of Spain in the United Kingdom, 1945–1969', in Carolin Viktorin (ed.), *Nation Branding in Modern History* (New York: Bergahn Books, 2018), p. 139.

Viktorin, Carolin (ed.) *Nation Branding in Modern History* (New York: Bergahn Books, 2018).

Villamediana González, Leticia, *Anglomanía: la imagen de Inglaterra en la prensa española del siglo XVIII* (Madrid: Támesis, 2019).

Vries, Jan de, 'Playing with Scales: The Global and the Micro, the Macro and the Nano', *Past & Present*, 242: 14 (November 2019), 23–36.

Waddell, David A. G., 'British Neutrality and Spanish-American Independence: The Problem of Foreign Enlistment', *Journal of Latin American Studies*, 19 (1987), 1–18.

Waldren, Jacqueline, *Insiders and Outsiders: Paradise and Reality in Mallorca* (New York: Berghahn, 1996).

Wawro, Geoffrey, *Warfare and Society in Europe, 1792–1914* (London: Routledge, 1999), p. 169.

Weber, David J., *Spanish Bourbons and Wild Indians* (Waco: Baylor University Press, 2004).

Webster, Charles K., *The Congress of Vienna 1814–1815* (Oxford: Oxford University Press: 1918).

Webster, Charles K., *The Foreign Policy of Palmerston, 1830–41* (London: G. Bell, 1951), Volume 1.

Whelan, Frederick G., 'Eighteenth-Century Scottish Political Economy and the Decline of Imperial Spain', *Journal of Scottish Historical Studies*, 38:1 (2018), 55–72.

White, Hayden, *Metahistory: The Historical Imagination in Nineteenth-Century Europe* (London: Johns Hopkins University Press, 1973).

Whitehead, Jonathan, *Spanish Republicans and the Second World War: Republic across the Mountains* (Barnsley: Pen and Sword, 2021).

Wilson, Ben, *Empire of the Deep: The Rise and Fall of the British Navy* (London: Orion, 2013).

Yamamoto, Koji (ed.), *Stereotypes and Stereotyping in Early Modern England: Puritans, Papists and Projectors* (Manchester: Manchester University Press, 2022).

Young, Patricia T., and Levy, Jack S., 'Domestic Politics and the Escalation of Commercial Rivalry: Explaining the War of Jenkins' Ear, 1739–48', *European Journal of International Relations*, 17: 2 (June 2011), 209–32.

Zaagsma, Gerben, *Jewish Volunteers of the International Brigades and the Spanish Civil War* (London: Bloomsbury, 2017).

Zamowski, Adam, *Holy Madness: Romantics, Patriots and Revolutionaries, 1776–1871* (London: Viking, 2000).

Zoffmann Rodríguez, Arturo, '"The Anarchist Feedback Loop": Spanish Solidarity Campaigns in London and the Birth of Revolutionary Syndicalism, 1896–1913', in Graciela Iglesias-Rogers (ed.), *The Hispanic Anglosphere from the Eighteenth to the Twentieth Century: An Introduction* (London: Routledge, 2021), pp. 188–202.

Index

afrancesado 30, 61, 64, 70
Africanista 114, 118
Álava, Ricardo de 68, 80
Alesón, Ramón 69
Alexander, Bill 122, 138
Alfonso XII 108, 113, 114
Alfonso XIII 111, 113, 114, 115, 116, 118, 158
Alhucemas Bay 118
Almansa 28
Almenar 30
Amadeo I 107
American Revolutionary War 43, 44, 46, 65
anarchism 106, 112, 117, 156
Anglo-Spanish League of Friendship 152
Anne, Queen 29, 33
Annual, battle of 117, 118
Apostles (Cambridge University) 71, 72
Appeasement 123
Armada 5, 17, 18, 20
asiento 35, 38, 39
Atlantic 14, 21, 25, 38, 43, 49, 64, 67, 100, 120, 142, 147
austracismo 34
Austria 8, 25
Azaña, Manuel 9, 149
Aztec 16

Bacon, John Francis 88
Bailén, Battle of 62
Barcelona, siege of 33, 34
Baroque 8
Basque country 4, 34, 47, 60, 75, 81, 82, 87, 88, 90, 92, 93, 99, 103, 110, 156
Battle of Leipzig 57
Bebb, Cecil 123
Bentham, Jeremy 67
Bevin, Ernest 149, 151
Bizet, Georges 114
Black legend 1, 2, 4, 9, 14, 15, 16, 17, 21, 23, 26, 29, 37, 38, 39, 41, 42, 43, 44, 45, 46, 53, 56, 58, 59, 62, 70, 71, 113, 114, 118, 121, 124, 131, 144, 153, 154, 162
Blanco White, Joseph 52, 61, 70, 77
Blázquez, José Martín 137
Bone, Muirhead 118, 119
Borrow, George 78, 79, 87, 101
Bourbon reforms 37
Brenan, Gerald 6, 148, 150
Brexit 1, 163, 164
British auxiliary legion 80, 81, 82, 84, 86, 89, 90, 91, 92, 93, 94, 102
British unification (1707) 23, 24, 25, 28, 34
British way of war 52
Brome, Vincent 134
Buckley, William 153
Bullfighting 3, 80, 113
Bulwer, Henry 103
Byron, Lord 55

Cable Street (battle of) 122
Cabrera, Ramón 77, 78, 94, 99, 102
Cacique 111
Calpe Hunt 115
Canary Islands 14, 19, 86, 120, 145
Canning, George 67
Carlist 5, 68, 69, 71, 73, 75, 76, 78, 79, 81, 82, 85, 86, 87, 88, 89, 90, 91, 92, 93, 94, 95, 100, 101, 102, 104, 105, 107, 108, 149, 161, 162
Carlos III 40, 41, 44, 45, 46
Carlos IV 48
Caro Baroja, Julio 80
Casas, Bartolomé de las 16
Catalonia 4, 6, 25, 26, 33, 34, 85, 86, 90, 98, 99, 103, 106, 109, 112, 117, 118, 119, 121, 125, 131, 136, 138, 139
Chalmers Mitchell, Peter 120, 121, 155
Charles I 20, 21, 22
Charles II (of Spain) 24
Charles III (Habsburg pretender) 31, 32
Churchill, Winston 123, 127, 141, 145, 153
Clarke, Bob 130, 133

Clarke, Edward (Earl of Bristol) 40
Cobden, William, 103
Copeman, Fred 138
Coleridge, Samuel 61
Columbus, Christopher 17
Communism 122, 124, 125, 127, 128, 134, 135, 136, 137, 138, 151, 159
Composite monarchy 1
Congress of Vienna 64, 65
Conquista 21
Constitution of 1812 61, 62, 63, 65, 66, 67, 68, 86, 87
Cornford, John 122, 127
Cortes, Hernán 8
Costa, Joaquín 111
Costello, Edward 79
Crimean War 104, 128
Cristino 75, 76, 77, 80, 81, 84, 86, 88, 89, 91, 92, 97, 101, 105
Cromwell, Oliver 21, 23, 124
Cuba 26, 39, 40, 101, 104, 107, 108, 109, 110

Dampier, William 22
Darién 23, 24
Democrats 106, 107, 123, 125, 126, 157, 158, 159
Disaster (*Desastre*) 109, 110, 111, 113, 114
Disraeli, Benjamin 71, 105
Downie, John 52, 56, 57, 100
Drake, Francis 16, 18, 19

Eliot Treaty 83, 85, 86
Elizabethan England 3, 15, 16, 17, 18, 19, 20
Enlightenment 2, 41, 42, 43, 44, 45, 112
'English Armada' 18
entangled history 4, 5
Espartero, Baldomero 78, 87, 92, 93, 95, 97, 98, 99, 101, 102, 103, 105
Espoz y Mina, Francisco 63, 76
Estala, Pedro 48
European integration 151, 152, 159, 163, 164
exile 2, 11, 64, 66, 67, 68, 72, 93, 94, 95, 127, 139, 147, 152

Falklands war 160
Family Compact 44, 51

fascism 118, 122, 123, 125, 126, 127, 137, 142, 143, 146, 147, 149, 151, 152, 153
Ferdinand VI 37
Ferdinand VII 48, 53, 61, 62, 63, 65, 66, 67, 68, 69, 70, 71, 72, 73, 75, 153
Fernández de Moratín, Leandro 47
Ferrer, Melchor 94
Ferri, José 147
fiction 6, 17, 54, 55, 76, 77, 111, 125, 126, 127, 131, 152, 159
First Spanish Republic 107, 115
First World War 113, 116, 124, 131, 152
Fiscal-military state 43, 45
Flamenco 3, 113
Flinter, George Dawson 100, 101
Flórez Estrada, Álvaro 49
Florida 40
Ford, Richard 46, 48, 76, 99
Franco, Francisco 5, 6, 8, 15, 76, 120, 123, 126, 129, 136, 137, 138, 141, 142, 143, 144, 146, 147, 148, 149
Franco regime 150, 151, 152, 153, 154, 155, 156, 157, 158, 159, 160
French Foreign Legion 83, 84, 95, 140
French Revolution 40, 42, 51, 64, 67
'fueros' 34, 47, 82, 90

Gardiner, Robert 115
Geddes, John 47
George I (Elector of Hanover) 33, 37
Germany 29, 64, 107, 137, 139, 144, 145, 147, 153, 164
Gernika 34
Gibraltar 5, 7, 25, 27, 28, 33, 35, 43, 44, 46, 54, 68, 71, 72, 87, 99, 104, 107, 114, 115, 116, 121, 126, 137, 141, 142, 143, 145, 150, 160, 162, 163
globalization 1, 40
Glorious Revolution (1688) 23
'global turn' 2, 19
Godoy, Manuel de 48
Golden Age 9, 13
Gondomar, Count (Diego Sarmiento de Acuña) 20, 21
Goya, Francsco de 106, 125
Grand Alliance 24
Gregory, Walter 130

Gregory, William 133
Guerrilla 27, 30, 31, 51, 53, 55, 56, 58, 59, 60, 63, 65, 69, 76, 77, 83, 84, 107, 139, 140, 161
Gunpowder Plot 20, 29
Gurney, Jason 131, 135
gypsy 113, 114

Hannay, David 98
Henty, George 26, 53
Hernani 91
Hispanism 6, 7, 29, 52, 53, 54, 55, 62, 67, 71, 72, 98, 100, 106, 113, 115, 124, 148, 152, 154, 158, 163
Hobbes, Thomas 22
Holy Alliance 67
Home Guard (Local Defence Volunteers) 139, 140
Howard, John 44
Human rights 155, 156
Humboldt, Alexander von 41
Hume, David 42, 43
Hundred Days 63

India 65, 68, 78, 99, 100, 115, 147, 149, 156
Indians (Americas) 22, 26, 42
Informal empire 105, 109, 111, 114, 115, 116, 117
Inglis, Henry David 71
Inquisition 26, 41
International Brigades 125, 126, 129, 130, 131, 132, 133, 135, 136, 137, 138, 156, 161, 162
Ireland 17, 34, 49, 58, 88, 91, 143
Isabella II 97, 98, 99, 107
Islamic Spain 2, 7, 71

Jacob, William 54
Jacobite 33, 34, 37, 39
James VII (James I) 19
Jamestown 19, 20
Jarama, battle of 130, 133
Johnson, Hewlett 128
Johnstone, Nancy 122
Jones, Jack 126
Jovellanos, Gaspar Melchor de 45, 55
Juderías, Julián 15

Kemble, John 71
Kennett-Barrington, Vincent 108
King's German Legion 58

La Granja 86
Labour Party, 149
Lacy Evans, George de 80, 82, 83, 84, 85, 89, 91, 92, 93, 95
Langdon-Davies, John 6, 125, 140
Latin America 4, 8, 9, 14, 17, 20, 21, 26, 32, 33, 35, 38, 39, 40, 41, 42, 48, 49, 51, 54, 61, 64, 65, 66, 68, 100, 101, 109, 152
League of Nations 149
Lee, Laurie 120
León, Diego de 98, 99
Leslie, Charles 54, 63
Liberalism 51, 60, 61, 62, 66, 67, 69, 70, 71, 72, 85, 97, 98, 99, 102, 103, 104, 106, 107, 126, 137
Londragon, John 131
Louis XIV 22, 23, 24, 25, 28, 29
Lunn, Arnold 153

MacDonald, Ethel 136
Machado, Antonio 127
MacKay, Hugh 133
March, Juan 146
Mary I 15, 16
Maulets 27
May Days (137) 135, 136
Mayflower 19
Mayhew, Henry 94
Medina Campo, Treaty of 14
Memoirs 53, 54, 58, 64
Mendizábal, Juan Álvarez 68, 78, 85, 100, 101
Metternich, Klemens von 64, 102
Migration 10, 67, 116, 121, 155
Mill, John Stuart 90, 91
Mina y Larrea, Martín Francisco Xavier (Xavier Mina) 52, 63, 64
Miranda, Francisco de 48, 49, 56
Molotov-Ribbentrop Pact (1939–41) 137, 138
Moore, John 57, 59
More, Thomas 14
Morocco 14, 18, 19, 105, 114, 117, 118, 152
Mosley, Oswald 122, 151

Napier, William 62
Napoleonic 7, 10, 24, 32, 40, 42, 48, 49, 51, 52, 54, 57, 58, 59, 60, 61, 62, 64, 75, 80, 89, 92, 93, 95, 105, 107
Narváez, Ramón 102, 103
National Catholic 15, 146
Navalism 65, 87, 104
Netherlands 8, 17, 19, 20, 22, 24, 25, 26, 33, 37, 44, 46, 57, 64, 149
Nine Years War 23
Non-Intervention 123, 137, 149
Nueva Planta decrees 25, 28, 34

O'Donnell, Leopoldo 91, 104
'Ominous Decade' 69, 85
Operation Mincemeat 146
Oriamendi, battle of 82, 88
Orientalism 10
Ortega y Gasset, José 111, 113
Orwell, George 3, 125, 132, 135, 136, 148, 151

Palmerston, Lord (Henry John Temple) 76, 80, 89, 90, 92, 102, 103
Panama 19, 23
Pan-Hispanism 100, 105, 144, 160
Pelham Thomas 45
Peake, Osbert 140
Peninsular War 5, 27, 45, 49, 51, 52, 53, 54, 55, 56, 57, 58, 59, 60, 61, 62, 63, 65, 66, 68, 75, 79, 81, 82, 84, 106, 115, 145, 161, 162
People's Olympiad (1936) 122, 123
Pepys, Samuel 27
Perfidious Albion (Anglophobia) 16, 26, 37, 41, 44, 47, 48, 49, 60, 99, 101, 134, 143, 147, 163
Phillip, John 105
Philip II 5, 8, 15, 17, 19, 25, 37, 44
Philip V 25, 28, 31, 32, 33, 34, 37
photojournalism 128, 129, 138
piracy 4, 16, 17, 19, 22, 23
Pirala y Criado, Antonio 81
Pitt, William 48
Politt, Harry 124, 135
Portugal 7, 18, 29, 30, 31, 51, 52, 54, 56, 57, 58, 59, 60, 64, 79, 80, 101, 105, 107, 110, 124, 144, 151, 156
Potsdam declaration 149

Primo de Rivera, Miguel 116, 118, 119
Prisoners of war 39, 40, 46, 63, 80
Pritchett, Victor Sawdon 120
Progressive Biennium 103, 104
Pronunciamiento 61
Propaganda 8, 11, 16, 33, 60, 108, 112, 119, 125, 129, 136, 143, 144, 145, 151, 162
protestant 1, 16, 17, 21, 22, 23, 24, 26, 27, 29, 31, 33, 34, 58, 59, 78, 153

Quadruple Alliance (1718–20) 37
Quadruple Alliance (1834) 80, 84, 102

racism 49, 110, 123
Raleigh, Walter 16, 20
reconquest 8
regeneration 71, 110, 111, 113, 117
Revolutions of 1848 102, 108
Revolution of 1868 106, 108
Revolutionary crisis of 1917 108, 121
Richards, Marianne 94
Riego, Rafael del 66
Rio Tinto Company 112, 117, 119
Robertson, William 42
romantic 1, 5, 6, 52, 53, 54, 55, 71, 72, 76, 78, 80, 81, 93, 98, 99, 114, 122, 124, 125, 127, 154, 162
Romilly, Esmond 126
Ross Campbell, John 136
ruralism 124
Rust, William 131, 132, 134, 135, 137, 138

Santiago the Apostle 20, 62
Schiller, Friedrich 56
Second of May (1808) 52, 106, 124, 162
Second Spanish Republic 118, 119, 120, 124, 125, 130, 133, 136
Second World War 5, 7, 121, 127, 128, 138, 139, 139, 140, 141, 142, 143, 144, 145, 146, 147, 148, 149, 150, 151, 152, 162, 163
Serviles 62, 63, 66
Seven Years' War 39, 40
Sfakia, battle of 141
Shakespeare, William 13
Sheridan, Richard Brinsley 54
slavery 4, 16, 35, 38, 80, 100, 101, 106
Smith, Adam 43

socialism 106, 112, 126, 130, 133, 136, 137, 150, 155, 157
Social Darwinism 110
South Sea Bubble 38
Southey, Robert 55, 56, 63
Spanish Civil War 5, 6, 10, 75, 81, 117, 119, 121, 122, 123, 124, 125, 126, 127, 128, 129, 130, 131, 132, 133, 134, 135, 136, 137, 150, 155, 161, 162
Spanish Exhibition (1889) 109
'Spanish Match' 20
Spanish Succession War 5, 6, 10, 23, 24, 25, 27, 30, 34, 35, 37, 48, 53, 57, 59, 161, 162
Stanhope, James 25, 27, 29, 30, 31
Strubell, Michael 33
Swinburne, Henry 45, 46

Talavera, Battle of 59
Tangier 27
Tennyson, Alfred Lord 72
Tercio 21
Thackeray, William Makepeace 77
Thirty Years War 22
Thomas, Fred 132
Thomas, Hugh 6
Tories 25, 27, 29, 31, 37, 62, 63, 70, 71, 81, 84, 88, 89, 90, 91, 92, 93, 105, 110, 129, 137, 151
Torrijos, José María 72, 73
Townsend, Joseph 41
Townsend Warner, Sylvia 125
Trade 38, 39, 40, 41, 43, 46, 48, 49, 68, 98, 103, 109, 115, 117, 128, 152, 157, 164
'Tragic Week' (1909) 112
travel 5, 9, 10, 35, 42, 44, 45, 46, 47, 54, 55, 56, 58, 70, 71, 72, 76, 77, 78, 79, 80, 81, 88, 99, 100, 109, 112, 113, 115, 117, 119, 121, 144, 154, 155, 162, 164
Treaty of London (1604) 19
Treaty of Utrecht (1713) 25, 32, 33, 38, 115
Triple Alliance 114

Tudor 13, 14, 15
Turner, William, 81, 82, 88, 91, 93
'Two Spains' 51, 153

Unamuno, Miguel de 127
Union of Crowns (1603) 19, 20
United Nations 147, 149, 150, 151
USA 4, 9, 15, 64, 94, 95, 101, 110, 116, 117, 144, 145, 150

Vassall-Fox, Heny (Lord Holland) 52, 55, 63, 67
Velázquez, Diego 56, 76, 105
Vichy France 140, 141, 144, 145, 146
Victoria, Queen 102, 114
Villiers, George 77, 85, 92, 100, 101, 103

Walcheren expedition 57
Walpole, Robert 37, 38
War of Jenkins' Ear (War of the Asiento) 39
War of the Austrian Succession 39
War of the Three Kingdoms (British Civil Wars) 21, 22, 23, 35
Waugh, Evelyn 141, 142
Wellington, Duke of (Arthur Wellesley) 4, 49, 53, 54, 56, 57, 58, 59, 61, 68, 69, 70, 79, 80, 83, 84, 85, 92, 93
Whig 23, 25, 27, 29, 33, 37, 54, 62, 63, 65, 70, 89, 90, 91, 105
Whittingham, Samuel Ford 62
William and Mary 23
Winter War 138
Wintringham, Tom 139
Woodville, William 100

Xenophobia 10, 31, 39, 52, 58, 59, 70, 103, 162

Young, Arthur 46
Young England 71, 94

Zumalacárregui, Tomás de 75, 77, 87

www.ingramcontent.com/pod-product-compliance
Lightning Source LLC
Chambersburg PA
CBHW071828300426
44116CB00009B/1476